PRAISE FOR *THE EXPERIMENT*

'A sympathetic, lucidly written and
first Georgian Republic, which mak ... .ve use of the accounts
of foreign observers as well as some of the major leading figures.'
Donald Rayfield, author of *Stalin and His Hangmen*

'Covering a crucial but strangely overlooked period in the fevered
evolution of socialism, we've been waiting for this book for a long
time. Fortunately, it arrives excellently written and researched.'
Peter Nasmyth, author of *Georgia: In the Mountains of Poetry*

'In a clear and succinct style, Eric Lee paints a sympathetic portrait of
this remarkable experiment in democratic socialism. Lee has brought
this almost unknown story out of the shadows, giving it its proper
place in the historiography of socialism and the Russian Revolution.'
Stephen Jones, author of *Socialism in Georgian Colors*

'Eric Lee has skilfully shown in this thoroughly-researched book how
a century ago Georgia created the first democratic socialist republic –
and laid the basis for Georgian democracy today.'
H.E. Ambassador Tamar Beruchashvili

PRAISE FOR ERIC LEE'S PREVIOUS BOOK *OPERATION BASALT*

'Riveting'
Wall Street Journal

'An authentic and compelling read'
Damien Lewis, best-selling author of *The Nazi Hunters* **and**
Churchill's Secret Warriors

THE
EXPERIMENT
GEORGIA'S FORGOTTEN
REVOLUTION 1918–1921

ERIC LEE

BLOOMSBURY ACADEMIC
LONDON • NEW YORK • OXFORD • NEW DELHI • SYDNEY

BLOOMSBURY ACADEMIC
Bloomsbury Publishing Plc
50 Bedford Square, London, WC1B 3DP, UK
1385 Broadway, New York, NY 10018, USA
29 Earlsfort Terrace, Dublin 2, Ireland

BLOOMSBURY, BLOOMSBURY ACADEMIC and the Diana logo
are trademarks of Bloomsbury Publishing Plc

First published in Great Britain 2017 by ZED BOOKS LTD
Reprinted by Bloomsbury Academic 2022

Cover design: David A. Gee
Cover image © National Archives of Georgia: Chkheidze,
member of the Russian State Duma, president of the Petrograd Soviet
of Workers' and Soldiers' Deputies, and later chairman of the
Constituent Assembly of the Georgian Republic.

A catalogue record for this book is available from the British Library.

A catalog record for this book is available from the Library of Congress

ISBN: HB: 978-1-7869-9093-8
PB: 978-1-3503-5604-7
ePDF: 978-1-7869-9094-5
ePub: 978-1-7869-9095-2
mobi: 978-1-7869-9096-9

Typeset by in Bembo Std by seagulls.net

Printed and bound in Great Britain

To find out more about our authors and books visit
www.bloomsbury.com and sign up for our newsletters.

Dedicated to the memory of Karl August Wittfogel (1896–1988), Max Shachtman (1904–1972), Arieh Yaari (1918–2005), Michael Harrington (1928–1989) and Tom Milstein (1943–2012).

CONTENTS

TIMELINE

1783   Georgia signs the Treaty of Georgievsk, putting it under Russian protection.

1801   Russia begins the annexation of Georgia.

1868   Birth of Noe Zhordania.

1878   Birth of Joseph Stalin.

1892   *mesame dasi* (The Third Group), Georgia's first Marxist organisation, is formed.

1904   Outbreak of a peasant rebellion in the western Georgian province of Guria.

1905–6   Russian Revolution; in Georgia, Guria falls under the complete control of the Social Democrats.

1906   "Gurian Republic" ends as Russian troops re-occupy the district. Elections to the first State Duma; in this and future Duma elections, the Social Democrats win large majorities in Georgia.

1917   In March, the tsar abdicates. The Provisional Government asserts its authority over all of Transcaucasia. In November, the Bolsheviks seize power in Petrograd. Elections take place across the former Russian empire for the Constituent Assembly; in Georgia, the Social Democrats win a large majority. The People's Guard is formed in Georgia and seizes weapons from the Tiflis arsenal in a daring raid.

1918   In January, the Bolsheviks disperse the Constituent
        Assembly by force. Transcaucasia declares independence,
        but the federation lasts for just one month. On 26 May,
        Georgia declares independence. Peace agreement signed
        with Turkey following mediation by the Germans,
        who then occupy Georgia. In December, a brief war
        breaks out with Armenia. The First World War ends in
        a German defeat; Britain begins to move forces into
        Transcaucasia.

1919   Elections to the Georgian Constituent Assembly;
        several parties compete and the Social Democrats win
        a landslide victory. The British occupation of Georgia
        begins. General Denikin's Volunteer Army engages
        in border clashes with the Georgians. Rising tension
        between the British, who support Denikin, and the
        Georgians. On 7 November Georgian Communists
        make a failed coup attempt.

1920   On 2 May, the Communists make a second failed coup
        attempt. Shortly afterwards, Russia and Georgia sign a
        peace treaty. In exchange for Russian recognition, the
        Georgians legalise the Communist Party. The British
        forces complete their withdrawal from Georgia. The other
        two Transcaucasian republics, Armenia and Azerbaijan, fall
        under Soviet rule. In September, a delegation from the
        Second International arrives in Georgia.

1921   In February, the Russian army invades Georgia and after
        several weeks of fighting establishes Soviet rule, forcing
        the Georgian Republic's leaders into exile. Sporadic
        rebellions break out against Soviet rule, most notably in
        the province of Svanetia.

1923   The Georgia Social Democratic Party is forced to
       dissolve – but continues its existence underground. Key
       Georgian Menshevik leaders return covertly to the
       country from exile.

1924   Under the leadership of the Social Democrats, armed
       rebellion breaks out across the country. It is bloodily
       suppressed and Soviet rule firmly established.

1953   Stalin and Zhordania die.

1956   Following Khrushchev's "secret speech" at the 20th
       Congress of the Communist Party of the Soviet
       Union in which Stalin was denounced, pro-Stalin
       demonstrations break out in Georgia and are bloodily
       suppressed.

1978   Demonstrations break out in Tbilisi following a Soviet
       constitutional reform that removed Georgian as the
       official state language; the regime concedes to the
       protestors' demands.

1985   Mikhail Gorbachev begins a process of democratic
       reform in the Soviet Union, and names Georgian
       Communist leader Eduard Shevardnadze as his foreign
       minister, to preside over the end of the Cold War.

1989   Pro-independence demonstration in Tbilisi ends with
       twenty dead and hundreds wounded as Soviet troops
       open fire.

1990   Georgia holds its first free elections since 1919 as a pro-
       independence party wins and the Communists receive
       only 30% of the vote.

1991   On 9 April Georgia declares independence, reviving
       the 1921 Constitution and the national flag of that
       period. On 26 May, the 73rd anniversary of Georgian

independence, presidential elections are held. The newly elected president, former dissident Zviad Gamsakhurdia, lasts barely seven months in power before being overthrown in a coup. Former Georgian Communist Party leader Shevardnadze comes to power the following year.

1992   Fighting erupts in Abkhazia; the following year, Georgian forces suffer military defeat and are driven out of the province, together with a large number of Georgian civilians.

2003   The "Rose Revolution" deposes Shevardnadze, replacing him with a government led by Mikheil Saakashvili.

2008   Georgia and Russia go to war over South Ossetia. In the end, Russian forces remain in control of both South Ossetia and Abkhazia.

2013   Giorgi Margvelashvili is elected Georgian president, and first truly peaceful and orderly transition of power in modern Georgian history takes place.

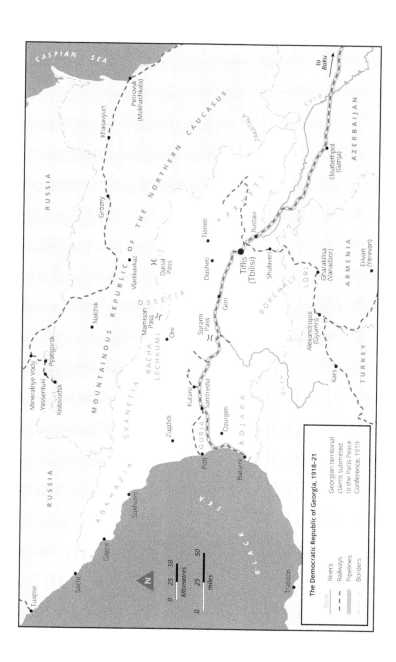

The Democratic Republic of Georgia, 1918–21

Georgian territorial claims submitted to the Paris Peace Conference, 1919

Kura   Rivers
- - -   Railways
▓▓▓   Pipelines
- · - · -   Borders

CASPIAN SEA

RUSSIA

MOUNTAINOUS REPUBLIC OF THE NORTHERN CAUCASUS

AZERBAIJAN

ARMENIA

TURKEY

BLACK SEA

ABKHAZIA

SVANETIA

RACHA-LECHKUMI

OSSETIA

KAKHETI

BORCHALI

LORI

GURIA

ADJARA

Tuapse
Sochi
Gagra
Sukhumi
Zugdidi
Poti
Ozurgeti
Batumi
Trabzon

Mineralnye Vody
Yessentuki
Kislovodsk
Pyatigorsk
Nalchik

Grozny
Khasavyurt
Petrovsk (Makhachkala)

Vladikavkaz
Darial Pass
Mamison Pass
Oni

Samtredia
Kutaisi
Surami Pass
Gori
Dusheti
Tianeti

Tiflis (Tbilisi)
Rustavi
Shulaveri

Elisabethpol (Ganja)

Gharakilisa (Vanadzor)
Alexandropol (Gyumri)
Erivan (Yerevan)
Kars

to Baku

Kura
ZAKATALA

N

0 25 50
kilometres

0 25 50
miles

PREFACE

I have spent most of my life as an activist in the labour movement and on the democratic left. I grew up in America, during the Cold War, a time when "socialist" was a dirty word, and was closely identified with the regime established by Lenin and Stalin in the Soviet Union.

I was never enthusiastic about that regime and at a young age was happy to discover that there was a movement on the left which did not accept that the Soviet model was a positive one. We called ourselves "*democratic* socialists" and we challenged the claim that the Soviet Union was in any way a socialist society. But people would ask: so where is this democratic socialism of yours? It was a difficult question to answer, then and now.

Of course we could point to the Nordic countries, and certainly a few decades ago, countries like Sweden and Denmark did seem to be far more liveable, humane and decent societies than the ones on either side of the Iron Curtain. They were, and are, democracies. They had, and have, very powerful labour movements. They achieved a degree of social justice and equality that was unimaginable in places like the United States. But they remained capitalist countries, and the Social Democratic parties which led them for so many decades had little ambition to transform them into anything other than a decent and humane form of capitalism.

If we were looking for a more advanced model of democratic socialism, there was always the example of the kibbutz movement in Israel. The kibbutzim took socialist ideals and realised them to a degree not seen anywhere else. Communal dining rooms and laundries, collective child rearing, direct democracy through weekly meetings of the entire community – these were revolutionary ideas rooted in classical socialist writings. But the kibbutzim for all their strengths never amounted to more than 3-4% of the population of the small Jewish state. They punched above their weight, providing the country with many of its leading politicians, generals and cultural figures. But the country as a whole was no more socialist than Denmark.

If one looked around for examples of countries where socialist parties came to power and carried out far-reaching reforms aiming to create socialism while defending democracy – and that means multi-party elections, freedom of speech and the press, free and independent trade unions and so on – there were hardly any to be found.

There were plenty of interesting experiments in workers' rule during the twentieth century. Among these were those carried out by anarchists, syndicalists and independent socialists in Spain during the civil war, or Austria's great experiment in socialist urban living known as "Red Vienna." But a Marxist party carrying out a democratic socialist revolution in an entire country? I know of only one example: Georgia.

PROLOGUE

BRUSSELS, 29–30 JULY 1914

It was the eve of the First World War, a war Europe's socialists had vowed to prevent.

The leading figures of the socialist parties in Germany, Austria, Russia, Italy, France, Britain and elsewhere were meeting at the Maison du Peuple in the Belgian capital. Austria-Hungary had already declared war on Serbia, and Russia was mobilising its army. Germany was only days away from joining in the fray. The world stood on the brink of catastrophe.

It would turn out to be the very last meeting of the International Socialist Bureau. The historian of the international socialist movement, Julius Braunthal, described the meeting as "the most fateful conference in its history."[1]

That Bureau was the permanent leadership of the Second International, the global federation of socialist parties founded in Paris in 1889. The successor organisation to Karl Marx's International Workingmen's Association (known as the First International), the Second International was far more powerful, more global and more in line with Marxist thinking about socialist politics.

The parties affiliated to the Second International believed that they understood how the world worked, what was broken and how to fix it. They welcomed liberal capitalism as an improvement over the feudal society that had preceded it. They believed that the extension of democracy into all spheres of public life, including the economy, would create a new kind of society, one in which exploitation, inequality, poverty, even social class, had no place. They called the envisioned new society "socialism" and while advocating for it, they supported reforms that would at the very least make life under capitalism more bearable for working people. Their first worldwide campaigns took place in the early 1890s around the first of May, and their principal demand was the eight-hour working day. They were also strong opponents of war and militarism, as well as committed internationalists who rallied under the slogan "workers of the world, unite."

No socialist party had yet come to power anywhere in the world, but by the summer of 1914 it seemed like the day was not far off when at least one of them might win an election and be able to test socialist values in the real world.

The German socialists were already the largest party in the country's parliament. In the January 1912 elections, the last held before the war, they had won over 4.2 million votes, nearly 35% of those cast, and captured the largest number of seats in the Reichstag. Meanwhile, the socialists were the second largest party in France, winning 17% of the vote in the 1910 elections. Even in the United States, the only major industrial country where no mass socialist movement ever emerged, the Socialist Party of Eugene V. Debs seemed on the cusp of making a breakthrough. It achieved its greatest electoral success in 1912, with over 900,000 votes, nearly 6% of the total. In addition, the party won hundreds of local election victories, with mayors, state legislators, and even a couple of members of congress. It was the high-water mark of American socialism, never to be repeated.

For years, the leaders of the Second International had been discussing what to do in case of the outbreak of war. At their regular international congresses, the socialists were generally in agreement that the international working class should do all in its power to prevent war, with debates revolving around just how far socialists were willing to go.

In August 1907, the world's socialists met in Stuttgart, Germany, in the largest gathering ever of the movement. Nearly 900 delegates, from 25 different countries, were in attendance. The congress aimed to coordinate the work of the various socialist parties and focussed on several key themes: militarism, colonialism, women's suffrage, immigration, and the relationship between trade unions and socialist parties. Of these, the discussion of militarism was to prove the most contentious. Three different resolutions had been proposed. A commission consisting of delegates from every country present was appointed to debate this issue and it did so for five full days. On the sixth day, the entire congress also debated the question of militarism.

At the instigation of Polish-born revolutionary Rosa Luxemburg and the Russian Social Democrats Julius Martov and Vladimir Ilyich Lenin, leader of the Bolshevik wing of the Russian Social Democratic Party, the congress voted not only to struggle against war, but declared that in the event war broke out, the socialists were committed to bringing that war to a speedy end, using the political and economic crisis "to hasten the breakdown of the predominance of the capitalist class." As Lenin put it, "The essential thing is not merely to prevent war, but to utilise the crisis created by war in order to hasten the overthrow of the bourgeoisie."[2] Revolution seemed to be on the agenda.

Seven years after Stuttgart, those in attendance at the July 1914 Brussels meeting of the International Socialist Bureau were a veritable Who's Who of the European socialist movement.

They included Rosa Luxemburg and Karl Kautsky from Germany. The Socialist Party they represented was the most successful in the world, which was only as to be expected. After all, socialism was predicted to triumph first in the wealthy industrial capitalist societies like Germany, France, and Britain − countries considered "ripe" for socialism. Countries like Russia were, at the time, considered a backwater.

The German party was seen everywhere as a model. Its theoretical journal, *Die Neue Zeit*, edited by Kautsky, was where Marxists debated the issues that mattered. Kautsky himself had been nicknamed the "Pope of Marxism" and had authored the first genuinely Marxist programme for the German Social Democrats. He was the executor of Marx's and Engels' literary estates and had completed the editing of Marx's unfinished multi-volume work *Theories of Surplus Value*. In the debates within German social democracy, and in particular the fight over "revisionism" (which proposed that socialists give up the idea of revolution in favour of a slow process of reform), Kautsky defended Marxist orthodoxy. He was described in later years as "a kindly old man with a white beard", a description that seems to describe Kautsky for much of his earlier life as well.[3]

Rosa Luxemburg, born to a Jewish family in Poland, was the party's leading left-wing firebrand. Though personally close to Kautsky, Luxemburg found herself to Kautsky's left on many key questions. She was a keen advocate of the general strike (which right-wing social democrats liked to call "general *nonsense*") and a proponent of revolution. She held unorthodox views on issues like Polish independence (which she opposed), how capital accumulated (she thought Marx had got it wrong), and was also a vigorous opponent of Lenin's views on the structure of socialist parties (she feared the very dictatorship that would later turn Lenin's dream into a nightmare).

France was represented by Jean Jaurès, the leader of the *Section Française de l'Internationale Ouvrière* (SFIO), as the French Socialist Party was then known. An accomplished orator, he became fixated on the problem of militarism and war in the years leading up to 1914 and authored a book, *The New Army*, which influenced socialists around the world.

The local socialists in Belgium playing host to the meeting were represented by Emile Vandervelde and Camille Huysmans. The balding Vandervelde, who sported a pince-nez, a thick black moustache, and a grey goatee beard, was the chairman of the International Socialist Bureau and a leading figure in the *Parti Ouvrier Belge*, the Belgian Labour Party. The narrow-faced Huysmans was the secretary of the International, a post he would hold from 1905 until 1922. He was a leading figure in both the Belgian unions and the Socialist Party.

To socialists and working people across Europe, many of these were household names. The movement they headed seemed to be on an unstoppable upward trajectory toward ever-increasing numbers of supporters, more and more seats in parliaments, and a rapid climb toward political power. But they all proved to be powerless in the face of greatest war the world had ever seen.

The meeting opened on an optimistic note as Keir Hardie, who represented the British Labour Party, told delegates that it was quite out of the question that Britain would be involved in the coming war. One of the German delegates insisted that the Kaiser opposed the war because he feared the consequences. Jaurès insisted that the French government desired peace. But Austria's Victor Adler set a depressing tone as he told the delegates in Brussels that there was nothing to be done to stop the war Austria-Hungary had unleashed on Serbia in retaliation for the killing of the Archduke Franz Ferdinand in Sarajevo on 28 June that year. Socialist leaders from other parts of the Hapsburg empire (Hungarians and Czechs) agreed with Adler.

Despite the growing sense that there was nothing the socialists could do to stop the descent into war, the meeting of the Bureau was used by the local Belgian socialists to hold a rally at the Cirque Royal attended by thousands in support of peace. Demonstrators chanted "War on War!" Jaurès gave a rousing speech with his arm placed symbolically around the shoulders of his German colleague Hugo Haase. The gesture echoed the famous handshake between the Russian socialist Plekhanov and his Japanese colleague Katayama at an international socialist congress held in Amsterdam during the Russo-Japanese war of 1904–5.

But the time for gestures of this kind had passed. War was imminent and with nothing further for the socialist leaders to do, the meeting broke up after just one day.

The war that followed was nothing like what the socialist leaders, or anyone else, had imagined. Europe had just experienced something like a century of peace. Both sides in the impending conflict expected a short, sharp campaign that would result in a swift victory for their side. The German Kaiser told his soldiers as they went off to war in August, "You will be home before the leaves have fallen from the trees."[4] As Professor David Stevenson put it, "Even the direst military predictions … failed to foresee a conflict lasting four and a half years that would claim at least 10 million lives."[5]

Angelica Balabanov, representing the Italian socialists, wrote that she felt "hopelessness and despair" at the apparent inevitability of the war.[6] Rosa Luxemburg felt the same way, returning to Berlin just as the country declared war on Russia and then France.

Jaurès returned to Paris where the following day he was assassinated in a cafe. His murder marked the end of an era as one by one the socialist parties which had pledged to bring the war to a speedy end, and even to use the opportunity to overthrow the capitalist system, caved in to nationalist pressure.

The German socialists in the Reichstag voted to approve war credits on 4 August. Hugo Haase was a strong opponent of war, but he put loyalty to his party first and backed the decision. His declaration that "we won't abandon the Fatherland in the hour of danger" signified the complete abandonment by mainstream socialists of their values.[7]

Emile Vandervelde supported the Belgian government and the Allies during the war and became the country's first socialist minister. He had the full support of his comrades in the Belgian Workers' Party, which issued a manifesto on 3 August asserting the country's right to self-defence in the face of German aggression. The party called upon the Belgian working class to defend "our neutrality and the very existence of our country." The defence of Belgium, it proclaimed, was part of the fight for "the cause of democracy and political liberties in Europe … against militaristic barbarism."[8]

Victor Adler chose to publicly support Austria during the war (though he privately opposed it). His son Friedrich, meanwhile, decided to show his militant opposition to the war when in

1916 he shot and killed the minister-president of Austria in a Viennese hotel – a crime for which he was sentenced to death, but later had his sentence commuted by the emperor. The Social Democrats, led by his father, were shocked at what he had done and condemned the assassination. Friedrich Adler denounced his former comrades who had betrayed the International's opposition to war.

Not all the parties took a pro-war position. The Americans, and even the Serbian socialists stood by their pre-war commitment to struggle for peace. American socialist leader Debs went to prison as a result of his anti-war activities. In his famous Canton, Ohio speech, Debs could not have been clearer: "Every solitary one of these aristocratic conspirators and would-be murderers claims to be an arch-patriot; every one of them insists that the war is being waged to make the world safe for democracy. What humbug! What rot! What false pretense!"[9]

Even in the parties which supported their countries during the war, there were individuals who spoke out against it, including Friedrich Adler, Rosa Luxemburg and Keir Hardie. Speaking in the House of Commons as the world war broke out, Hardie, whose Labour Party now supported the war, thundered:

Our honour is said to be involved in entering into the war. That is always the excuse. I suppose our honour was involved in the Crimean War, and who to-day justifies it? Our honour was involved in the Boer War. How many to-day will justify it? A few years hence, and if we are led into this war, we shall look back in wonder and amazement at the flimsy reasons which induced the Government to take part in it.[10]

But it was not enough, and the International had ceased to exist. As Rosa Luxemburg would later write,

Violated, dishonored, wading in blood, dripping filth – there stands bourgeois society. This is it. Not all spic and span and moral, with pretense to culture, philosophy, ethics, order, peace, and the rule of law – but the ravening beast, the witches' sabbath of anarchy, a plague to culture and humanity. Thus it reveals itself in its true, its naked form. In the midst of this witches' sabbath a catastrophe of world-historical proportions has happened: *International Social Democracy has capitulated.*[11]

Six years later, with the war now over, much of Europe in ruins and in the wake of revolutions which toppled centuries-old empires in Germany, Austria-Hungary and Russia, three of the participants in that July 1914 Brussels meeting gathered together again, this time in Paris. Karl Kautsky, Emile Vandervelde and Camille Huysmans had been instructed by the newly revived International to travel across Europe to pay a visit to a country which under the leadership of Marxists was creating a new kind of society. It was a society which one member of their delegation would later describe as "the most perfect Socialism in Europe."[12]

Their journey would take them not to Russia, then under the control of Lenin and the Bolsheviks, but to the provincial backwater known as the Georgian Democratic Republic.

1

FOUNDING FATHER

Georgia is an ancient land situated on the crossroads between Europe and Asia. To its north is the Caucasus mountain range; to its west is the Black Sea. Its neighbours today include Russia, Azerbaijan, Armenia and Turkey. For centuries, powerful empires fought over it, including the Ottomans and Persians, and it was not until 1783 that Georgians could finally feel a degree of safety. In that year King Erekle II signed a treaty with the Russian empress Catherine the Great which turned this proud country into a Russian protectorate. Eighteen years later, the Russians decided to extend that protection without asking anyone's permission, and annexed Georgia. From then onwards it was a province of their vast and growing empire.

Though deprived of their statehood, for more than a century Georgians could feel relatively secure knowing that a Russian army stood between them and their neighbours. But the country also suffered because it was a remote outpost of the empire, and the vast majority of its inhabitants lived in poor rural communities. Nevertheless, as Russia itself began to slowly modernise during the nineteenth century, so did Georgia - fuelled in part by the discovery of oil in neighbouring Azerbaijan. The oil pipeline from

Baku to the Georgian port of Batumi and the railways that spanned the Transcaucasian region began to transform the country.[1]

In 1868, in the small village of Lanchkhuti in the province of Guria in western Georgia, a baby son was born to the Zhordania family.[2] His name was Noe and he would go on to become the leader of the Georgian socialists and later the president of his country. But at the time of his birth, Zhordania's family lived in a modest one-storey wooden house with a covered porch, built on a stone platform. In 1990, after the collapse of communism, Zhordania's son Redjeb returned from France, where his family had gone into exile in 1921. He paid a visit to Lanshkhuti. All that remained of the house was the stone base and a magnolia, which according to local legend Noe Zhordania himself had planted.

Noe Zhordania described the backwardness of the province in which he was born. "All the villagers in Lanshkhuti, and probably all the Gurians, had a fantasmatic view of the world," he wrote. "They were convinced that the universe was populated by invisible beings that were constantly fighting against the humans and confusing them as to their destiny. And who were these beings? They were demons, devils, monsters, ghouls, incubus, succubus, witches, warlocks and many others."[3]

Like so many other Georgian revolutionaries, including a young Stalin several years later, Zhordania escaped village life by enrolling in the Tiflis Seminary, where he trained to be a priest.[4] But the young Noe was already starting to have his doubts about religion and the monarchy. He read illegal publications and like many other young students across the Russian empire, he fell under the influence of the Narodniks, the populist rebels who were the forerunners of Russia's modern socialist movement. The Narodniks were already being challenged by the likes of

Georgi Plekhanov, who introduced Russians to the writings of Karl Marx. In Georgia, intellectuals got hold of and began to read Marx's *Das Kapital*. In 1886, a favourable review of Volume II of the book appeared in a Georgian journal called *Teatri*. Plekhanov's writings too began to be circulated in Tiflis.

It became clear that the young Zhordania was never going to become a priest and instead he travelled to Poland to study veterinary science in Warsaw. There he was introduced to the writings of Karl Kautsky. Zhordania was hooked, his faith in the Narodnik world view now completely shattered. He no longer believed that Russia's salvation would come from the peasants, and he welcomed the growth of capitalism in the country. He rejected the Narodnik insistence that the leaders of the revolution would come from an intelligentsia that would "go to the people," and he dismissed their conviction that a new socialist society could easily grow out of the village communes, without passing through a modern capitalist phase. "I now realized for the first time," he wrote, "that Russian socialism was a thoroughly utopian and reactionary movement, and that if it should ever be put into operation anywhere, we should be plunged back into barbarism."[5]

In Warsaw, Zhordania found himself in a Western setting for the very first time, and encountered an industrial working class he would not have found in his impoverished homeland. He also discovered Polish nationalism and anti-Russian sentiment on a scale he had not experienced in Georgia. He began thinking about revolution, the working class and the national question. "In subjugated countries there must first of all take place a political revolution," he wrote. "Democracy must be established first, and only afterwards, by the furtherance of economic progress and by extensive organizational work, can we proceed towards social revolution."[6]

In just a few words, Zhordania had summed up the essence of what would later become known as "Menshevism" - the view that in a backward country like Russia or Georgia, first of all democracy needed to be established, and only later would a social revolution come. As historian David Lang wrote, "the achievement of democratic socialism through the agency of a mass of benighted *muzhiks* [peasants] seemed to the young Zhordania a highly dubious undertaking."[7]

Zhordania also rejected Georgian separatism, believing that Russians, Poles and Georgians needed to work together to overthrow tsarism. This was a view he shared with Rosa Luxemburg, whose opposition to Polish nationalism put her in a small minority in her home country. The rejection of separatism among the Georgian Social Democrats grew so strong that eventually their speeches to peasant audiences would end with "'Down with Georgia! Long live the Russian Social-Democratic Workers' Party!'"[8]

While in Warsaw, Zhordania set up a socialist group for the Georgian students living there, among them his friend Pilipe Makharadze. Makharadze, like Zhordania, was born in 1868 in the province of Guria, had studied at the Tiflis Seminary and had been radicalised. Zhordania and Makharadze worked together for years, but their paths would part later when the latter joined the Bolsheviks. While in Warsaw, Zhordania also corresponded with comrades back home, including Sylvester Jibladze and the writer Egnate Ninoshvili, to whom he sent subversive literature.

In August 1892, the twenty-four-year-old Zhordania returned to Georgia. There, he and a couple of close friends founded the organisation that would become the country's first Marxist group, known as *mesame dasi* (Third Group). The group had its first meeting in December of that year, organised by Ninoshvili and held in Zestafoni, in western Georgia.

Zhordania's attempts to persuade the group – which was still under the influence of the Narodniks – to embrace Marxism failed at first. He decided to write a comprehensive analysis of Georgia from a Marxist perspective entitled "Economic Progress and the National Question." He presented this to the group in February 1893 at their meeting in Tiflis. This time, Zhordania's view won unanimous support. But Zhordania couldn't stick around to lead the organisation whose loyalty he now commanded.

After just nine months in the country, the young radical was warned that he faced imminent arrest by the tsarist authorities, leading him to flee to Europe in May 1893. In retrospect, his flight was fortuitous, and during his four-year stay in Europe he managed to meet many key figures in the European socialist movement.

Zhordania's travels took the young Georgian Marxist to Switzerland, where he met emigre Russians including Georgi Plekhanov and Vera Zasulich. A couple of years later he travelled to Paris, where he met the French socialist firebrand Jules Guesde and Karl Marx's son-in-law, Paul Lafargue. He also travelled to Stuttgart, where he visited Karl Kautsky, who became a great supporter of the young Georgian socialist movement.

"Kautsky," Zhordania recalled, "made a deep impression on me by his modesty, simplicity, clarity of thought and great knowledge."[9] One of the more colourful characters Zhordania met in Germany was Alexander Helphand, known as Parvus, who would later play a key role in efforts by the German High Command to take Russia out of the First World War using Lenin and the Bolsheviks. By 1897, Zhordania was in London where, like Marx several decades earlier, he was a regular visitor to the British Museum. His reports for newspapers in Tiflis were quite favourable, and in them he contrasted the London "bobbies" with their Russian counterparts.

Upon his return to Georgia in 1897, Zhordania assumed a leading position in the Social Democratic Party which had grown out of *mesame dasi*.[10] Based on what Zhordania and others had learned in their travels, the focus of the group was now primarily on organising the growing urban working class in Tiflis, Batumi and other cities. The Marxist position was triumphant. No longer focussed on the peasants, the Social Democrats were busy organising study circles and strikes among Georgia's small urban working class.

Zhordania's experience of village life in Lanshkhuti seemed to be part of a distant past. Little did he or anyone else expect that within a few short years, the Social Democrats would be leading an extraordinary revolutionary battle not of industrial workers, but of that "mass of benighted muzhiks" in Zhordania's birthplace, Guria.

2

DRESS REHEARSAL

During the nearly seven decades that separated the publication of the *Communist Manifesto* in 1848 and the Russian Revolution in 1917, there were only two examples of socialists seizing political power and attempting to realise their vision of a new society. One was the Paris Commune of 1871, which Marx and later Lenin described as a kind of prototype for a future socialist society. The other was the "Gurian Republic" of 1902–6, widely known at the time but utterly forgotten today.[1]

This is understandable. Paris was perhaps the most important city on the European continent in 1871, and the events that took place there were naturally the focus of international attention. Guria, on the other hand, was a desperately poor district in western Georgia, then a poor province on the borders of the Russian empire. But the Gurian Republic is worthy of some attention not only because it offered an example of popular revolutionary self-government like the Paris Commune, but also because it foreshadowed the later triumph of democratic socialists throughout Georgia.

Though the Paris Commune may not be as well remembered today, back in 1871 and for decades thereafter it was seen as a historical watershed. The "Second Empire" of Napoleon III had been defeated by Prussia in a short war, the emperor had fallen into the hands of the victorious Germans, and a republic was proclaimed in Versailles. But in Paris, a restive population had taken power into its own hands, creating an experiment in participatory democracy the likes of which the world had never seen.[2]

The commune was run by a council whose delegates could be immediately recalled by electors, and who combined legislative with executive functions. In the few weeks of its existence, the commune passed a number of reforms, including banning night work in bakeries, separating church and state, and allowing workers to take direct control of businesses abandoned by their owners. It is estimated that around 10,000 *Communards* lost their lives defending their experiment in social democracy, in a week of fighting against troops of the French Republic known as "*la semaine sanglante.*"

The Paris Commune lasted barely ten weeks, and though its leaders and martyrs were publicly defended by Marx, they were by and large not Marxists themselves. In the months and years following the violent suppression of the commune, much was made in the right-wing press of the role of Marx and the First International which he founded and led. But as Marx was the first to acknowledge, he had little influence over, let alone control of, the Communards in Paris.

This did not prevent Marx from hailing their heroism and highlighting the world-historic importance of their bold attempt to create a new society. Marx's close friend and partner Friedrich Engels once used the example of the Paris Commune to answer critics of the concept of the "dictatorship of the proletariat," a phrase which appears only a few times in Marx's writings. Engels wanted to make it clear that Marx never called for anything like the dictatorships of his time – or the even more horrific ones which followed in the twentieth century. The "dictatorship of the proletariat" that Engels imagined would include free elections, an accountable government, freedom of speech and association.

Twenty years after the fall of the Paris Commune, he wrote: "do you want to know what this dictatorship looks like? Look at the Paris Commune. That was the dictatorship of the proletariat."[3]

Barely a decade after Engels wrote those words, and 3,000 kilometres away from Paris, the Gurian Republic was born, led by an orthodox Marxist party. Instead of a few weeks, it lasted for several years. As a test of Marxism in theory and practice, it can be argued that it was even more important than the Paris Commune. And unlike the Paris Commune, the Gurian experiment had a second act.

The brutal suppression of the Communards ensured that right-wing parties would continue to rule France for many decades afterwards. The Gurian Republic, on the other hand, prefigured Georgia's experiment with democratic socialism little more than a decade after its violent suppression by the tsarist government.

By the time the French Left finally came to power under the Popular Front in the 1930s, the Paris Commune was a distant, if revered, memory. But the socialists who led the Georgian Democratic Republic in 1918, among them the head of government Noe Zhordania, the interior minister Noe Ramishvili, and the minister of agriculture Noe Khomeriki, were natives of Guria and applied lessons learned there.

The Gurian Republic had its origins, as revolutions often do, in a minor affair, beginning in May 1902 in the village of Nigoiti with a dispute over grazing rights. How it began and who led it ensured that this would be no ordinary peasant rebellion, of which there had been plenty in the tsarist empire.

The Gurian peasants suffered from an acute land hunger. As a popular saying went, "If I tie up a cow on my bit of land, her tail will be in someone else's!"[4] As a result, many Gurian peasants were compelled to take occasional jobs in cities, including Russian towns like Odessa and Rostov. Some of them had been working in the nearby Georgian seaside town of Batumi and had participated in strikes there, organised and led by the Social Democrats. The tsarist authorities crushed those strikes and expelled some of the strikers from the city. They returned to their villages in Guria and back at home they incited the peasants to action. It is possible that they were also inspired by peasant rebellions in other parts of the empire, including in Ukraine, Tambov and Saratov. In any event, their political education in Batumi was certainly a factor in their rebellious frame of mind.

The result was a mass meeting in Nigoiti of some 700 peasants who drew up a list of demands that included free grazing rights, a reduction in rent, and no more payments – known as *drami* – to local priests. They then agreed on an oath of secrecy, which was a common feature of these kinds of meetings. Other meetings followed, and the movement started to spread across the province. Even though the Gurian peasants were keen to stop paying their priests, they were not anti-clerical or anti-tsarist at this stage. They remained wedded to a mystical way of thinking and tended to treat the emerging revolutionary committees, which were led by the Social Democrats, as holy bodies. One Georgian social democrat described a meeting he attended of some 700 peasants as "semi-religious." The meeting ended as propagandists held an icon of sorts in their hands.

Another meeting was led by a priest, and the participants stood before a cross and bible.

When news of the first peasant meetings reached the Social Democrats in the nearest towns, Batumi and Kutaisi, most of the party leaders were indifferent. Some were even hostile. Karlo Chkheidze, the future leader of the early Soviets and chairman of the Georgian parliament, dismissed the rebellion by saying "we cannot have a peasant movement under our banners."[5]

But Noe Zhordania was a native of Guria. He immediately grasped the significance of the unrest in the province. The poor peasants, he said, were no different from other workers. Zhordania's sympathy for the Gurian peasants was to prove decisive not only over the course of the next four years of revolution, but also during the period of Georgian independence which was to come. It flew in the face of traditional Marxist indifference or even hostility toward the peasants, who were seen as a reactionary class. The view embraced by Zhordania and the party he led was eventually adopted by Lenin as well, and turned out to be critical to the Bolsheviks' later success. In a backward country like Georgia (or Russia), only if the peasants were viewed as workers, and allied to the urban proletariat, could the revolution triumph.

The Gurian peasants were not the ones caricatured by vulgar Marxists, fond of citing Marx's reference to "the idiocy of rural life."[6] These peasants had a very high degree of literacy, and more schools per head than Georgia's urban centres. Every Gurian village had a library of its own, and a regular postal service ensured that villages received deliveries of newspapers not only from the Georgian capital Tiflis, but also from Russia.

Many children of Gurian peasants went on to study in the city of Kutaisi, then a hotbed of revolutionary sentiment. When the students would strike, as was often the case during the turbulent years leading up to 1905, the authorities would send them back to their villages. In the villages, with their many schools, there were also a disproportionate number of teachers, who were often sympathetic to the revolutionaries. The tsarist authorities were suspicious of those teachers, and in the first round of arrests in 1902 teachers made up the largest single group of those jailed.

The Gurians, like others on the margins of the tsarist empire, also had a long tradition of resistance to imperial rule. The nineteenth century saw at least three armed rebellions in the province.

In the first decade of the twentieth century, the Gurians therefore had several key ingredients in place to become the focus of revolutionary activity. The rebellion which began in the village of Nigoiti soon spread across the province. Within a year, half of Guria was involved, and by 1904 twenty of the twenty-five rural societies were participating in boycotts and other measures.

The Russian authorities responded with repression. There were at least 300 arrests and the governor of Kutaisi warned of the "severest measures." Among those arrested, many of whom were sent into Siberian exile, were the Social Democrat leaders Zhordania and Khomeriki. But the repression did not succeed in restoring order and if anything contributed to increasing violence – in particular, terror, arson and blackmail – on the part of the rebellious Gurian peasants. Meanwhile, word of the rebellion was spreading far beyond the borders of Guria. Even *Iskra*, Lenin's underground newspaper published abroad and smuggled into Russia, began to run extensive accounts of what was happening in Red Guria.

A year into the rebellion, in May 1903, the Social Democrats in western Georgia held a conference, and took a stand firmly in support of the peasants. They formed several committees, one of which was called the committee of "agricultural workers" for Guria. The choice of words was important. This was an attempt to re-brand the peasants as "workers" and was a significant step for an orthodox Marxist party which had historically been focussed almost exclusively on the urban working class.

Not long after that conference, Gurian Social Democrat leaders including Noe Ramishvili, who would later be the first head of government of independent Georgia, and Noe Khomeriki, the future architect of independent Georgia's land reform, met to discuss a number of issues. One of those was the use of terror against the authorities, which as Marxists they were against. The Marxists had historically opposed individual acts of terror which an earlier generation of Russian revolutionaries including the Narodniks had embraced. Though the Bolsheviks would later engage in various forms of terrorism, particularly in Georgia, the Georgian Social Democrats were adamant on this point. Class struggle, not terrorism, was how they intended to overthrow tsarism and create a new society.

The peasants were not at all happy with the condemnation of terror but eventually accepted their leaders' arguments.[7] None-theless, terror, and in particular arson, continued to be sporadically employed.

At this time all Russian Social Democrats, including those in Georgia, agreed that under the conditions of tsarist rule, a Social Democratic Party would of necessity be a relatively small one, consisting primarily of the urban working class. They disagreed over precisely who could be members of such a party, and what the responsibilities of membership entailed, but no one could imagine a mass-based socialist party in Russia any time soon, let alone one with thousands of peasants as members. And yet that is precisely what began to happen in Guria.

Initially, the Georgian Social Democrats rejected this new model. They decided to set up two parallel organisations, one for the rebellious peasants, the other for proper Social Democrats. Regional organisations were established across the province, with a Gurian Social Democratic Committee at the top. Each village held a "People's Meeting," a form of direct democracy. But the peasants were not happy at being excluded from the party, and Khomeriki among others argued that it was impractical to maintain two separate structures. He insisted that the peasants be allowed to join the party en masse, and by November 1905, the Third Congress of the Social Democrats in Guria confirmed the transformation of their party from a small, elitist group based on urban workers into a mass party of the people. Later efforts, after the collapse of the 1905 revolution, to "purify" the party and purge it of "petit bourgeois elements" failed in Guria, where the Social Democrats were to remain a mass, and largely peasant-based, party for the next two decades.

In August 1903, the Russian Social Democrats held their party congress in western Europe (they could not meet in Russia, where the party remained illegal). At the congress, which lasted for more than three weeks and which took place first in Brussels, then in London, the party split.

One faction, headed by Lenin, was convinced of the need for a small, illegal organisation of professional revolutionaries working under an iron party discipline. The other faction, headed by Julius Martov, was more inclined to support a mass Social Democratic party such as already existed in Germany and other European countries. At the time, Plekhanov, the grand old man of Russian socialism, supported Lenin. Trotsky supported the Mensheviks. In later years, both men would switch sides.

The atmosphere at the meeting was toxic. As Lenin described one incident: "Martov then got up and, in his own name and that of his colleagues, declined to stand for election, uttering all sorts of dreadful and wretched words about a 'state of siege in the Party' ... and 'emergency laws against particular individuals and groups'."[8]

At the time of the split, the differences between Lenin and Martov were quite small, but these grew over the next few years. Despite many attempts to bring the two factions back together, the split eventually became permanent.

Lenin's faction was known as the Bolsheviks (from the Russian word for majority) and Martov's group was known as the Mensheviks (from the word for minority). Following the Bolshevik seizure of power in November 1917, the split became extremely acrimonious and spread far beyond Russia's borders. Eventually, socialists in all countries had to choose sides between what became known as Communist parties (successors to Lenin's Bolsheviks) and Socialist parties, sometimes known as "democratic socialists" or "social democrats." Following that initial 1903 split, the Georgians under Zhordania's leadership sided overwhelmingly with the Mensheviks. There were a few Georgian Bolsheviks, Stalin and Makharadze among them. But on one question at least, the Georgian Mensheviks seemed to side with Lenin: the potential of the peasants as a revolutionary class.

While the Social Democrats grappled with questions of party membership, the nature of the peasantry and so on, the revolution in Guria continued to spread. By 1904, the province was already no longer in any meaningful sense under the control of the tsarist authorities. This reality was recognised at the national level by the

Mensheviks in their decision at the height of the 1905 revolution to endorse the idea of "revolutionary self-government." They did so because revolutionary self-government, then emerging in different parts of the Russian empire, had already been a reality in Guria for nearly three years. Guria had become an island of democracy in the autocratic Russian empire.

Long before the outbreak of revolution across the Russian empire, the Gurian Social Democrats were already taking bold steps toward revolutionary self-government. At their Second Conference, they voted to extend the boycotts which had targeted landowners and now focussed on the tsarist government and the church as well, calling for the "revolutionary seizure" of landowners' and government lands.

They were doing all this nearly two years into their rebellion at a time when most parts of the vast Russian empire were still in the iron grip of the despotic tsarist regime and its feared secret police, known as the Okhrana. It was only a year later, in January 1905, following the events of "Bloody Sunday" in the imperial capital, St Petersburg, when soldiers massacred unarmed protestors, that revolution exploded across the empire. The details of what actually happened on that cold January day in St Petersburg are still not entirely clear, but it seems that soldiers of the tsar's Imperial Guard fired upon demonstrators led by radical priest (and secret agent of the Okhrana) Father Gapon. The demonstrators had assembled to present a petition to the tsar demanding an end to the war with Japan, labour reforms and universal suffrage. Somewhere between 96 and 4,000 protestors were killed. The massacre shocked people across the country, and triggered strikes and protests throughout the empire.

The Gurians were years ahead of the rest of the country, though the 1905 revolution gave everyone else a chance to catch up. By the end of that revolutionary year, the tsarist regime was tottering.

A structure had already existed in Guria since the emancipation of the serfs four decades earlier which provided the basis for their revolutionary self-government. This structure consisted of such institutions as the village meeting and peasant courts. The village meeting sometimes doubled as a court and constituted the supreme authority. From the beginning, the vote was extended to women. Alexandra Kollontai, who later became a prominent Bolshevik, wrote: "The Guria peasant women at village meetings in the Kutaisi province adopted resolutions demanding political equality with men."[9]

One foreign journalist who visited Guria at the time, Luigi Villari, was extremely impressed with the People's Courts. Though the death penalty had not been abolished (this would not happen until Georgia broke free of Russian rule in 1918), it was never used. The preferred form of punishment was the boycott, the exclusion of the convicted person from village life. That said, the People's Courts, though certainly free of some of the corruption and cruelty of the tsarist courts, were hardly models of a more humane and liberal system, as will be seen below. But they were enormously popular, and very quickly the locals stopped using Russian courts entirely, with the Russian criminal justice system collapsing as the disempowered police no longer carried out arrests.

The institution created by the peasants was known as the "*narodny sud*" (popular tribunal). Despite the absence of an effective police force or criminal courts, "brigandage and robbery have greatly decreased in the region," Villari wrote.[10] Such crimes had previously been quite common and justice was rarely dispensed by the tsarist police and courts. In the absence of "brigandage and robbery" the courts increasingly inquired "into the private morals of the inhabitants."[11]

Villari gave examples of their judgments which impressed him, several of these revolving around adultery. This focus on adultery was, in his view, a peasant reaction against the "loose morals" of the Russians. "Any man committing adultery or living with a mistress," wrote Villari, "is liable to prosecution and punishment."[12]

In addition to the boycotts, "other curious forms of punishment have also been introduced," Villari noted.

> A peasant of the district of Sharopany having committed adultery with a woman of the place, he and his paramour were summoned before the Narodny Sud. They pleaded guilty, and were condemned to ride through the village stark-naked on the back of a donkey; during their progress they proclaimed their sin before all the assembled villagers, declared their contrition, and vowed to lead a pure life in future.[13]

Villari managed to attend one sitting of a popular tribunal in a village called Ekhadia. The meeting consisted of some 200 people, both men and women, mostly peasants but with a few "intellectuals" as well. There were none of the formal trappings of a courtroom, neither judge nor lawyers nor prosecutors. One of the participants was elected to chair the meeting, but had no particular power. Every participant had the right to speak and to vote.

At issue was the case of a merchant from Guria's largest town, Ozurgeti. He had been found guilty of committing adultery at a previous sitting of the tribunal, and sentenced to its most severe punishment: perpetual boycott. After several weeks of this, he could bear it no longer and was appealing the sentence.

Villari described the merchant as tall, about forty years old, his beard and hair tinged with grey, wearing a very sad expression on his face. "I admit my sin," he told the members of the community, and even admitted that the punishment had been just, but insisted that he felt remorse and promised in future to lead a virtuous life. Perpetual boycott was, he felt, an even harsher sentence than the death penalty and he could not bear it.

The audience listened attentively to his appeal and there followed a long discussion. Speakers came out on both sides, with some talking about the man's past history of adultery, and insisting that he was too old to reform. But others supported his appeal and according to Villari, "quoted obscure German philosophers" (one wonders which ones) and "Socialist writers" on the subject of a scientific approach to the man's sin and his repentance. After an hour, a vote was taken and the appeal accepted. The adulterous merchant was re-admitted to his community. One of Villari's friends, proud of what had happened, asked the writer: "Is it not better to be tried in this way than by three scoundrels in black robes?"[14]

When the village meetings were not hearing cases of adultery, they were busy creating new laws, such as bans on expensive funerals and weddings, or drunkenness. The ban on drunkenness was a common feature of peasant rebellions at the time. Historian Stephen F. Jones writes: "Such 'puritanism' was characteristic of other rebellious peasant communities in 1905. The peasant assembly of Rakitinskaia volost' in the Ukraine, for example, ordered an end to drunkenness and theft. Liquor stores were frequently closed or even burnt down to prevent drunkenness undermining the social discipline required for successful self-government."[15]

The meetings discussed curricula for the schools, and the appointment of teachers. According to Villari, "native schools have taken the place of Russian ones, and the children are taught the three R's combined with Socialist principles in the Georgian tongue."[16] In some villages, religious ceremonies were replaced with secular ones. The peasants worked together, in shifts, to maintain the provincial infrastructure including roads and bridges.

By the time revolution had broken out across the empire in 1905, the village meetings in Guria had become well-established weekly affairs. One of those who witnessed them was Nikolai Marr, who was a Guria native himself. Marr became an important linguist in Soviet times, though after his death Stalin famously attacked him in his book *Marxism and Problems of Linguistics*. Marr was amazed at "the intense public life in the villages."

> Meeting follows meeting, and you would be surprised how the peasants, burdened by their work in the fields, hurrying everywhere, take active part in the debates, sitting for long hours, sometimes days, at meetings. Today the court, tomorrow discussion of the principal social questions with a well-known travelling speaker, the day after tomorrow decisions about local affairs: schools, road, land, etc., etc.[17]

According to Marr's account of such village meetings, workers from the cities played the most active roles in the debates. The Gurian peasants were mostly concerned with day-to-day matters and were largely indifferent to national questions, which the Social Democrats helped them to interpret. For example, after the "Bloody Sunday" massacre in January 1905, Gurian peasants decided to refuse to pray for the imperial family, and destroyed portraits of the tsar.

By the end of 1904, before the revolution broke out across the rest of the Russian empire, the Social Democrats led the Gurian peasants in the organisation of "Red Detachments." These armed self-defence forces were financed by a tax on villagers and effectively displaced the tsarist army and police in the province. They trained in the art of insurrection, learning how to construct barricades and rob trains. According to a Soviet-era history of the 1905 revolution in Georgia written half a century later, one former member of the Red Detachments recalled special missions such as one to Tiflis in December 1905 to aid the workers' uprising there.[18]

Villari's friends in Guria had complete confidence that the Red Detachments could withstand an attack by the tsarist army. "I was told," he recounted, "of frequent gatherings of thousands of armed Gurians who practice military manoeuvres, shooting, and other warlike exercises, including ambulance service. Gun-running is carried on extensively both over the Turkish frontier and by sea, and the Gurians have even sometimes got hold of Government stores of arms."[19]

The "Red Detachments" were probably more impressive on paper than in reality, and while a few hundred armed men could be effective against local landowners, they would turn out to be no match for the tsar's army.

By 1905, with the entire Russian empire in turmoil, the tsarist authorities in Georgia began to turn their attention to crushing the Gurian Republic. The procurator of the Kutaisi District Tribunal complained to his superior in Tiflis about Guria on 2 February of that year:

> Over the past fortnight the situation in the Ozurgeti district has begun to deteriorate so rapidly that at present virtually complete

anarchy prevails there. The entire territory of the region is now completely in the hands of the Committee and its agents, and only where a substantial armed detachment of police guards or cossacks make their appearance is the influence of our government momentarily restored.[20]

Five days after the procurator sent this letter, Lieutenant-General Malama, who the Russians had left in charge of the Caucasian provinces, telegraphed the minister of the interior in St Petersburg, writing:

> The situation in the Ozurgeti district and the surrounding areas is assuming the character of a rebellion, finding expression in open defiance of authority, the murder of government officials, squires, priests and persons not in sympathy with the revolutionary movement. The population is repudiating the oath of allegiance to the crown and pledging fidelity to the revolutionary committee. Officers of the government are fleeing. All measures hitherto taken, including the co-operation of the army, have failed to produce any results.[21]

Malama decided to send a strong force of troops into Guria, ordering Major-General Alikhanov-Avarsky to put an end to unrest in the province, and giving him artillery to help carry out his task. But before Alikhanov had a chance to attack the rebels, his expedition was cancelled. The tsar had appointed a new viceroy for the region, the liberal Count Illarion Ivanovich Vorontsov-Dashkov, who decided that what was needed was a fact-finding mission.

Vorontsov-Dashkov was later described by Pilipe Makharadze as the "most sensible representative of autocracy in Caucasia" and his liberal reputation was deserved. He appointed the liberal Privy Counsellor Prince N.A. Sultan Krym-Girey to head off to Guria and report back on what he learned. Krym-Girey had been a prominent member of the Caucasian Society for Agriculture, and was "considered suitable for the job on account of both his non-Russian descent and connections and his opinions."[22]

Even before Vorontsov-Dashkov arrived in the region to take up his post as viceroy, Krym-Girey was off to Guria to find out what he could, with a number of journalists from the major newspapers coming along on the trip. From the point of view of the tsarist regime, Krym-Girey's tour was a disaster. Part of the reason for this was that reporting restrictions had been lifted and journalists were free to write about what they saw. In the tsarist empire, this was a new phenomenon, as there had never been a free press. Liberal politicians like Vorontsov-Dashkov and Krym-Girey were experimenting with trying to open things up a bit, an early version of glasnost. The experiment failed, however, as the opposition Social Democrats seized the opportunity to get their message out to a much wider audience, and not only in Guria. In those parts of the country not yet gripped by rebellion, a spark was ignited. Even the eastern part of Georgia, now informed for the first time about what had been happening in Guria, was soon in turmoil.

Peasants speaking at meetings attended by the prince were often surprisingly articulate, their demands combining local concerns with broader political matters. Before Krym-Girey arrived, the local peasants met and chose delegates to address him. When he appeared, they would engage in the formality of an "election." The delegates chosen to be the local spokespeople were invariably reliable Social Democrats. But it was not only the trained Social Democratic leadership who spoke – as Jones tells it, "Spontaneous interventions by peasants at the meetings show many were politically sophisticated."[23]

At one such meeting in Jvartsma, attended by 1,000 peasants, a list of fifteen demands was presented. In addition to purely local issues, the list also included such things as the formation of a constituent assembly, freedom of speech and assembly, separation of church and state, free compulsory education and the abolition of the standing army. Though a liberal himself, Krym-Girey was shocked by all this, and said that the French Republic's own constitution would not have satisfied the Gurians, which was true.

The demands varied from village to village. In Bakhvi, government taxes were a top priority, while in many villages there was strong resentment against conscription. However, the one thing that was strangely absent in the demands was Georgian nationalism or any kind of anti-Russian sentiment. The Gurian peasants, like the Georgian Social Democratic movement as a whole, were happy to remain part of the same country as their Russian brethren. As Zhordania himself recalled, the Georgians welcomed the presence of the Russian army, if not the tsarist officials, as a way of keeping the country safe from the neighbouring Turks. Though the Gurians clearly wanted more local autonomy, no one was dreaming of an independent Georgian state – yet.

Sultan Krym-Girey reported back to his superiors, suggesting that some concessions needed to be made to the peasants. But no one was listening, as revolution was now spreading across the Russian heartland. The tsarist regime had decided to hit back, and the days of the Gurian Republic were numbered.

The new viceroy, whose choice of Krym-Girey did little to strengthen tsarist rule in Georgia, made another odd choice in mid-1905. Instead of naming a hard-liner to crush the insurgency in Guria, he appointed Vladimir Aleksandrovich Starosel'skii, a forty-five-year-old liberal, as the new governor of Kutaisi province. The son of a judge, Starosel'skii was a trained agronomist, having graduated from the Moscow Agricultural Academy. He moved to Georgia in 1888, where he participated in a programme to eliminate phylloxeras – an aphid-like insect that attacks grape vines. As Georgia then (and now) was famous for its vineyards, this was a very important mission.

Starosel'skii heard the warnings from the tsarist police that things had been out of control in Guria for too long. The head of the police in Kutaisi reported that the revolutionary movement resembled "a huge cauldron filled with water and hermetically sealed and suspended above an enormous furnace. Beyond a doubt, when the sides of the cauldron can no longer withstand the pressure of the steam which is formed by the heating of the water and has no other outlet, they will burst into splinters and fly in all directions as a result of the force of the blast." [24]

The tsarist police were often the only ones with a true grasp of what was going on, but Starosel'skii ignored their warnings and allowed the Gurians to do as they wished for most of 1905. He did not merely adopt a hands-off attitude. According to some reports, he released prisoners, attended meetings with revolutionaries, and even travelled in trains under the protection of the Social Democratic committees. According to official Soviet sources writing years later, "He used his position to aid the revolutionary movement and was nicknamed the Red Governor."[25]

As the revolutionary year of 1905 drew to a close, all of western Georgia was in the hands of the revolutionaries. No train passed through the province without the permission of the Social Democratic committee. Attempts by tsarist troops to restore order were defeated by the rebels. In a clash at Nasakirali, a platoon of Cossacks was pinned down for two days by as many as 4,000 rebels.

By October, even the liberal viceroy had had enough and ordered General Alikhanov to crush the Gurians. But Starosel'skii and others protested and the troops were withdrawn. For the Gurians, it was too good to last. Starosel'skii was removed from his post as governor of Kutaisi in January 1906.

Starosel'skii wound up in Ekaterinburg, far from the Caucasus, and was briefly secretary of the local Social Democratic committee there. Later, he was a delegate to the Fourth Congress of the Social Democrats, held in Stockholm, where it is likely he met Stalin, who also attended the meeting. In 1908, he escaped Russia, fleeing to Paris, where he joined the Bolsheviks in exile. He wrote books on the history of the revolutionary movement and viticulture, and died in obscurity in 1916.

Count Vorontsov-Dashkov had made two disastrous appointments with the liberals Krym-Girey and Starosel'skii. One had managed in the course of a fact-finding mission to unintentionally spread the Gurian rebellion to other provinces; the other had earned the nickname of the "Red Governor." But this was soon to change.

The Moscow uprising had ended in defeat in December 1905 and the revolution was in retreat across the Russian empire. A workers' uprising in Tiflis had also been defeated. It was finally time for the regime to unleash General Alikhanov, described as "famous as a crusher of revolt," and his men against Guria.[26] The whole of Kutaisi province was given over to his command, with the "Red Governor" sent packing.

Alikhanov gave orders to disband the revolutionary committees, destroy the Red Detachments and shoot anyone who resisted. The Gurian Social Democrats decided to make a stand at the Surami Pass where a railway tunnel passed under the mountains.

But they failed to hold Alikhanov's forces back, and the tsarist troops began the re-conquest of Guria at the beginning of 1906. At this point, Alikhanov issued a seventeen-point declaration demanding, among other things, "the return of all monies unpaid, the rebuilding of all burnt government offices, an end to the boycott and the surrender of all revolutionaries."[27]

Alikhanov was a merciless conqueror. As one Social Democratic newspaper reported at the time, "It is terrible in Guria today. The town of Ozurgeti no longer exists … in the villages, hundreds of houses are in ashes … The soldiers plunder the villages by day and night."[28] The Russians had entered Guria with nearly twenty battalions of troops, twenty-six cannon and a squadron of Cossacks. The Red Detachments were no match for them.

Though there does not appear to have been a formal surrender at any stage, the Social Democratic committees, which still dominated the peasant masses, urged the peasants to cease resistance. The Social Democratic newspaper *elva* wrote: "The Gurian who had proudly resisted the bureaucracy's every unconscionable act today hangs his head and with a tricolored flag, a picture of the sovereign, and with 'bread and salt' greets his bloody enemy."[29]

By the end of March 1906, the Gurian Republic no longer existed. Some 300 rebel leaders were deported to Siberia. The peasants remained strong supporters of the Social Democrats, voting for them when they could, and in some cases standing up to unimaginable repression at the hands of the tsarist authorities. In one village, local residents were flogged for twenty days by the invading soldiers, but never revealed the names of their leaders.

The Gurian Republic, like the Paris Commune three decades earlier, ended in the victory of reaction, with a bloodbath. But unlike the commune, it turned out to be a harbinger for a much larger experiment in "revolutionary self-government," one that would last for several years and take place across an entire country. Neither the Communards in Paris nor the Social Democrats in Guria created a utopian society, nor were they trying to. Both groups spent much of their time trying to survive, facing the inevitability of invasion by far larger military forces. In the end, the achievements of both were modest. The Paris Commune handed some abandoned factories and work-shops to the workers, banned night work in bakeries, separated church and state, and paid public officials a worker's wage – and that was it.

The Gurians helped to solve the land problem by redistributing land directly to the peasants, and curtailed the power of the tsarist state and the church. They instituted a kind of direct democracy in the villages, with their weekly meetings. They established a system of justice which while primitive was nevertheless an improvement over the previous regime. They created a public space for women to air their views, help set the agenda, and vote. These were no small accomplishments, particularly as most of them happened at a time when the tsarist regime was still strong, long before the 1905 revolution.

More than a decade after the crushing of the Gurian Republic, Lenin was preoccupied with thinking about the question of the state. His short book, *State and Revolution*, summed up his views. He discussed the Paris Commune at some length, but had nothing to say about Guria. This doesn't mean, however, that Lenin was unfamiliar with the Gurian experience.

In an Afterword Lenin wrote that he had planned a chapter on the experiences of the 1905 and 1917 Russian revolutions. "But apart from the title," he wrote, "I had not succeeded in writing a single line of the chapter" due to the revolution. "Such a hindrance," he added, "can only be welcomed."[30]

It seems unlikely that Lenin would have said much about Guria in any event. His bitterness toward the Mensheviks was by this stage quite pronounced. A detailed account of the Gurian Republic might not only cast the Mensheviks in a positive light, but could show where they and Lenin agreed – on the question of land. As Stephen F. Jones has written, "Lenin did not miss the significance of Georgian social democracy's success in Guria. Although his ultimate aim was the nationalization of land, he understood the Georgian insistence on incorporating the peasantry into the Social Democratic revolutionary strategy."[31]

If Lenin had little to say publicly about the peasant rebellion in Georgia, others did comment on the meaning of the Gurian Republic. Count Leo Tolstoy wrote:

> What is happening in Guria is an event of immense importance. Although I am aware that the Gurians have not even heard of my existence, I have nevertheless a great desire to express to them the ideas and sentiments which they have awakened in me by their admirable movement. Tell them, "There is an old man who for twenty years has been ceaselessly repeating that all the evils of humanity are due to the fact that men are always expecting to find some external aid with which to organize their lives; and when they see that the authorities do not aid them and do not create order, they begin to accuse them, to condemn them, to revolt against them." What should be done is exactly what the Gurians are doing, viz., to organize life in such a manner that there should be no need for any authority.[32]

Tolstoy died four years after the Gurian Republic was crushed, and thus did not live to see what succeeded it: the Georgian Democratic Republic, founded in 1918. For men like Zhordania,

Khomeriki, Ramishvili and the others, Gurians all, Georgia's experiment in democratic socialism was going to take the lessons of the Gurian Republic and apply them across an entire country.

3

THE EXPERIMENT
BEGINS

The years between the crushing of the Gurian Republic in early 1906 and the fall of the tsarist regime in March 1917 were tumultuous ones across the Russian empire. By the end of 1905, the tsar had been compelled to offer concessions, including an elected parliament, of sorts, called the Duma.

In Georgia, the Mensheviks won landslide victories in elections to the Duma. Most of the prominent Menshevik leaders became Duma members, including Zhordania, Tsereteli, and Ramishvili. Zhordania was even elected as the head of the Social Democratic faction in the short-lived First Duma. He was succeeded by another Georgian Menshevik, Irakli Tsereteli, as head of the much larger Social Democratic faction in the Second Duma. Eventually, though, the tsar ordered the arrest and exile to Siberia of the Social Democratic Duma members, in what was became known as the "coup" of June 1907. The tsar and his prime minister, Pyotr Stolypin, were not pleased by the very large socialist contingent elected to the Second Duma. Looking for a pretext to dissolve the Duma, they came upon the ongoing agitation in the army by Social Democrats and accused them of preparing an armed uprising against the regime. The government demanded that the Duma revoke parliamentary immunity for the fifty-five socialist deputies, but it refused to do so. On 3 June, the deputies were arrested anyway and the Duma dissolved. There would never again be such a large group of socialists in Russia's parliament. Afterwards, Zhordania split his time between Finland, St Petersburg, Baku and Georgia, suffering occasional arrest and imprisonment.

Meanwhile, the Georgian Bolsheviks remained a small group with few supporters, and concentrated their efforts on Baku. The split between the two factions deepened and by the time the world war broke out in 1914, Lenin's party was entirely separate from the Mensheviks, both in Georgia and across the entire Russian empire. Though the split had begun as a small disagreement over the wording of what precisely membership in the Social Democratic Party entailed, the split deepened into a chasm over the next several years. Lenin believed in a highly disciplined, centralised organisation whose members would be "professional revolutionaries." The Mensheviks preferred a mass party modelled on the German Social Democrats. Lenin's followers increasingly took the view that with the fall of the tsarist regime, it would be the turn of the socialists to take power, and through a process known as "permanent revolution" lead the transition of Russia from a pre-capitalist society into a post-capitalist one. The Mensheviks took a more orthodox Marxist position, arguing that historic stages could not be skipped at will, and Russia, like all other countries, would need to pass through a bourgeois democratic phase. After a decade of acrimonious factionalism, the small group of socialists who had introduced

Marxism to Russia, and who had published the highly influential underground newspaper *Iskra*, including Lenin and Martov, were no longer on speaking terms.

During the First World War a number of the Georgian Mensheviks, Zhordania among them, were sympathetic to the Allied cause. The Bolsheviks under Lenin's leadership were implacable opponents of the tsarist regime, and called for the transformation of the "imperialist war" into a civil war, a position known as "revolutionary defeatism."

The tsarist regime was finally brought down by a popular revolution in March 1917. But in Georgia that regime simply evaporated. On the fringes of empire, including the three Trans-caucasian countries of Georgia, Armenia and Azerbaijan, the unexpected fall of the monarchy created a political vacuum. The Georgian Social Democrats learned of the fall of the tsar in a cryptic telegram sent by Karlo Chkheidze, who was then in Petrograd, to Zhordania. "Mr Governmentson," it said, "has died; inform friends relatives."[1] Zhordania, Ramishvili, and others came immediately to the viceroy's palace, where Grand Duke Nikolai Nikolaievich announced that he would be leaving Tiflis – but expressed confidence that the Social Democrats could be trusted with power. As he put it, the Social Democrats were "on the side of order."[2] The Social Democrats were the only mass party in the country, with support among intellectuals, urban workers and peasants. Their leaders had a classic Marxist interpretation of their historic task, and did not believe it possible to create a post-capitalist society in a society which had not yet experienced capitalism. As they were well aware, Marx and Engels had warned about the tragedy which occurs when revolutionaries try to take power and transform a society when it is not yet ripe for transformation. As Engels wrote in *The Peasant War in Germany*, "The worst thing that can befall a leader of an extreme party is to be compelled to take over a government in an epoch when the movement is not yet ripe for the domination of the class which he represents and for the realisation of the measures which that domination would imply."

Neither Georgia nor Russia were ripe in 1917 for anything other than what Marxists called a "bourgeois revolution" – starting with the establishment of a democratic republic. If the Georgian Social Democrats were forced by circumstances to take political power, they had no intention of using it to prematurely create socialism. Instead, they accepted the *Communist Manifesto*'s assertion that "the first step in the revolution by the working class is to raise the proletariat to the position of ruling class to win the battle of democracy."[3]

They also had no intention of seceding from Russia. There were nationalists in Georgia and they had political parties of their own. The Social Democrats, however, had among their leaders men who had played very prominent roles in Russian politics, leaders of the Russian Social Democratic faction in the State Duma and later of the Petrograd Soviet and the Provisional Government. The overthrow of the tsar opened up new possibilities for democracy and a federal state. Georgian independence was thus not on the agenda.

For the first several months in 1917, events in Georgia paralleled those in Russia. Soviets – elected councils of workers, peasants and soldiers – were formed, and in Georgia the Social Democrats were the dominant force in these. The Georgian Bolsheviks were then, and remained, a tiny and ineffectual force. Unlike in Russia, where a widening gap between the soviets and the government created a situation that Trotsky described as "dual power," in Georgia the soviets and the national government were both controlled from the beginning by the same people, the Georgian Social Democrats. There never was a situation of "dual power" and the successful Russian Bolshevik slogan "All power to the soviets!" would have made no sense in Georgia.

The Provisional Government in far-away Petrograd struggled to assert its authority in Russia's borderlands, including Georgia. There and in the other Transcaucasian countries, Armenia and Azerbaijan, the local populations gradually began creating the institutions for a new society. The special committee appointed by the Provisional Government in Petrograd to oversee Transcaucasia, known as the *Ozakom*, was powerless.

The Tiflis Soviet, established on 16 March 1917, was far more important. It made clear from the outset that it had no intention of separating from Russia, with a founding declaration announcing that its aim was "to assist in the establishment in Russia of a democratic republic."[4]

Two days after the formation of the Soviet, Zhordania made clear how the Georgian Social Democrats viewed the revolution. "The present revolution in its content is not the affair of some class; the proletariat and the bourgeoisie are together directing the affairs of the revolution."[5] This was the classic Menshevik take on the nature of the revolution in both Georgia and in Russia. This was to be a bourgeois democratic revolution, not a socialist one. The Tiflis Soviet was dominated by the Mensheviks, as were the soviets in Kutaisi, Batumi and elsewhere.

Long before there was a Georgian state, an army began to form. On 5 September 1917, the People's Guard (known at first as the Worker's Guard or Red Guard) was founded in Tiflis.

These armed urban workers were the Praetorian Guard for the Social Democratic Party, fiercely loyal to it. Their leader was the thirty-year-old Vladimir "Valiko" Jugeli. It was ruled by an elected congress, and its general staff was elected to a one-year term. There was also an educational and agricultural wing to the Guard. When Georgia became an independent state, the Guard was under the direct control of the Menshevik-dominated parliament rather than the minister of war, and was eventually renamed the National Guard.

Meanwhile, in early November 1917 the Military Revolutionary Committee in Petrograd, under Trotsky's leadership, seized power. Under cover of a Congress of Soviets, the Bolshevik Party declared the formation of a new government, the Council of People's Commissars, with Lenin at its head. Though the coup was successful in Petrograd, where the Provisional Government showed a complete inability to fight back, it struggled to spread throughout the rest of Russia and the empire. As Soviet power was proclaimed in one city and province after another, it did not spread south of the Caucasus mountain range. In Georgia, the Social Democratic leaders, who had been awaiting elections to the Constituent Assembly, were shocked by the coup, and determined to have no part in it.

Initially, they assumed that the Bolsheviks would not last in power for very long. On 8 November, just one day after the coup in Petrograd, a meeting of the regional centre of soviets and the executives of both the Social Democrats and Socialist Revolutionaries passed a resolution demanding "a peaceful liquidation of the rebellion," the "democratization of the regime," and the convocation of the Constituent Assembly. Three days later, Zhordania addressed representatives of all the revolutionary parties in Tiflis. He began by saying that for a hundred years the Transcaucasian region had worked closely with Russia and considered itself part of Russia. "Now a misfortune has befallen us," he said. "The connection with Russia has been broken."[6]

The first step facing the local authorities in the region was therefore to ensure that the thousands of Russian troops still in the country, many of whom had Bolshevik sympathies, did not attempt a military coup. To prevent this, and to ensure that the democratic forces in Georgia had a well-equipped military force of their own, Jugeli, a former Bolshevik himself, and the People's Guard raided the Tiflis arsenal, which was guarded by Russian soldiers with strong Bolshevik leanings. Jugeli passed on orders in the name of the Tiflis Soviet to surrender, and the soldiers gave up after offering token resistance. When Lenin learned about this raid he was extremely displeased.

So successful was this daring raid in which the Bolshevik Russians were disarmed, that for some years afterwards 12 December was celebrated as a national holiday, second only to Independence Day. Despite this success, the presence of a large number of armed Russian soldiers continued to represent a security threat to the local authorities for some time to come.

Even though the Bolsheviks had come to power through a military coup, elections to the Constituent Assembly went ahead as planned across the former Russian empire. The first free elections in the country's history, and the last until the 1990s, they did not produce the results the Bolsheviks desired. Lenin's party received less than a quarter of the votes, with the Socialist Revolutionary Party emerging as the clear winner.

The number of votes cast was over 48 million. Here are the main results across the entire former Russian empire:[7]

Socialist Revolutionary Party: 19,110,074 (39.5%)

Bolsheviks: 10,880,437 (22.55%)

Kadet (Constitutional Democrats): 2,180,488 (4.5%)

Social Democrats (Mensheviks): 1,522,467 (3.2%)

Labour Populist Socialists: 439,200 (0.9%)

Socialist lists of non-Russian nationalities: 7,030,000 (14.6%)

Non-socialist lists of non-Russian nationalities: 4,670,000 (9.6%)

All others (right liberals, conservatives, Cossacks, religious groups etc.): 5%

While the Mensheviks had done poorly compared to the Bolsheviks, in Transcaucasia it was another story entirely. There the Bolsheviks received just 86,935 votes compared to 662,000 votes for the Mensheviks. Not only had the Social Democrats emerged as the largest party in Transcaucasia, but the Transcaucasians provided nearly half of the entire Social Democratic vote across the former Russian empire.

The Constituent Assembly eventually did convene in January in Petrograd, but its session lasted for less than a day as the Bolsheviks decided to rid themselves of a body they no longer considered legitimate or representative. Following its dispersal by armed Bolshevik soldiers, border regions which were not yet under the control of the Petrograd government had to decide on their next steps. In Transcaucasia, the three regions of Georgian, Armenia and Azerbaijan decided to cooperate.

The dominant political parties in all three countries had a great deal in common. In Armenia, the main party was the Dash-naktsutiun (Armenian Revolutionary Federation), a member party of the Second International since 1907, committed both to

Armenian liberation from Turkey and also a version of Marxism. The Marxism of the Dashnaks probably didn't run as deep as their nationalism and in particular their hatred of Turkish rule.

In Azerbaijan, the leading party was the Musavat, formed by local intellectuals. Like the Armenians and Georgians, they did not at first advocate independence for their country and instead imagined a future as part of a Russian federation.

For several months, the three countries maintained a temporary governing body, the Transcaucasian Commissariat, which handled such important matters as agreeing a truce with the Turkish armies threatening from the south-west. Though no longer under any form of effective control from Petrograd, and rejecting the legitimacy of the Bolshevik government there, it took several more months for the local political leaders to reach the conclusion that Transcaucasia and Russia needed to part company. During this entire period, they remained committed to a pluralist, multi-party democracy based on free elections.

By mid-April 1918, the three countries that made up Transcaucasia realised that they would not be re-joining Russia any time soon, as Lenin and the Bolsheviks were solidifying their grip on power. Any hopes that the Bolshevik "usurpers" would soon be ousted from power had faded. The Russians were also showing signs of wanting their borderlands back. And the Ottoman empire, no longer constrained by the tsarist army blocking its way, was setting its sights on the resource-rich countries to its north-east.

On 22 April, the three countries proclaimed their independence, as a new state with the unwieldy name of the Democratic Federative Republic of Transcaucasia. It was not to last, though the idea of a Transcaucasian federation persisted for many more years.

The initiative for setting up the federation, whose creation was made necessary by the negotiations with Turkey, appears to have come from Azerbaijan, a Muslim majority country, which was considerably friendlier to the Turks than Georgia and Armenia were. And it was precisely this difference in opinion regarding Turkey that planted the seed for the Transcaucasian Republic's swift collapse. Under pressure from Turkey, Azerbaijan would not put up a united front against the country with the other two republics.

Armenia also had good reason to reject the federation with its neighbours and was reluctant to join. Convinced that the Allies would win the war, Armenian politicians anticipated that large swathes of Turkish territory would soon be handed over to them by the victorious British and French.

On 25 May 1918, less than five weeks after the Transcaucasian Republic was founded, it was dissolved. The Transcaucasian Sejm (its parliament) held its final meeting, while the Georgian National Council also met to plan its next steps. The following morning, at 11:00, the Sejm voted to dissolve the republic.[8]

Less than six hours passed before the National Council of Georgia convened a special session in the former residence of the tsar's viceroy in Tiflis. The 120-member council consisted not only of ethnic Georgians, but representatives of the various national minorities living in the country including Russians, Armenians, Azeris, Abkhazians, Ossetians and Jews. The council had been elected by the Georgian National Congress which had met for the first time in December 1917 and included all the Georgian political parties, representatives of the soviet, the army, the trade unions, various minority groups (including Jews and Muslims) and others. That congress had named Zhordania as chairman of the National Council.

Seventy-eight people were in attendance, including forty-two full members and thirty-six candidate members of the council. Noe Zhordania, as chairman of the council, presided. He read out the proposed Declaration of Independence.[9] It was greeted with applause, and was later also read aloud to large crowds of people waiting outside in the street. Support for the act of independence was almost universal in Georgia, with nearly all political parties approving it, the Georgian Bolsheviks being the exception. They considered themselves to be part of the Russian Bolshevik Party, opposed independence and supported reunification with Russia.

The Declaration of Independence began with the new country's leadership's interpretation of history. "For several centuries Georgia existed as a free and independent State," it read.

> At the end of the eighteenth century, Georgia voluntarily allied herself with Russia, with the stipulation that the latter should protect her against enemies from without. In the course of the great Russian Revolution, conditions arose which resulted in the disorganisation of the entire military front and the abandonment of Transcaucasia by the Russian Armies.
>
> Thus, left to their own devices, Georgia, and with her all Transcaucasia, took into their hands the direction of their affairs, creating the necessary organs for these purposes; but under pressure from exterior forces [the Turks] the links which united Transcaucasian nationalities were broken and the political unity of Transcaucasia was thus dissolved.
>
> The present position of the Georgian nation makes it imperative that Georgia should create a political organisation of her own in order that she may escape from the yoke of her enemies and lay a solid foundation for her free development.[10]

The declaration laid out seven articles which reflected the Social Democrats' vision for the new state.

1. *In future the Georgian people will hold sovereign power, and Georgia will be a state enjoying all the rights of a free and independent state.*
   This was a significant shift for the Social Democrats, who had long held the view that Georgia saw its future as part of a democratic, federal Russian state. Six months of Bolshevik rule in Russia had changed their view of things.

2. *Independent Georgia's form of political organisation will be a Democratic Republic.*
   There were a small number of monarchists in Georgia, who were keen to restore the Georgian kings. Some of them tried to use the turmoil of the First World War to trigger the restoration of the monarchy with German help. However, they had no influence in the new Georgian state.

3. *In case of international conflicts, Georgia will always remain neutral.*
   This sentence was not some vague aspiration referring to some imaginary future conflict. Georgia was born during a world war, facing enemies on all sides. The country would come under pressure from the Germans to provide assistance to them in their war effort, and from the Russians as well. Though many Georgians harboured some sympathy for the Allies in the war, the Social Democrats were planting the flag of neutrality from day one. It would be difficult to fulfil this commitment and critics of the Georgian Republic, mostly notably Trotsky, later focussed on this issue, claiming that the Georgians were not neutral at all in the Russian Civil War, and provided assistance to the Allies and their White Russian clients.

4. *The Georgian Democratic Republic will apply itself to establishing friendly relations with all nations, and especially with neighbouring nationalities and states.*

This statement was soon tested, as within just a few months Georgian troops would find themselves embroiled in a war with Armenia. But Zhordania and his comrades meant what they said, and genuinely sought diplomatic solutions to problems with their neighbours, as even the conflict with Armenia was to show.

5. *The Democratic Georgian Republic guarantees to all citizens within its territory all civil and political rights without distinction of nationality, religion, social position or sex.*

This sentence too would be challenged by a number of ethnic minorities in the country. But the announcement on the very first day of Georgia's independent existence that women were to be guaranteed "all civil and political rights" was a breakthrough. Women not only voted for, but were also elected to, Georgia's parliament.

6. *The Democratic Georgian Republic offers to all inhabitants of its territory a wide field for free development.*

One wonders what exactly the founders had in mind. It sounds as if they were already showcasing Georgia's differences from the Bolsheviks to the north, who in setting up a brutal dictatorship were doing little to encourage the "free development" of anyone.

7. *Until the convocation of the Constituent Assembly, the National Council, with the addition of representatives of the minorities and the*

Provisional Government responsible to the National Council, is at the head of all Georgian administration.

To a certain degree, the Bolsheviks too had accepted the provisional character of their own government when they seized power in Petrograd in November 1917. But while they allowed elections to the Constituent Assembly to be conducted unhindered across Russia, they dissolved that assembly as soon as it met. In contrast, the Georgian Social Democrats meant what they said. The Georgian Constituent Assembly did convene and did draft a constitution for the Georgian Democratic Republic.

Following the announcement of independence, the Social Democrats quickly formed a new national government. At its head was Noe Ramishvili, who was effectively the country's first prime minister. Ramishvili was thirty-seven years old at the time, and had served as the interior minister in the Transcaucasian Republic. But he didn't last; the Social Democrats wanted to strengthen the ties between the party and the government and brought in Noe Zhordania to take charge. Replaced on 24 June, Ramishvili returned to his post as the interior minister. For a time, he also served as minister of education, and defence minister too.

Zhordania, who now headed up the Georgian government, held at various times the posts of head of the Social Democratic Party and chairman of the Tiflis Soviet. Wladimir S. Woytinsky, a Russian Menshevik who came to Georgia after the Bolshevik coup, knew all the local Social Democratic leaders. Referring to Zhordania, he wrote that

My recollections of Tiflis are inseparable from the memory of this man. I had met him occasionally in Petrograd and Finland after the first revolution, but he had not impressed me. In Georgia he looked taller, his voice was stronger, and a slight stammer added weight to his words. There seemed to be the halo of the tribal prophet around his majestic head with its thin gray hair and full beard. Indeed, he was more than the head of a political party. He was the uncontested leader of his small nation, surrounded by love and devotion, and the remarkable unity of the Georgian people stemmed largely from his influence.[11]

The first Georgian foreign minister was Akaki Chkhenkeli. In the short-lived Transcaucasian Republic, he served as minister for foreign affairs and headed the Transcaucasian delegation in its peace talks with the Turks and their German allies. Chkhenkeli was closely identified with the government's supposed orientation towards Germany in 1918, and when the Allies won the war later that year, he was replaced by Evgeni Gegechkori.

Noe Khomeriki, a veteran of the Gurian Republic of 1902-6, was named minister of agriculture and given the critically important task of implementing land reform.

The group had their work cut out for them, and began building a new society in a country that had never known democracy.

Elections for the new Georgian Constituent Assembly were held in February 1919. Suffrage was universal, equal and secret, and strict proportional representation determined the makeup of the Assembly. Turnout was high – about 60% – despite heavy snow. Fifteen parties ran candidates, but the Social Democrats won an overwhelming victory. A total of 505,477 votes were cast, the breakdown for the major parties being as follows:

409,766 Mensheviks (109 of 130 seats in the chamber)
33,721 Socialist Federalists (8 seats)

30,154 National Democrats (8 seats)

21,453 Socialist Revolutionaries (5 seats).[12]

The Social Democratic vote was even higher than it had been in the 1917 elections for the Russian Constituent Assembly. Several months later, areas of south-western Georgia which had been in the hands of Turkey and Armenia also held elections which produced similar results.

Seventeen women were among the candidates for seats in the assembly and five of them were elected. All were members of the Social Democratic Party. Kristine Sharashidze was the youngest of the group, just thirty-two years old, and was chosen to serve as a member of the Presidium of the Constituent Assembly, in the role of secretary. When the international socialist delegation visited in 1920, British Labour Party leader Ethel Snowden was impressed by Sharashidze and described her as "very able." Sharashidze was a political veteran, having joined the Social Democratic Party when she was just eighteen years old. She was also a survivor. Following the defeat of the Georgians in 1921, she remained in the country and, despite being arrested several times in 1921 and again in 1922, she continued to live and work in Georgia up until the 1970s.[13]

Snowden wrote that "Distinctions of sex do not exist in Georgian politics or in Georgian industry. Equal pay for equal work is the ruling economic dictum."[14] Sara Huysmans, who also participated in that socialist delegation, added that "Women were indeed granted the right to vote and they were entitled to some benefits, such as for example ten weeks of fully paid maternity leave – four weeks before delivery and six weeks after – plus a small bonus out of a special fund."[15]

On 12 March 1919, the Georgian Constituent Assembly met for the first time and continued to meet over the course of two years, eventually passing over 100 laws. Its main task was the drafting of a constitution, and this was completed in the republic's final days in 1921.

Meanwhile, the country needed a regular army to defend itself, and one was duly formed, side by side with the People's Guard. The regular army was only partially mobilised in peacetime, with the majority of its forces held in reserve. Commanded by General Giorgi Kvinitadze, those reserves would be called up and armed as needed. Kvinitadze – a life-long soldier who rose to the rank of major general in the tsarist army – had a difficult relationship with the Social Democrats, occasionally resigning his post as military commander, and then returning to it. He was very critical of both the left-wing politics of the government and of its failure, in his eyes, to properly prepare the country for defence. As his daughter wrote to me, "My father wanted to create a regular army knowing that the Bolcheviks [sic] would attack Georgia, and was hoping to resist just like Marshal Mannerheim did in Finland … or Pilsudski in Poland. But our government did not believe the Bolcheviks would attack a social-democratic government."[16]

The army and People's Guard consisted of infantry, artillery brigades, cavalry regiments, a military school, a motor squadron, an air detachment and some armoured trains. The army had about 27,000 men mobilised, with another 60,000 in reserve. There was also a tiny Georgian navy consisting of one destroyer, four fighter aircraft, four torpedo boats and ten steamboats. The Georgian leadership would later be criticised for maintaining such a small armed force, especially considering that there were nearly 200,000 Georgian First World War veterans from the Russian army, including many skilled officers.

Regardless, they now had a state of their own for the first time in more than a century and it was the democratic republic they had promised, one with a multi-party system, free and fair elections, freedom of speech and assembly, an independent judiciary, and local government.

With Turkish forces pressing on Georgia's borders, the first task of the new government was to make a deal that would ensure the country's survival as an independent state.

4

THE TURN
TOWARDS GERMANY

The Georgian Social Democrats were pragmatists. Though their ideology was rooted in the writings of Karl Marx and they dreamed of a world in which "all men are brothers," they very much lived in the real world. In that world, both in 1918 and today, small nations can only defend themselves if they have strong allies. The Georgian Social Democrats understood this from the very beginning, as Georgia itself had been living under the protection of the Russian tsars for over 130 years by the time the country declared independence. Without that protection, Georgia would have been torn apart by invading Turks and Persians.

Until May 1918, the Georgian Social Democrats had always assumed their country would form part of a democratic and federal Russia after the revolution. Independence, and with it the need to defend their own borders, came to them as a complete surprise.

During the four years leading up to Georgian independence, the country was on the very front lines of the First World War, as the tsar's army battled the Turks. When the war began in the summer of 1914, a "Germanophile mood dominated in Georgia," according to Noe Zhordania.[1] Some pro-German nationalists dreamed of joining the Germans in a bid to oust the Russians, but the vast majority of Georgians, including the Social Democrats, would have no part of it. Some of them, including Zhordania and the future foreign minister Akaki Chkhenkeli, expressed sympathy for the Allied cause, as did a number of Russian Mensheviks, among them Plekhanov.

A year after the abdication of Nicholas II, the newly independent Georgian Republic found itself sharing a border with Turkey, with no Russian army to speak of standing between the two countries. What remained of that army, now a hungry and undisciplined mass, was engaged in a disorderly retreat through Georgia, a security problem of not inconsiderable magnitude.

Other security problems were to arise later on, including a border dispute with Armenia and a growing threat from the north as Russian armies (both White and Red) cast their hungry eyes over the three Transcaucasian republics. But in early 1918, the Turkish army was on the march and posed the gravest threat to Georgian independence. The Georgians, lacking a powerful military of their own, needed a protector that could help the new republic defend itself from the Turks. The most suitable candidate for that role seemed to be Germany.

The Georgians also needed to urgently reach agreement with the Germans following the disastrous Brest-Litovsk peace agreement signed by the Soviet government. In addition to giving away vast swathes of Russian territory, including Ukraine, to the Germans, the Bolsheviks also gave large chunks of Georgian territory to the Turks. These included Batumi, Akhaltsikhe and Akhalkalaki, all historical Georgian districts, and more recent conquests including Artvin, Ardahan, Kars and Erzurum.

Zhordania called these "the strategic keys to Transcaucasia."[2] "A century's re-conquest of historic Georgian territory was undone at the stroke of a pen," wrote historian Donald Rayfield.[3] The Georgians had no say in any of this and Brest-Litovsk was one more reason the Georgians were ready to part ways with Russia.

The Germans, meanwhile, had interests of their own in the region. Germany in May 1918 was not yet defeated. It still had the strength to launch offensives on the Western front, and its armies had decisively defeated the Russians. In June 1918 German artillery bombarded Paris; while Baku fell to the German-allied Turks in September. Germany desperately needed oil from Azerbaijan and metals to help in steel production, the latter of which Georgia produced in abundance. As Donald Rayfield wrote, "For Germany in 1918, access to Georgia was a matter of life and death."[4]

General Erich Ludendorff, one of the Kaiser's more successful commanders, later wrote that he supported German forces occupying Georgia, primarily in order to acquire both raw materials from Georgia and oil from Azerbaijan. Even though Germany hardly had the troops to spare in the middle of a world war, Ludendorff felt that Turkey was not a reliable ally. "That we could not rely on Turkey in this matter had been once again demonstrated by her conduct in Batum," he wrote, "where she claimed the right to retain all the stocks for herself. We could expect to get oil from Baku only if we helped ourselves."[5]

Negotiations with the Germans began even before Georgia was an independent state, led by the Transcaucasian Commissariat. These talks were closely linked to the negotiations with Turkey to end the war on the Caucasian front. The Georgians and their Armenian and Azerbaijani partners were compelled to sue for peace following the Brest-Litovsk deal and the renewed threat of a Turkish invasion.

On 26 May 1918, the day that the Transcaucasian federation broke apart and Georgia declared its independence, it faced an ultimatum from Turkey which demanded even more territory than the Bolsheviks had conceded at Brest-Litovsk. Now was the time to quickly reach a deal with the Germans to pre-empt the Turks before they moved to seize more Georgian territory.

Field Marshal von Hindenburg and General Ludendorff, men who would later become notorious for their role in bringing Hitler to power, ordered Freiherr Friedrich Kress von Kressenstein, a Bavarian general, to head a military mission to Georgia. In addition to access to Georgia's raw materials and Baku's oil, Ludendorff hoped Georgia could be used by the Germans for an eventual attack on British India.

The Turks were impatient, and they forced Georgia to capitulate in Batumi. The German officers coming in from the Black Sea were forced to land further north, in Poti, to avoid falling into the hands of their Turkish allies. The Georgians, meanwhile, protested to the Turks that they had gone too far in overstepping the Brest-Litovsk treaty, but to no avail.

The Georgian diplomats now reached a separate agreement, unknown to the Turks, which was signed by the Georgian foreign minister Chkhenkeli and the German General Otto von Lossow on a ship, the *Minna Horn*, in Poti. General von Lossow warned the Georgians that Turkey and Soviet Russia were likely to conclude a secret pact, which would have been a disaster for the small country.

The first document the Georgians and Germans signed recognised the Brest-Litovsk agreement. The Georgian Social

Democrats had been furious at the Russian Bolsheviks for signing away their territory without even asking their opinion. But in the meantime, facts on the ground had changed. The Germans and Turks were in a far better bargaining position, and without an intact Russian army to hold them at bay, the Georgians had no choice but to agree to Brest-Litovsk.

That agreement also gave the Germans the right to use the Georgian railroads until the end of the war. Use of these railroads was essential if Germany was to extract manganese and other raw materials from the country.

There were other economic parts of the new agreement too. A Georgian-German Mining Joint Stock Company was set up with equal rights and shares for both countries. The Germans were given the right to purchase all excess output from Georgia's mines, to regulate the country's naval communications, and to ease the importing of basic commodities. Germany's currency, the mark, was to be legal tender in Georgia. Most of these concessions proved to be theoretical, though, as their implementation was thwarted by the sudden end of the war and Germany's defeat in November 1918.

In exchange for those concessions, the Germans agreed to help mediate between Georgia and Turkey. This was quickly accomplished with the signing of an agreement on 4 June 1918 between the new Georgian prime minister Noe Ramishvili and the Turks in which latter formally recognised the Georgian state. It was a victor's peace with the treaty allowing Turkey to determine the size of Georgia's army and to deploy Turkish troops inside Georgia to protect the railways if needed. Georgia promised to expel all officers from Allied powers, and to disarm and intern any Russian ships in its ports. As Firuz Kazemzadeh summed it up, "Georgia was losing much of her independence at the very moment she proclaimed it."[6]

Immediately after signing the agreement with the Germans, Chkhenkeli travelled to Berlin together with von Lossow, Nikoladze (the mayor of Poti) and Zurab Avalishvili, a Georgian diplomat, remaining in the German capital for several months. There they proposed bringing Georgia under German protection as a "dominion" of the German Reich, but apparently the Kaiser vetoed this. Perhaps, had Germany won the war, a German protectorate might eventually have been formally established. It is also not clear how the German government viewed a country ruled by Social Democrats, as many of the German Social Democrats, Kautsky among them, had proven to be "disloyal" to their country during the world war.

Years later, Trotsky sought to explain the decision of the Georgian Social Democrats to make a deal with the German imperialists. It was not enough for Trotsky to oppose their decision, accusing them of betraying the working class and colluding with imperialism. Trotsky also needed to explain *why* the Georgian Mensheviks reached out to the German imperialists. In his view, it had nothing to do with Germany's need for Georgia's manganese or Baku's oil, nor did it have anything to do with Georgia's need for a protector against the Turks, as the Germans and Georgians were saying. Instead, he insisted, "the German troops were brought into Georgia, as into Finland, the Baltic countries and the Ukraine, *chiefly against the Bolsheviks*."[7]

The Bolsheviks, who in 1918 and for years afterwards were a tiny, ineffectual group with hardly any influence in Georgia, were, in Trotsky's view, the real reason behind the Georgian–German alliance. Having exposed the "real reason" behind the deal with Germany, Trotsky berated the Georgians for hypocrisy:

> When they held the posts of Ministers in an All-Russian government, the Georgian Mensheviks accused us of being in alliance with the German General Staff, and through the Tsarist courts charged us with high treason. They declared that the Brest-Litovsk Peace, which opened "the gates of the revolution" to German imperialism, was a betrayal of Russia. It was precisely with this cry that they called for the overthrow of the Bolsheviks, and, when the revolution became too hot for them, split Trans-Caucasia away from Russia, and later Georgia from Trans-Caucasia, thereby really opening wide the gates of "democracy" for the troops of the Kaiser.[8]

While some of this is nonsense, Trotsky had a point about Brest-Litovsk. The Georgians, and indeed all three Transcaucasian republics, had felt betrayed by the Russians for their concessions to the Germans at Brest-Litovsk. To come back just a couple of months later and agree to the very same concessions (or worse) does seem, on the face of it, to be a bit hypocritical. In reality, though, compared to where things stood just a few months later, the defeated Russians were in a position of relative strength when negotiating at Brest-Litovsk. By June 1918, with almost nothing standing between the Turkish army and Tiflis, Brest-Litovsk was starting to look to the Georgians like a good deal.

Trotsky's description of the German occupation of Georgia became a part of Soviet-era history, long after his exile and murder at the hands of Stalin, and was the view taught to Georgians during the seven decades of Soviet rule. Trotsky dismissed the idea that Georgia invited the Germans to help protect the country against the Turks, writing:

The role of the German troops in the border states of Russia during 1918 was quite definite. In Finland they acted as the executioners of the workers' revolution, in the Baltic states they did the same. They passed through the whole of the Ukraine, breaking up the Soviets, massacring the Communists, and disarming the workers and peasants. Jordania had no reason to expect that they would enter Georgia with any other aim. But it was precisely for this reason that the Menshevik government invited the troops of the indomitable Hohenzollerns – that as against the Turkish troops they had all the advantage of discipline.[9]

The Georgia Trotsky described was one in which the Social Democratic government was faced by constant unrest, with peasant uprisings, worker rebellions and so on, and with a powerful Georgian Bolshevik party ready at any moment to wrest power on behalf of the working class. We will see when we explore the Georgian Bolsheviks later in this book how much of this is true. Without the Germans around, Trotsky was convinced, the Social Democrats would have soon lost their grasp on power – and not to the Turks, but to the working class:

> One can … state quite confidently that in spite of the White terror, supplemented by paper flowers of rhetoric, the Menshevik dictatorship would have been swept away, without leaving a trace, by the rapid current of the revolutionary movement, had it not been for the presence of foreign troops in the country. It was not the German Marx that helped the Mensheviks to maintain themselves through that period, but the German Von Kress.[10]

In the Russian Bolshevik view, the Georgian Social Democrats were solely concerned with crushing the Bolsheviks, and faced no other threats of any significance, such as Turkey or even General Denikin's White armies. Zhordania, according to Trotsky, would have used those German troops to break up soviets (in which the Social Democrats had large majorities), disarm the workers (though presumably not the armed proletarians in the People's Guard, which was fanatically loyal to the Social Democrats) and massacre Communists. If those were Zhordania's expectations, he would surely have been disappointed, as none of those things were done by the German occupation forces when they arrived in Georgia. The Soviets were not broken up, the workers were not disarmed, and the repression of Georgia's tiny and ineffectual Communist Party was left to the hands of the Georgian police and People's Guard.

An alternative view, and a more accurate one, of how the Georgians and Germans came to be partners for a few months in 1918 was given by Karl Kautsky. Kautsky began with a longer historical view, noting that "the Germans have been popular in Georgia for a long time, thanks to the Wurttemberg colonists who settled there a hundred years ago, as peasants, and retained their nationality until to-day, earning for themselves a good reputation."[11]

To the Georgian socialists, Germany was the land of Marx, Lasalle, Bebel and Liebknecht. It was the heartland of social democracy, with the most powerful socialist party in the world and the strongest trade unions.

This view of Germany was shared to a certain degree by the Bolsheviks as well. Not only did Bolshevik leaders like Lenin base many of their ideas on things they had learned from German Social Democrats, but when they also found themselves in need of European allies, Germany seemed a good choice. While Trotsky railed at the Georgian Social Democrats for betraying the revolution by cosying up to Berlin, his own comrades were putting the final touches to the Treaty of Rapallo, signed in 1922, which marked the beginning of a Soviet-German *rapprochement* which continued right up to the 1930s. And of course senior Bolshevik leaders, Lenin among them, did travel to Russia in early 1917 on the infamous "sealed train" provided by the German High Command, which was convinced that if Lenin were allowed to return to Petrograd, he would work to bring Russia out of the war, thus contributing to a German military victory. Lenin's collaboration with the German military command and rumours of large quantities of German gold in his party's coffers caused a major scandal in 1917.

Kautsky, though a life-long opponent of the Kaiser's regime, supported the Georgian decision to turn toward Germany in 1918. The Germans, he wrote, "came to Georgia not as plunderers but as organisers of its productive forces, as they needed the Georgian products, especially manganese, and also its railways. Thus they brought to Georgia precisely what was most lacking in the country, and what it could only obtain speedily by foreign assistance, namely economic organisation."[12]

The deal made between Germany and Georgia forced the Russians to sign an amendment to the Brest–Litovsk treaty on 27 August 1918. It stipulated that Russia consented to Germany's recognition of Georgian independence. In a sense, this meant Russian recognition of Georgia's independence too, though this would not become formal until the Georgian–Russian peace treaty in May 1920. This was not necessarily a massive concession by the Soviets, as Lenin had already acknowledged in principle the right of the border states of the Russian empire to secede, and had accepted this in practice in the cases of Finland, Poland and the three Baltic republics – Estonia, Latvia and Lithuania.

German troops arrived in Tiflis just two weeks after Georgia had proclaimed independence and were welcomed as protectors from the Turks. Three days after their arrival the Social Democratic government issued a declaration, informing the population that those troops were there at the invitation of the government "for the purpose of defending the frontiers" of the country. The Workers' and Soldiers' Soviet in Tiflis voted to back the deal.

Within a month, the Germans had taken control of the country's ports and railways from the hands of the Turks. They began work on exporting hundreds of thousands of tons of manganese from the mines in Chiatura to Germany. They lent 54,000,000 Deutschmarks (at a very high rate of interest) in order to back the new Georgian currency. They also began planning to develop the port of Poti, to lay a cable under the Black Sea and to build an oil pipeline from Batumi to Poti.

But all did not go smoothly, despite the Georgian government's commitment to the relationship. The Georgian workers, who, unlike their comrades in Russia under Lenin, belonged to free and independent trade unions with the right to strike, had other ideas. According to Donald Rayfield, "On 27 June the first consignment of manganese left Poti for Germany, but the shortage of dockers, and the undernourished, strike-prone state of those that did work, left more manganese behind than could ever be shipped. Similar blockages prevented the export of Abkhaz tobacco, highland wool and Kakhetian copper, or the import of much-needed flour."[13]

The Germans were furious. Kressenstein demanded that the Georgian Social Democrats crack down on the workers, and one imagines that if the Germans had remained in Georgia after 1918 they would have lost patience with the country's militant workers, and possibly with their Social Democratic government as well.

Some senior German officers called upon Georgia to integrate its army with the armed workers of the People's Guard and to denationalise lands seized from the nobles and redistribute these to the peasants. In addition, they called on the government to deport several thousand stranded Russian soldiers to the Crimea, where they could join the fight against the Bolsheviks, and indeed wanted Georgia's help in the fight against Lenin's rule in Russia. There were even attempts by the Germans to see if the Georgian monarchy could be revived. (It couldn't.) According to a Georgian propaganda pamphlet from 1919, "Germany tried, in vain, to impose one of her Princes as ruler of the country, but it failed against the Socialistic majority, which presented a solid democratic front to the schemes of Germany."[14]

Meanwhile, the German occupiers were busy with other things as well. They offered scholarships to attend German universities and established a German gymnasium in Tiflis. They also revived a German-language newspaper that was quite anti-socialist, *Die kaukasische Post*. Its influence would no doubt have been limited both by the small number of German-speakers in Georgia and by the equally small number of anti-socialists.

Just five months after German troops entered Tiflis, the world war ended with a German defeat. The German soldiers in Georgia, who had previously been so well-behaved and therefore welcomed by most Georgians, "became an undisciplined rabble."[15] In early December 1918 the first British troops arrived, among them some Indian soldiers. The German military headquarters in the Palace Hotel was burned down, and before the year was over, German forces began withdrawing from the Georgian capital.

Early in the new year, the Georgian government held a welcoming banquet for the British military mission, while at the very same time the war minister also gave General Kress a farewell dinner. The Georgians were sad to see the Germans go, and not at all happy to be replacing them with the British. Kress and his men remained in Georgia until February, and were treated by the British as prisoners of war.

The Georgian Social Democrats were, if anything, practical people. Facing the imminent threat of Turkish invasion, and a possible Turkish-Soviet pact, they engineered a deal with Germany that guaranteed the country's borders and provided a measure of internal stability.

Donald Rayfield insisted that "there is no doubt that, by stiffening the administration and forming a regular army, in autumn 1918 the German military mission saved Georgia from internal chaos and from Turkish invasion and Armenian encroachments."[16] They also played a small role in assisting the Georgians in the first days of their conflict with Armenia at the end of the year.

As the Germans left Georgia, they were not viewed as hated occupiers. And the esteem in which they were held by most Georgians would only rise after the experience with their successors, the British.

5

AT WAR WITH ARMENIA

Georgia's main security concerns during its three years of independence were with Turkey to the south and Russia to the north. But oddly enough, its first shooting war came neither with the resurgent Turks nor with Denikin's Volunteer Army. Instead, it was little Armenia that chose to pick a fight, a fight that would raise serious questions about the Georgian socialists' promise, made in their Declaration of Independence, regarding "establishing friendly relations with all nations, and especially with neighbouring nationalities and states."[1]

Georgia had been independent for less than five months when it first accused the Armenians of illegally occupying some of its territory. On 18 October 1918, Armenian troops entered Georgian-controlled territory and occupied a couple of villages. German soldiers were still occupying much of Georgia at this time, and clashes took place between Armenian forces and the Germans. Fighting raged for more than a week until the Georgians sent an armoured train which shifted the balance of power to their side. The Armenian government then backed down, said it was all a misunderstanding, announced a withdrawal of its forces, and suggested a peace conference. Nine days after the fighting started, it was over. But not for long.

Keen to prevent any further fighting, and anticipating the imminent end of the world war (and the departure of the German troops), the Georgians proposed a regional peace conference which they would host in Tiflis. The Armenians, Azerbaijanis and representatives of the "Republic of Mountaineers of the Northern Caucasus" were invited. (The last of these was a republic situated to the north of Georgia and consisting of provinces such as Chechnya, North Ossetia and Dagestan; it fell to Soviet rule in June 1920.) In an invitation to the conference on 27 October 1918, the Georgians named four issues to be addressed:

1. Recognition of each other's independence.
2. Solution of all disputes, including those over the frontiers, through arbitration.
3. Mutual obligation not to enter into agreements detrimental to the interests of one of the Transcaucasian republics or the Union of the Mountaineers.
4. Mutual support and solidarity at the forthcoming peace conference (in Paris) in defence of the common interests of the republics of the Caucasus.

Both Azerbaijan and the Mountaineers were happy to attend the conference in Tiflis. But not the Armenians, who took issue with the Georgian claim that the country's borders should be based on the provincial borders inherited from tsarist Russia. Instead, the Armenians insisted that the ethnic composition of disputed regions be taken into account. Some border regions that were then held by the Georgians were largely populated by ethnic Armenians, with small Georgian minorities. The Azerbaijani government also disputed Georgia's claim to the territories, but chose not to fight a war over them.

There were reports in Georgian newspapers that Armenia had mobilised its army. The Armenians issued a formal denial of this and then agreed after a few days to attend the conference.

The peace conference opened in Tiflis on 10 November, but with no Armenian delegate anywhere in sight. The conference was delayed for a few days to allow the Armenians to arrive, but still they didn't show up. Eventually, the Armenians explained the reasons behind their non-attendance. They didn't agree to the Georgian proposal to settle territorial disputes by arbitration, fearing that the two other republics would take the Georgians' side and gang up on Armenia. They expected deals to be made in which Georgia would support, for example, Azerbaijan's claim to the disputed region of Nagorno-Karabakh. Armenia and Azerbaijan did not have the best of relations then – or now. They were also unhappy about how the Georgians chose the date and venue for the conference without consulting them first.

It was not only Armenia's fear that it would be ganged up on by the other three republics – the country's leaders were absolutely convinced that they, unlike Georgia, had the Allied powers on their side. After all, Georgia had invited the German army to occupy the country, and the Azerbaijanis and Mountaineers had a cosy relationship with Turkey. The Armenians, meanwhile, had remained loyal to the Allied cause.

As Kazemzadeh put it in his book *The Struggle for Transcaucasia*:

> Had not Armenia been faithful to Tsarist Russia, England, France, and the United States? Had she not fought the Turks and defied the Germans while Azerbaijan and Georgia were cringing before them? Had not the halls of the House

of Commons, the American Congress and the Chamber
of Deputies resounded with promises to redress Armenia's
wrongs? The Armenians thought that the hour had come
when their country would be compensated for the hundreds
of thousands of their dead, for all the miseries and privations
they had suffered. The Turkish and German troops had not yet
left when Armenia began to celebrate her triumph. Feeling
as the Armenians did, it is not surprising that they refused to
compromise.[2]

The Armenian leadership had tragically miscalculated and
that miscalculation would lead to war with Georgia. But it may
not have been entirely a case of human error on their part,
as it is also possible that the two regional imperialist powers,
Turkey and Russia, and possibly Great Britain as well, were
helping to provoke a war between the two newly independent
Transcaucasian republics.

During the same week as the abortive Tiflis peace conference
opened – without the Armenians – the First World War ended.
The German and Turkish forces in Transcaucasia would soon
need to withdraw, to be replaced by the victorious British.
In a last malicious act before leaving, the Turks informed the
Armenians that they would be vacating the territories they
held on 6 December. But in a message to the Georgians,
they announced they'd be pulling out two days earlier, on 4
December. As a result, when the Armenian forces marched into
two previously occupied districts which straddled the Georgian
border, Lori and Borchalo, they found Georgian troops already
there, waiting for them.

A day earlier, the Armenians informed the Georgians that they
wouldn't send troops to a third disputed district, Akhalkalaki.
But the Georgians pre-empted them, having already sent troops

there, while announcing Georgia's historic and other claims on the district.

In other words, with the defeated Turkish army now gone, Georgia had taken hold of all three disputed districts, while the Armenians had refused the offer of participating in a regional peace conference and the arbitration that might follow.

It was not only the Turks causing mischief in the region. The Georgians were convinced, and told the British, that Armenia was allied with General Denikin's Volunteer Army. General Anton Denikin led the most important of the White armies fighting against Bolshevik rule, based in south Russia. But it cannot be ruled out that while the Turks were provoking conflict by providing different dates of their withdrawal to the two sides, Denikin was encouraging the Armenians to fight against a regime – the Georgian Social Democrats – that he despised nearly as much as he hated the Russian Bolsheviks.

Finally, as the Germans and Turks withdrew, the British were just beginning to arrive in the region and they were not exempt from accusations of involvement in provoking the feud. Noe Zhordania reportedly claimed that some British officers "in their extreme hostility to Georgia, organized the Armenian advance over Lori."[3]

Zhordania's claim was surprisingly echoed years later by a Soviet historian who asserted that "British agents had incited the war in order to secure a firm hold in Transcaucasia."[4] This claim, based on a document supposedly unearthed in the Georgian state archives, argued that the British used their influence to provoke the Georgians, not the Armenians.

Whether the Turks, or the Russian General Denikin, or the British had anything to do with the outbreak of hostilities doesn't absolve the Georgians and Armenians of responsibility for a series of stupid and sometimes criminal acts that led to war.

The behaviour of the Georgians towards Armenians who lived within their borders was not above reproach. As historian Ronald Grigor Suny has written, the Armenians in Georgia "were subjected to a series of repressive measures – the suspension of their newspapers, arrests of Dashnak deputies to the city duma, extortion of money – in the name of state security."[5] Armenians residing in Georgia were treated as prisoners of war, and in one case were paraded through the streets.

Georgian hostility to Armenians living within their borders was not new, and did not start with the outbreak of fighting in 1918. There were large numbers of Armenians living in Georgian cities during the years of Russian rule, and they were often quite successful businessmen.

By early December, an armed conflict seemed inevitable. In Borchalo, one of the two districts abandoned by the Turks and occupied by Georgia, a rebellion broke out. Georgian diplomats proposed that a mixed commission be appointed to settle the dispute. But it was too late. The Armenian response to the Georgian proposal was to issue an ultimatum demanding that Georgian forces withdraw from the district.

On 9 December, Georgia complained to the Allies (who had by now replaced the German troops) that regular Armenian soldiers had attacked Georgian border guards. Meanwhile, in Lori, the second formerly Turkish-controlled area that was now in Georgian hands, an Armenian commander announced that his forces could not even wait for a Georgian answer to the ultimatum and would commence an attack on 14 December.

The Georgians tried to get the French to intervene with the Armenian leaders, because a French officer was the only Allied representative in the Armenian capital Yerevan. They did not succeed. A Georgian diplomat in Armenia tried to rush back to Tiflis to calm things down, but was stopped at the border by Armenian troops.

As late as mid-December, the Georgians could not believe that the Armenian government had anything to do with the fighting taking place in the border regions. Gegechkori, the newly appointed Georgian foreign minister who had replaced the "pro-German" Chkhenkeli, telegraphed his Armenian counterpart proposing a settlement of these land disputes by peaceful means. Speaking to the Georgian parliament on 14 December, he insisted that the Armenian government could not be held responsible for the border clashes. For saying this, he was booed by some of the more nationalist deputies.

So convinced were the Georgians that this could not be a planned attack by the Armenian army that they recalled units of the People's Guard from the disputed region to come to Tiflis to take part in a parade celebrating the first anniversary of the creation of their force. Eventually, though, the Georgians got hold of an order, captured from Armenian soldiers, which showed that attacks had in fact been ordered by the Armenian minister of war. There could no longer be any doubt of Armenian aggression.

Finally, the Armenians held out an olive branch. A note reached the Georgians in mid-December suggesting that everything could be settled if only the Georgians would withdraw their forces from the disputed territories. The Georgians replied, as before, with an invitation to a peace conference followed by arbitration to settle any disputes. Meanwhile, the Georgians shared their information on the situation with the victorious Allies, hoping they could use their influence to rein the Armenians in – just as they had relied a few months earlier on the Germans to restrain their Turkish allies.

It was no longer possible to pretend that the Armenian government was not behind the fighting, and Zhordania addressed parliament to explain this. In what has been described as a "stirring" speech, he said, "There has taken place that which should not have taken place. … The present Armenian government, in instigating this shameful conflict, has precipitated that which has never before occurred – war between Georgia and Armenia."[6] The Armenians had provoked that initial rebellion in Borchalo, he said, in order to justify sending in troops to occupy the district.

It may well be that someone in faraway Moscow was paying attention to this, for twenty-six months later the Bolsheviks would do *exactly the same thing*. A "rebellion" in the disputed districts of Borchalo and Lori in February 1921 would "force" the Russian army to intervene, leading to a collapse of independent Georgia. In that sense, the Armeno-Georgian war of December 1918 was a dress rehearsal for what happened in 1921.

Though Zhordania was finally willing to fully blame the Armenian government for the war, he too struggled to understand why they did it. He blamed the murder of one Karchikian, a moderate leader of the ruling Dashnak party, for this. Extremists, he believed, had taken over what was once a moderate socialist party.

It turned out that the Georgians weren't very good at defending their newly independent state, and the Armenian troops initially did rather well in the war, almost reaching Tiflis before they were finally defeated on 29 December in the town of Shulaveri, just 56 kilometres south of the Georgian capital.

While the Armenian forces were advancing, the British began to press seriously for an end to the fighting, and on 21 December they ordered the Georgian and Armenian army commanders to stop fighting. Neither side obeyed at first.

On the following day, the Georgians informed the British that they accepted the ceasefire, but with two conditions. The order to cease fire would be given to the Georgian forces by their own government and not by the British. The second condition was that both sides withdraw to their pre-war positions, leaving the Georgians in control of the disputed districts.

Three days later, the Allies once again pushed both sides to stop the war. This time they announced that a commission consisting of Allied officers and representatives of the Georgian government (but not the Armenian) would visit the front lines to oversee the execution of the order. They telegraphed the Armenian president, ordering his army to withdraw from all disputed territories. And to cap it all off, the message was signed not only by the Allied representatives, but by Zhordania as well. It was a complete Georgian diplomatic victory.

As Kazemzadeh wrote, "The position of the Armenians was pathetic. Had it not been for their faith in the Allies, they would never have attacked Georgia. They had been sure that Britain and France would not object to the punishment of a people which had collaborated with the Germans during the war. The West they felt owed them a debt."[7]

They were wrong. And yet despite Georgia's success, with Armenia agreeing to the Allies' terms on New Year's Eve, two things were to come back to haunt the Georgians. One was their own inflated expectations of Allied support and the other was the state of their national defences. They should perhaps have paid more attention to how little help the Allies were to Armenia, which felt entitled to their support. Meanwhile, a Georgian army which could barely beat back little Armenia was hardly likely to be an effective barrier to the Russians.

The story of the Armeno-Georgian war did not end with the British-brokered ceasefire, but continued inside the international socialist movement. Only a few days after the fighting had ended, the Georgian Social Democrats and Armenian Dashnaks brought their dispute to a conference of the Second International in Berne in February 1919. That conference called on all sides to respect the principle of self-determination, which seems to have been a demand of the Armenians. Afterwards, the Dashnaks complained that the Georgians were not abiding by the Berne decisions, and in May 1919 their case was taken up by the International's Executive Committee. Among those who sat on the Committee and who would decide for or against Georgia were several of those who travelled to visit the country during the following year, including future British Labour Prime Minister Ramsay MacDonald.

The Executive Committee proposed that it send a special commission to the region to preside over a plebiscite. This would seem to be what the Armenians wanted all along, but now they demanded the withdrawal of the Georgian forces *before* such a vote could take place. The leaders of the Second International told the Dashnaks they should trust them to sort things out. But as Kazemzadeh observed, "the Armenians refused to trust anyone but themselves. Such was their obstinacy that [Belgian socialist leader Camille] Huysmanns reproached them with a lack of desire to reach an agreement."[8] The issue continued to come before international socialist conferences including at Lucerne in August 1919. By then the socialist leaders had given up on a mission to the Armeno-Georgian borderlands and suggested that the League of Nations could hold a plebiscite.

In his book defending the 1921 Russian invasion of Georgia, *Between Red and White*, Trotsky wrote a single paragraph about the Armeno-Georgian war of 1918. Just five months after Georgia's independence, he wrote,

> and between democratic Georgia and equally democratic Armenia, a war breaks out over a disputed bit of territory. From both sides were heard speeches on the lofty aims of civilisation and about the treacherous attack of the enemy. Kautsky does not say a single word about this "democratic" Armeno-Georgian war. Under the leadership of Jordania, Tsereteli, and their Armenian and Tartar doubles, Trans-Caucasia was transformed into a Balkan peninsula, where national massacres and democratic charlatanry, have reached an equally highly flourishing stage.[9]

Was it fair of Trotsky to blame the Georgian Social Democrats for the "Balkanisation" of the Caucasus?

It is clear that the 1918 Armeno-Georgian war was triggered by Armenian aggression, and that the Georgian Social Democrats did try in good faith to get their Dashnak comrades to come to the peace table first. The initial refusal of the Georgian socialist leaders to believe that the Armenian government was involved in the fighting is also to their credit.

This is not to say that the Georgian Social Democrats were above criticism. There can be little doubt that their swift military occupation of districts claimed by the Armenians and their treatment of ethnic Armenians within their borders contributed to tensions.

The end of the war with Armenia coincided with the beginning of a new chapter in Georgian history – the British occupation had begun.

6

THE BRITISH
TAKE CHARGE

At the very end of 1918, following the German defeat in the world war, it was Britain's turn to occupy parts of Transcaucasia, including Georgia.

When writing his book about Menshevik Georgia, Trotsky would later complain that the information he had was incomplete, noting that "the most valuable material is inaccessible to us. This material consists of the most compromising documents, as well as the archives of the respective British and French institutions taken out of the country by the late Menshevik government."[1] If only we had access to those British archives, he seemed to be saying, we could know the true story of Menshevik Georgia. Today, nearly a century later, we actually do have access to those archives and can begin to reconstruct the real relationship between the Georgians and the British. It is one that bears little resemblance to the one Trotsky described.

The British arrived in Baku on 17 November 1918, less than a week after the Armistice, quickly making contact with the Georgian authorities in Tiflis. From the outset the British were suspicious of the Georgians; after all, Georgia was still occupied by German troops, who had been welcomed into the country as protectors.

The first meeting between Zhordania and the British did not go well at all. A British colonel, described as "a big man with a reddish face and blond moustache," arrived to meet Zhordania with an aide and a Russian interpreter. He told the Georgian president that his orders in Georgia were to maintain order, assure the regular operation of the country's railways, and complete the evacuation of the defeated Turkish and German forces. He warned that if his orders were not obeyed, or if the British troops were harmed in any way, he would hold the Georgian government responsible. Zhordania replied as follows:

> Colonel, I must brief you about our country. This is an independent land. We are not at war with your country and you are here not as a conqueror, but as a guest. I had expected you would show some sign of appreciation of the honour of being received by the head of state. I would have offered you hospitality and friendship and have asked you what I could do for you. This would have given you an opportunity to talk about the railroad and whatever else you had in mind. Would this not have been a proper procedure between civilized people?[2]

Georgians who learned about what Zhordania had said to the British officer expressed some concern, wondering if this was the right way to address the representative of a great power. But Zhordania had been right. Two hours later the colonel reappeared, was exceptionally polite and formal, and discussed his mission, asking questions about Georgia as well. At the end of the meeting, he asked Zhordania to forget his first appearance at the palace. Zhordania, it is said, slapped the colonel on the shoulder and told him all was forgotten.[3]

A British general, William M. Thomson, commanding the expeditionary force in Baku, told Zhordania what the British aimed to achieve as the new rulers in the region. He said that Britain wanted to free the whole region from both the Germans and the Bolsheviks, to re-establish order without interfering in the internal affairs of a sovereign state like Georgia, to re-open trade routes, and to use the railways to move Allied troops around. The Georgians had no problem with any of this. But General Thomson also said that his government would like to restore the post of viceroy, as had existed under the tsar, aiming to eventually restore Russian authority in the region. Unsurprisingly, this was not acceptable to the Georgians.

The British and Georgians had got off on the wrong foot and things were only going to get worse. Even before the Germans had left, Zhordania was missing them. In his memoirs, he recalled the "genuinely noble, profoundly friendly and respectful" manners of General Kress, comparing them to the first Britons to arrive in Tiflis, whom he described as "like a sergeant-major, coarse, rude, imperious and masterful."[4]

Some of the Georgians were so outraged at the behaviour of the British that they threatened to oppose their entry into the country by force. Calmer heads prevailed. The Georgians quickly changed their foreign minister from the "pro-German" Akaki Chkhenkeli to Evgeni Gegechkori, an experienced Menshevik politician who had served as a deputy in the Russian Duma and later led the Transcaucasian Commissariat. Gegechkori assured the British that "the Georgian government, animated by the desire to work in harmony with the Allies for the realization of the principles of right and justice proclaimed by them, gives its consent to the entry of the troops."[5]

The British government could not make up its mind about what to with Transcaucasia, which had fallen into its lap with the military collapse of Germany. There were those who supported independent states in the region, among them Lord Curzon, who within a year would be the foreign secretary. Curzon supported a strong British presence in Baku and also along the strategic Baku–Batumi railroad, with the oil fields of Baku being Trans-caucasia's main prize. Curzon wanted Britain to help get the young republics on their feet, presumably also as a bulwark against the Russian Bolsheviks.

Curzon was opposed by others in the cabinet, including the then foreign secretary, Arthur James Balfour. Balfour was dismissive of the Georgians, Armenians and Azerbaijanis, saying that "If they want to cut their own throats why not let them do it … I should say we are not going to spend all our money and men in civilising a few people who do not want to be civilised. We will protect Batum, Baku, the railroad between them, and the pipeline."[6] In the end, the cabinet decided to keep British forces in the region, but without being entirely clear about their mission or their relationship to republics.

Meanwhile, with the war ending in Europe and a peace confer-ence about to take place in Paris, the Georgians were desperate to win recognition from the victorious Allies. Above all, they wanted a seat at the table in Paris. Georgian diplomacy in the next few years was focussed almost entirely on that peace conference and the League of Nations which grew out of it. Ever fearful of a Russian attempt to recapture Transcaucasia, the Georgians felt that only recognition of their independence by the international community could guarantee the country's continued existence. But their working assumption was that the post-1918 world was one in which the "great powers" could make decisions about the very existence of nation-states, as they had done in the century leading up to the world war. They could not imagine a world in which there would be states like Soviet Russia which were outside of that system, and which the great powers could not control.

The Georgians won a very early diplomatic victory when on 30 December 1918 Louis Mallet, the former British ambassador to Turkey who was then serving in the Foreign Office as an under-secretary of state, wrote to the Georgian diplomats Zurab Avalishvili and David Ghambashidze: "I am authorised by Mr. Balfour to inform you that His Majesty's Government view with favour the creation of a Georgian Republic and are prepared to urge its recognition at the Conference and to support its desire to send Delegates to Paris with the object of presenting its claims." This was forwarded on to Tiflis where the new foreign minister, Gegechkori, responded with a telegram of thanks.

If the text of Balfour's message to the Georgians sounds familiar, it may be because the same Balfour had written a year earlier to Lord Rothschild saying that "His Majesty's Government view with favour the establishment in Palestine of a national home for the Jewish people, and will use their best endeavours to facilitate the achievement of this object."[7] As the Jewish leaders in Palestine would soon discover, Balfour's diplomatic language concealed a more complicated position based on perceived British interests in the region. This would turn out to be the case with Britain's view of Georgian statehood as well.

It was later made clear that Balfour's message to the Georgians was specific to them and there was no implied British support for any of the other Transcaucasian republics. The British were certainly not throwing their support behind Armenia, which had already been compelled to stop its war against Georgia by British officers in the area.

General George Francis Milne was the commander of British forces in the region. Now in his mid-fifties, Milne had served as a professional soldier in the British army across several continents, with tours of duty in India, South Africa, India, Malta, Salonika and France. A photograph of him at the time shows a typical British officer of the period, clean-shaven but for a silver moustache, his chest covered with medals. Like Balfour, he was not particularly fond of the peoples of Transcaucasia, writing that "the country and the inhabitants are equally loathsome." He conceded that a British withdrawal from Georgia "would probably lead to anarchy" but "the world would (not) lose much if the whole of the country cut each other's throats. They are certainly not worth the life of a single British soldier." The reference to allowing the local populations to "cut each other's throats" echoed the earlier comments made by the foreign secretary.

In late May, Milne sent a telegram to London asking about the pledge made by Balfour to the Georgians the previous year. "I am not clear how this telegram came to be dispatched," he wrote, but "in the circumstances the moment does not seem opportune for any explicit withdrawal of the above mentioned pledge." Though the timing was not right to withdraw Britain's commitment to Georgian statehood, Milne was certainly hopeful that at some point Britain would extract itself from this mess.

The Russian Civil War, and the growing strength of the anti-Bolshevik White armies, were making diplomacy more complicated, and undermining pledges made to Georgia and others. The British, together with other Allied powers including the French, were strongly committed to the Whites in their war against the

Red Army. This took priority over any support for the Georgians or any other newly independent states on the borders of the former empire.

Meanwhile, the Georgians were desperately trying to get the British on their side. On 8 February 1919, the Georgian delegation in Paris sent a four-page letter to the British delegation to the Peace Conference laying out the case for independence and recognition.

Four days later, in a handwritten note attached to the letter, Arnold J. Toynbee, the great historian who was then a young British diplomat, wrote that "The Georgian case put forward in this memorandum seems entirely reasonable. There is a danger of Georgia becoming alienated from us if her point of view is not considered – unless we can point to higher grounds of policy for overriding it." Toynbee was one of a number of British diplomats who showed real sympathy for the Georgian cause, unlike some of the military men posted to the region.[8]

Balfour himself remained less sympathetic than Toynbee. In his response to the Georgians, he wrote that he

> fully appreciates the importance of these claims of which he has taken note and sympathises with your desire that they should be brought at an early date before the Conference. He trusts however that you will realise that it is essential, with a view to secure an early settlement with the countries with which the Allies have been at war, that questions directly concerning these countries should first be treated by the conference.[9]

In other words, first of all the British needed to deal with the really important countries such as Germany and later, when there was more time, Georgia would be on the agenda. Unfortunately for Georgia, time was not on its side and the delays in winning recognition from the great powers and eventually the League of Nations took their toll.

Meanwhile, the Georgians were pressing for the British to recognise their representative in London, David Gambashidze.[10] In the archived documents discussing this issue, there is a hand-written note by E.H. Carr, another future historian then working for the Foreign Office. Like Toynbee, Carr was sympathetic to the Georgians and wrote:

> Finland, Esthonia [sic] and Latvia have representations in London who are received by the F.O. as "informal diplomatic representations" of their respective gov'ts which have been given a sort of informal recognition falling short of recognition as de facto gov'ts. It would be sufficient to suggest to the F.O. that M. Gambashidze should be treated on the same footing as the Finnish, Esthonian and Latvian representatives, if this is what is desired.

In this case, Balfour accepted Carr's view.

The British had only been in Georgia for a few weeks and relations were already strained. In late February, a British official in Batumi, Mr Stevens, sent a telegram to London saying that "Tiflis and Georgian Press as a whole antagonistic towards us and blames us for present situation and attacks by armed forces on Georgian Republic."[11] A few days later, Stevens acknowledged that things had calmed down and the Georgian press had become less antagonistic. "Georgian Press has adopted less unfriendly tone towards us," he wrote. "Some incorrect statements made last week regarding actions of our representatives are withdrawn. Slight decrease of anti-British propaganda perceptible last few days." Relieved that the problem of a critical local press had been taken care of, he then added: "I suggest that all transport, steamship and railway means be forthwith taken over by us."[12]

The British may have said things about urging the other great powers to recognise Georgia, but the fate of the Transcaucasian republics was a sideshow in the eyes of most of the leaders in London. The real fight in that part of the world was between the White armies, meaning primarily General Denikin and his Volunteer Army in southern Russia, and Admiral Kolchak's forces in Siberia, and the Bolsheviks. The British and French were backing Denikin and Kolchak.

Denikin would give no assurance to the Georgians that he recognised their right to self-determination. It seemed that he was committed not only to defeating the Bolsheviks and capturing Moscow, but also subduing rebellious national groups on the fringes of the old tsarist empire. Certain of victory against the Reds, Denikin had no intention of inheriting from them a much-reduced Russia. He wanted the empire back, all of it. Inevitably, his forces clashed with the Georgians.

On 7 April 1919 the Georgian government protested to the British that Denikin's forces had crossed the Georgian frontier in the district of Sochi. The Georgians were now engaged in fighting with Russian forces and they feared that if Denikin's men succeeded, Georgia would not survive as an independent country long enough to celebrate its first anniversary. Two weeks after the protest was delivered to the British, the headquarters of the People's Guard in Tiflis issued a stirring call for the Georgians to defend their country against Denikin's aggression. It is worth quoting at length for the picture it gives of how the Georgian Mensheviks viewed Denikin:

> A new danger is felt today: the dark shadow of General Denikin's forces overclouds Georgia; they have treacherously entered the

Sochi and Gagry districts and this threshold of our republic is at present in their hands; this threatens us with a new invasion, we are obliged to defend ourselves, saving our democracy and republic from the gory hands of Denikin which have turned Sochi district into a flaming fire, and have delivered all over to fire and sword. The population of Sochi district rose with arms in hand. Comrades! Hurry all to your arms, let all our armed forces be ready for defence.

We will defend ourselves from the terrible power of reaction from the old "gendarmerie" and from slavery, and we will preserve our literal existence from destruction. The aim of the treacherous foe is to knock out of our hands the valiant red banner, to establish despotism, the triumph of the forces of darkness and to crush our freedom and democracy.

The sacred blood spilt by our comrades on the field of battle, in defence of freedom and democracy, compels us comrades, to unite ourselves and closely surrounding the red banner with arms in hand to join battle to the death with the forces of reaction advancing against revolutionary Georgia.

Everyone should join the colours.

Our revolutionary obligation summons us.

Away with black reaction.

Long live revolutionary democracy!

Long live Socialism!

This is not how Trotsky and other Bolshevik propagandists would later portray the Georgian Mensheviks. In their view, the Georgian leadership colluded with Denikin and the British to fight the hated Soviet regime. Reading this declaration, however, one does begin to understand some of the concerns British officers may have had regarding the Georgian armed forces and government.

Some weeks later, on 9 May 1919, General Milne sent a message to the War Office in London that revealed a great deal about how he viewed the conflict between the Georgians and

Denikin. Milne began by insisting that the Georgian government – which had been elected by universal suffrage only a few weeks earlier – in "no way represents the real inhabitants of Georgia, but contains all the worst elements of Bolshevism, seems to have been considerably influenced by the unfortunate Bolshevik successes in South Russia."

He supported the imposition of a mandatory power urgently "as the incapacity of the Government is daily becoming apparent" – and not only in Georgia, but across all three Transcaucasian republics. The Georgian government's attitude toward the British is described as "truculent and hostile." The Georgians were also deemed guilty of taking action against Denikin despite orders from the British. Those orders, he wrote, were "flagrantly disobeyed and the attack made in spite of the presence of British troops." Milne was concerned that the Georgian army had become "a Bolshevik rabble who have hoisted the Red Flag and are openly insulting the British Troops." The People's Guard with their references to "the valiant red banner" were only confirming Milne's fears. Nothing seemed to be restraining the Georgians. Milne wrote that he had tried everything, "but to bring the Georgian Government to obedience stronger action is essential."

That "stronger action" was his request to be empowered to tell the Georgians that the British government "no longer regard the creation of the Republic with sympathy as was stated by the Foreign Office" a few months earlier. He also recommended the removal of the Georgian diplomats then based in London and Paris, suggesting that this might have a "sobering effect." Milne was acutely aware of how desperate the Georgians were to participate in the Paris Peace Conference and to win recognition from the Allies.

But that was all insignificant compared to what came next in Milne's telegram to London. "Once the western frontier between Denikin and Georgia is defined," he wrote, "I request I may be authorised *to instruct the Navy to open fire on any Georgian troops advancing north of it* and inform the Georgian Government accordingly." A handwritten minute scribbled onto this telegram reads: "I think the Georgians ought to be warned that they must behave themselves."

A few days later, the Director of Military Intelligence wrote to the Foreign Office expressing support for General Milne's suggestions, his only disagreement being the proposed expulsion of the Georgian delegates from Paris and London. No one, though, seemed particularly shocked at the suggestion that the Royal Navy might bombard Georgian troops resisting Denikin's advances into their country.

Relations between the British and the Georgians had reached a low point. But the British were also growing impatient with General Denikin, who was busy fighting the Georgians instead of marching on Moscow and overthrowing the Bolsheviks. Maybe the General found the tiny Georgian army an easier target than Trotsky's Red Army.

On 19 June 1919, the Georgian delegates at the Paris peace conference formally protested at Denikin's invasion of Georgian territory. The Georgians were particularly concerned about Denikin's order that Georgian troops evacuate territory between the rivers Mekhadyr and Bzyb on the Black Sea Coast, and urged that the Allies insist that Denikin's troops respect the Georgian frontiers.

On 17 July 1919 the War Office in London sent a secret memorandum to General Milne. It ordered him to tell General

Denikin that there was a line which he must not cross. "Denikin must be made to understand that the continued support of H.M. Government depends upon the loyal observance of this line," the memorandum stated.

> The Caucasian States must be informed that they are to abstain from all aggression against the Volunteer Army and cooperate with Denikin at least to the extent of supplying oil and other supplies for the Caspian Fleet and withholding them from the Bolsheviks. They should be warned that if they fail to comply with these conditions they will be deprived of British Goodwill and it will be rendered impossible for H.M. Government to insist upon the retention of Denikin's troops north of this line.

In other words, in exchange for Denikin halting his aggression against Georgia, the Georgians were ordered to supply Denikin's army with oil and other supplies and to deny these to the Bolsheviks. Agreeing to this, of course, would have been totally contrary to the Georgian commitment to neutrality.

Karl Kautsky later wrote that the British and their Allies "sought to entangle Georgia in the Russian Civil War, and to draw it into an alliance with Denikin against the Bolshevists." He neglected to mention that the Germans had done the same when they occupied the country, just as he didn't seem to have a negative word to say about the German occupation in general. He continued: "These overtures too were definitely rejected by the Georgian Government, which continued to maintain the strictest neutrality. That was not easy, as the conflicting classes in Russia adopted the attitude of who is not for us is against us."[13]

Georgia did try to stay neutral, but Kautsky may be slightly exaggerating when he used the phrase "*strictest* neutrality." Zhordania later wrote that when the German commanding general requested that Georgia support the Central Powers (Germany, Austria and Turkey) in the world war, he replied: "I have never considered the international position of Georgia as that of an *absolutely neutral* state, as the contrary is being proved by evident facts." Zhordania described Georgia's policy as being one of "limited neutrality." Georgia's neutrality, he wrote, was limited "by the very fact of the presence of General Von Kress and his soldiers on our territory during the world war." But Russia's neutrality was limited too, he said, "even to a greater extent, by the presence of [German ambassador] Count Mirbach in Moscow."[14]

The first few months of the British occupation had not gone well. But on 27 June 1919 things began to change when Balfour wrote to the Foreign Office supporting a proposal that Oliver Wardrop be dispatched to the region "with a view to prevent conflict between Georgia and General Denikin's army." Wardrop's mission was to be made broader than that, his brief being to work closely with the other Transcaucasian republics as well, which like Georgia were expressing alarm regarding Denikin's actions. Less than a month later, Curzon sent Wardrop to be the British chief commissioner to the three Transcaucasian republics.[15]

Wardrop was the perfect man for the job. He had visited Georgia on a couple of occasions in the nineteenth century, learned the local language and had written several books about the country including *The Kingdom of Georgia* in 1888. There were few people in Britain who knew the country as well. His sister Marjory translated Rustaveli's *The Knight in the Panther's Skin*, the great masterpiece of Georgian literature, into English. He was described as being "a slender, gentle-eyed fellow with a scholarly manner."[16]

Wardrop was given several objectives. These included reporting on the political situation in the region, preventing friction between

Denikin's forces and the Georgians, and advancing the interests of British trade. It was made clear to him that as long as the British maintained troops in the region, they would be under the authority of General Milne, with whom Wardrop could consult.

The friction between Denikin and the Georgians persisted. In July a British official wrote to the Georgian delegation in Paris assuring them that Denikin was not a threat.

> Although H.M.G. are aware that there have been difficulties as to the precise limits to be set to the zones on the Black Sea Coast occupied by General Denikin's forces and the Georgian military forces – difficulties which the British military authorities on the spot have done their utmost to overcome, H.M.G. have no information as to any plan of invasion of the Trans-Caucasian countries being entertained by General Denikin or his volunteer army.

If that wasn't sufficiently reassuring, they added that "On the contrary they have reason to believe that General Denikin is anxious to devote all his available military resources to his front against the Bolsheviks." This may have had something to do with the Red Army turning its attention to defeating Denikin, having already largely crushed Admiral Kolchak's White forces in Siberia.

Four months later, in a telegram Wardrop sent to the Foreign Office on 2 November 1919, he reminded the British government about continuing Georgian concerns about Denikin. Despite Denikin's forces now suffering a series of defeats that would end in a catastrophic defeat, he was still seen by the Georgians as a threat.

Meanwhile, Wardrop was considering what the British needed to be doing in Transcaucasia in general, and more specifically in Georgia. On 16 August 1919 he sent a long message to the Foreign Office laying out his views. He began by urging the

British government to reconsider the decision, already taken, to evacuate Transcaucasia. If this could not be prevented, he wanted the evacuation to be as slow as possible, and, as a minimum, to continue to hold onto Batumi and the surrounding district for as long as possible. Wardrop was clearly aware of the increasing danger to Georgia from both the Russians to the north and the Turks to the south.

To deal with the problem of the ongoing friction with Denikin, Wardrop urged that the Foreign Office dispatch "a carefully selected political officer responsible to the Foreign Service alone" to observe Denikin's Volunteer Army and advise him how to reduce friction with the Transcaucasian republics. "The political officer," he wrote, "should inform General Denikin that the continuance of supplies by him by His Majesty's Government is dependent on his strict observance of the principle of non-intervention in the internal affairs of the Republics and abstention from recruiting in their territories."

He called on Britain to either recognise the three republics or at least announce its intention to do so. The condition for this would be that those republics give "undoubted proof of their intention to live in peace and amity together and maintain a benevolent attitude towards General Denikin so far as his policy is directed to the support of a free, democratic government truly representative of a regenerated Russia." He also called upon the government to help get the republics recognised by other great powers, and admitted to the League of Nations.

Wardrop requested "a wireless installation of sufficient power" to allow him and his staff to communicate with Constantinople, with the British officer attached to Denikin in South Russia, and with the British forces in Mesopotamia (Iraq) and Tehran.

This request underscored the strategic significance of Georgia, which was located at the very heart of British interests in the Middle East.

Wardrop also proposed an intensification of trade between Britain and Transcaucasia, and the sending of expert technical advisors from Britain to the region. In addition, he suggested that "trustworthy representatives of trades unions should be allowed to travel to England and keep contact with the genuine British labour party."

He furthermore wanted to encourage the teaching of English to schoolchildren "and the establishment of an English boarding school of the Public School type with classical, modern, scientific and athletic teachers, and by helping carefully selected students of both sexes to secure admission to universities, high schools, schools of economics and commerce, working men's colleges etc. in Great Britain." He proposed cultural exchanges between Transcaucasia and England and even offered to personally help with this:

> I might arrange for the immediate application of the income of
> the Marjory Wardrop Fund in Oxford (now amounting to £3500)
> to the delivery of lectures on the history, literature and language
> of Georgia and I think I could bring about similar instruction
> in Armenian and Turkish subjects with the assistance of friends,
> without asking for any aid from the Treasury.

The Georgians were delighted to have Wardrop on their side.

While the government in London considered Wardrop's proposals, friction between the Georgians and Denikin continued unabated. On 26 December 1919, Wardrop found himself passing on to the Foreign Office in London a detailed Georgian government response to allegations made by a pro-Denikin newspaper in

Russia. The newspaper had claimed that the Georgians secretly negotiated with the Turks and the Bolsheviks, and that they had agreed with the Azerbaijanis to help them fight Denikin's army if it attacked, that they were planning to remove the Allies from the region entirely, that Georgia and Azerbaijan had secretly connived to gang up on Armenia, and so on. The Georgians insisted that none of this was true.[17]

The British occupation of Georgia was never popular with the local population. Over time, the British withdrew their forces to Batumi, but even this was not enough for the Georgian Social Democrats. They constantly demanded that Batumi too should be returned to Georgian sovereignty as soon as possible, and the British forces withdrawn. As David Lang wrote, "the purblind patriots in the Georgian government resented even this last British bridgehead as an affront to their national dignity." Lang was convinced that faced with threats from both the Bolsheviks and Turkey, calling for a British withdrawal from Georgia was counter-productive.[18]

In early July 1920, the British finally withdrew. In Batumi, people celebrated, and the streets were festooned with Georgian national flags as the British troops withdrew to the port, while Georgian General Giorgi Kvinitadze marched his forces into the city.

A year earlier, in April 1919, Louis Mallet met with a couple of Georgian leaders who expressed concern about a possible Russian invasion. At that time, their fear was General Denikin and his Volunteer Army. Mallet reassured them, saying that "if the British forces were to leave the Caucasus at some future date, their place would be taken by other Allied troops." And throughout the preceding several months, there had been various proposals of this sort, including an abortive attempt to create an Italian mandate. In the end, though, when the British forces withdrew from Batum, they left Georgia alone and vulnerable.

"Georgia hailed the disappearance of the British imperialists as a major triumph," wrote David Lang, "without giving much thought to the even more formidable foes which now ringed about her."[19]

7

GEORGIA'S AGRARIAN REVOLUTION

Nothing the Georgian Social Democrats did could compare in importance to their agrarian reform. In a poor, rural society like Georgia it was at the heart of their democratic socialist project to transform the country.

Years before the Social Democrats ever came to power in Georgia, they had a powerful learning experience in Guria, where a rebellious population took control over an entire province for several years. There, land-poor peasants took advantage of a tottering tsarist regime which had lost the ability to rule large parts of the country, and seized land from the landowners.

Later, when the Russian Social Democrats (including their members in Georgia) debated the best way to deal with the "agrarian question," they considered a whole range of options including full nationalisation, municipalisation, and redistribution of land to the peasants. For the rebellious Gurian peasants, only the last option was appealing.

According to Marxist theory, the urban proletariat would provide the leadership of the upcoming Russian Revolution, with the peasants following. But the Gurian peasants didn't play according to those rules, and didn't wait for party congresses and Social Democratic intellectuals to make decisions for them. They demanded to be treated as equals, to take their place as full members of the Social Democratic Party, and to be heard. In this they succeeded, changing how the Georgian Social Democrats viewed the peasants as a class and their role in the revolution. They influenced not only the Georgian Social Democratic leaders, but Lenin as well. The Bolshevik leader grew to understand the central role that would be played by the peasants in the upcoming revolution. But while both the Bolsheviks and Mensheviks became increasingly focussed on the peasants and their demands, their approaches to the agrarian problem were strikingly different.

After the defeat of the 1905 revolution in Russia, the Russian Social Democratic Labour Party (RSDRP) held its congress in Stockholm in late April and early May of 1906. Though the Bolsheviks and Mensheviks had split into two separate parties several years earlier, in the aftermath of 1905 they attempted to put that split behind them. Stockholm was therefore branded as a "unity congress," and involved not only the two main Social Democratic factions, but also parties from Poland, Lithuania, Finland, Bulgaria and even the Jewish Bund. One of the key questions the party needed to discuss, drawing upon the lessons of the failed revolution, was what to do about the agrarian question. In the run-up to the party congress, the leading lights on both sides laid out their views on the subject.

Lenin, leading the Bolsheviks, supported the full nationalisation of the land. He was convinced that for the Social Democrats to win and retain power, they needed not only the support of the small urban proletariat, but of the millions of land-poor peasants.

To win their support, he thought making nationalisation of the land part of the party programme would help.

Speaking for the Mensheviks, Georgi Plekhanov challenged Lenin's view, rejecting nationalisation of land. Plekhanov, then fifty years old, was the grand old man of Russian Marxism. The argument he made against the nationalisation of the land deeply troubled Lenin and not only because the Bolshevik leader had once seen himself as a student of Plekhanov.

According to Karl August Wittfogel, "Plekhanov branded the idea of a socialist seizure of power as premature and the plan to nationalize the land as potentially reactionary. Such a policy, instead of discontinuing the attachment of the land and its tillers to the state, would leave 'untouched this survival of an old semi-Asiatic order' and thus facilitate its restoration."[1]

Wittfogel wrote many years after the fact, but it is worth taking a moment to discuss who he was and how he is relevant to this story. Wittfogel's name will not be familiar to most people today, but in the 1920s he was the international Communist movement's leading expert on the subject of Asia. A German Marxist, Wittfogel took an interest in the largely unknown writings of Marx on the subject of what he called "the Asiatic mode of production" or, sometimes, "Oriental despotism."[2]

Wittfogel rediscovered a whole body of work describing a type of society that did not fit into the usual Marxist historiography. The opening sentences of the *Communist Manifesto* famously describe how the various stages of class society evolved, from ancient slave societies, through feudalism to modern capitalism. To most Marxists, this remains a more or less accurate picture of European history. But parallel to this, in large parts of the world (and not only in Asia), societies existed in which there were no social classes in the European sense, and no class struggle either. These were countries in which the state was stronger than society, and where instead of progressive historic changes, the only changes seemed to be dynastic.

These societies, which Wittfogel characterised as "hydraulic," were based on large-scale irrigation works, including canals. Civil society was weak, the regimes were brutal and despotic, and the land was nationalised. The Russian empire, which had been under the rule of the Mongols for a time, was described by Marx as being "semi-Asiatic" and this label had long been accepted by most Russian Marxists. Their society was not feudal and never had been. Rather, it was "semi-Asiatic," characterised by a powerful despotic state, weak social classes, and very little private ownership of land.

This is what Plekhanov was referring to in his opposition to Lenin's 1906 proposal to nationalise agricultural land in Russia. According to Wittfogel, Lenin himself used a variety of expressions to refer to what Plekhanov warned against: "'the restoration of the Asiatic mode of production,' 'the restoration of our old "semi-Asiatic" order,' the restoration of Russia's 'semi-Asiatic nationalization,' 'the restoration of the semi-Asiatic order,' 'the return to the *Aziatchina*,' and Russia's 'Asiatic' restoration'."[3]

They all meant the same thing: the possibility that a revolution aimed at overthrowing the old tsarist regime could result in a system that was infinitely worse, far more repressive and barbaric. Lenin was aware of this possibility, and was troubled by it. He remained troubled by it even after the Bolsheviks under his leadership seized power in 1917, and his fears about the revolution giving birth to something monstrous continued right up to his death.

As Wittfogel put it, "With these experiences in mind, Plekhanov fought Lenin's program to establish a dictatorial government based on a small proletarian minority that could do little to prevent restoration. Instead he advocated the municipalization of the land, a measure that would place 'organs of public self-government … in possession of the land' and thus 'erect a bulwark against reaction'."[4]

In other words, the debate over whether to nationalise the land, or turn it over to local organs of self-government (or even over to the peasants directly), was not just about what would benefit the peasants themselves, or would be the most efficient way to run an agricultural society. The agrarian question went to the very heart of what kind of society Russia was – and what it could become.

Lenin did not leave Plekhanov's analysis unchallenged. Writing later, he applied his cutting sarcasm to the man who was once his mentor. "When Plekhanov speaks," Lenin wrote, "he is brilliant and witty, he crackles, twirls, and sparkles like a Catherine-wheel. The trouble starts when the speech is taken down verbatim and later subjected to a logical examination."[5]

The Bolshevik leader conceded that of course there was a risk that following a revolution there might well be a restoration of the old order in Russia. "We are not in a position to call forth at our own will a socialist revolution in the West," he wrote, "which is *the only absolute guarantee* against restoration in Russia." Those words would come back to haunt the Bolsheviks once it became clearer that there would be no Communist revolutions anywhere else for some time, and that they were on their own, attempting to build "socialism in one country," in Stalin's phrase. In any event, Lenin stood his ground, insisting that "it is nationalisation [of the land] that far more radically eliminates the economic basis of Asiatic despotism" – thereby acknowledging that Russia was in fact "Asiatic" and that the risk of a restoration following a revolution needed to be addressed.

Plekhanov's warnings that a "premature" seizure of power by the Social Democrats and the subsequent nationalisation of land would not produce a socialist paradise but something far worse turned out to be prescient. As Wittfogel summed it up:

> Plekhanov certainly was on firm ground when he pointed to Russia's Asiatic heritage and when he stressed "the necessity to eliminate that economic foundation through which our people have approached more and more closely the Asiatic people." This formulation implies what Plekhanov in the same debate and in conformity with Marx' and Engels' views said explicitly – that in Russia, Oriental despotism, although very much weakened, still persisted after the Emancipation [of the serfs in 1861]. And he was only drawing the logical conclusion from this premise when he warned that the decay of the hoped-for revolution would lead to an Asiatic restoration.[6]

These ideas – in particular the possibility of an "Asiatic restoration" – were to prove anathema to Stalin and the rising Soviet Communist bureaucracy, for reasons which now seem clear. Wittfogel was eventually expelled from the ranks of the German Communist Party, and at an infamous meeting in Leningrad in 1931 the Soviet leadership put an end to all discussion of the "Asiatic mode of production." Russia until 1917 was now rebranded as having been "feudal" all along, and the most extreme form of nationalisation imaginable – the forced collectivisation that Stalin imposed at an unimaginable human cost – was therefore perfectly acceptable.

The debate which took place in 1906 certainly influenced the thinking of the Georgian Mensheviks when they came to power after the fall of the tsarist regime. Lenin's Bolsheviks were willing to risk an "Asiatic restoration" with their premature seizure of power and a nationalisation of the land that provided the social basis for despotism, confident that a revolution in the West would save their revolution. Zhordania and his comrades had something entirely different in mind.

Karl Kautsky described agrarian reform as "the most important task of the new government" in Georgia, though he characterised this as "clearing away the remains of feudalism." In this sense he was being somewhat imprecise in his use of language, for the issue was clearing away the remains of "Oriental despotism," as Marx would have put it.[7] Kautsky noted that the result of the freeing of the serfs by the tsar, which took place in 1861 in Russia and slightly later in Georgia, caused the peasants to actually lose land. The landlords retained most of their lands, and peasants were compelled to lease land from them. In Kautsky's view, this system of small landholdings "makes any rational agriculture impossible, and yields a scanty living to the countryman."

The revolution was therefore tasked with giving land to the peasants. This was not a step towards socialism, in Kautsky's view, but it was necessary. Kautsky was unflinching in his description of what giving land to the peasants actually meant: "This was no socialistic but a middle-class revolution, but the conditions rendered it necessary, and it took place. We Marxians are distinguished from utopian socialists by the fact that we recognise that Socialism is only possible under specific circumstances."[8] Kautsky shared the view of the Georgian Mensheviks that the country needed first of all to become a liberal capitalist society before it could transition to socialism. And the first steps in this direction included the agrarian reform.

One of the Georgians' main complaints was not only that land had been taken away from the peasants, but that it had been concentrated in the hands of the Russian state during the century-long tsarist occupation of the country. According to a Georgian government publication, "On these lands whole villages of Russian and other foreign colonizers have been settled by the Government. In many Georgian provinces the Government has even prohibited the Georgian peasants from buying any land from these so-called Imperial possessions."[9] In other words, the land question was intimately linked to the national question. Land reform was part of the process of the liberation of the Georgian people from Russian imperial rule.

Long before the Social Democrats had a chance to pass any laws, the peasants took the law into their own hands, as they had done in Guria in 1902–6. As Ronald Grigor Suny wrote, "The fall of the monarchy had led to a general questioning of authority, and Caucasian peasants had almost immediately ceased paying their redemption payments and other taxes to the state and either refused altogether to pay dues to the landlords or demanded that they be reduced."[10]

The landowners protested to the local representatives of the Provisional Government. Peasants were illegally cutting down forests, and were using private land and state-owned land to graze their animals without permission. In response, government officials issued a decree demanding that the peasants behave, and pay their debts.

In the Gori district, the peasants complained directly to the Menshevik party chairman who sent delegates to meet with Zhordania in Tiflis. The result was not the enforcement of the decree, but the sacking of the government official who had attempted to enforce it. No further efforts were made to collect taxes and rents from the peasants.

While this incident showed a degree of sensitivity towards the peasants and their needs, the initial reaction of the Georgian Social Democrats to the revolution was to revert to old Marxist formulations naming the moving forces of the revolution as the proletariat, the army and the liberal capitalists. Zhordania did not mention the peasants as a "moving force" of the revolution, at least not in its very early stages, and almost certainly saw them as a potentially reactionary force.

Though the Georgian Social Democrats had learned many lessons from the Gurian Republic of 1902-6, they seemed to have forgotten some of these by 1917. Nevertheless, they remained the dominant party among the peasants. Their Bolshevik rivals seemed readier to opportunistically support rebellious peasants and to include them among the revolutionary forces in their rhetoric, but they had very limited success in drawing support from rural workers. The Socialist Revolutionaries, which was the dominant party among peasants across the Russian empire, also had little influence in Georgia.

In the first few months of the 1917 revolution in Transcaucasia, a series of conferences adopted a wide range of differing positions on the agrarian question in the region. A Socialist Revolutionary-dominated conference of soldiers demanded the socialisation of the land. The Social Democrats had advocated the confiscation only of church and state lands, but later amended this to include the transfer of some lands that had been given to the nobles in the emancipation which would be given back to the peasants. Church and state lands could then be rented by the peasants.

Decisions at this stage were being made in common across all three Transcaucasian countries. The Georgians and Azerbaijanis generally supported the Social Democratic proposals while the Armenians and Russians in the region backed the proposals for nationalisation of the land. Everyone agreed that a final resolution of the agrarian question would have to be made by the Constituent Assembly.

It took Lenin's seizure of power in Petrograd to move the Transcaucasian politicians to action. It was now clear that the Constituent Assembly had been pre-empted by the Bolshevik coup (and would later be dispersed by Bolshevik soldiers). It could not and would not solve the agrarian problem. The first Provisional Government in Transcaucasia issued a decree on the land on 16 December 1917, and passed a law in the Transcaucasian parliament on 7 March 1918. These measures were intended to be carried out across the region, but in reality were only realised in Georgia, where peasants suffered from greater land hunger than in the other parts of Transcaucasia. The laws were passed with the support of Azerbaijani politicians, landowners among them, who had no intention of ever implementing them.

Every large landowner had land taken away from him, without compensation. Large landowners could retain only as much land as they could till (with their families), and were reduced to medium-sized peasant holdings. The maximum amount of land each family could own was limited to 17.5 acres of gardens or vineyards, 37.5 acres of arable land or 100 acres of pasture. Anything above those amounts was seized by the state as part of a national land reserve. Some exceptions were made for larger holdings which had special value for the national economy. The private market in land was essentially eliminated, though buying and selling of land went on in the black market.

British officers in the region did not trust the Georgian Mensheviks. Admiral of the Fleet Sir Somerset Arthur Gough-Calthorpe, who commanded the Royal Navy fleet in the Mediterranean, sent a telegram to the Foreign Office in which he warned about the agrarian reform then underway in Georgia. "If by Bolshevism is meant the nationalisation of land leaving property without compensation using force when necessary to do this," he wrote, "the Georgian Government of which these men are heads and representatives cannot be exonerated from holding Bolshevik opinions." The Foreign Office was forced to reply and explain to the admiral that this was not the case: "Nationalization of land, even by forcible measures, does not necessarily imply co-operation or even sympathy with Russian Bolsheviks."

Karl Kautsky, who was aghast at the inefficiencies of the traditional Georgian landowning system, noted that, as a result of this reform, "Well conducted, intensive large-scale cultivation is maintained as far as possible, and is either carried on under the auspices of the State, or devolved upon the local assemblies."[11]

Poor peasants were entitled to lease land - but not to buy land - from the new state-owned land reserve. Gardens and arable land were given over to peasants who cultivated it. Pastures were generally turned over for common use.

Peasants in many districts were not happy with this first attempt at agrarian reform. In the northern mountainous districts of the country there were signs of peasant unrest. Sometimes the cause was the transfer of large estates not to the peasants directly, but to state control. The Georgian Bolsheviks, looking for any opportunity to win popular support, agitated in support of the peasant demands, including creating armed detachments of peasant rebels. They were particularly successful in South

Ossetia, where an incendiary mix of national resentment and peasant discontent led to open rebellion. This in turn caused the government in Tiflis to send units of the People's Guard to put down the rebellions, which was done with brutal force in the winter of 1918.

Trotsky quoted People's Guard commander Jugeli in order to illustrate the brutality of Menshevik rule. In his published memoir, Jugeli wrote "Ossetian villages are burning all round us … In the interests of the struggling working class, in the interests of the future socialism, we will be cruel. Yes, we will. I can look on with imperturbed soul and clear conscience at the fire and smoke of the burning houses … I am quite calm, quite calm indeed."[12]

The Georgian Social Democrats had shown more than a decade earlier that they could, over time, hear what the peasants were saying. The growing unrest in some parts of the country led them to adopt a new law on 29 January 1919 which gave peasants the right to purchase land from the state at a moderate price.

As Karl Kautsky put it, "This is certainly not a Socialistic step, but it was rendered unavoidable by the pressure of the peasants."[13] The state, though, reserved for itself the right of first purchase.

Faced with an ongoing economic crisis as well as unrest in the countryside, the Georgian Social Democrats were looking for ways to increase the production of food and other agricultural products. They hoped that selling land to peasants would give them incentives to make improvements and rationalise production. Tenant farmers, it was felt, were less likely to do this than landowning peasants.

The result of this was that 5 million acres of gardens and arable land, pastures and woods were purchased by peasants. In addition, the woods and lands formerly owned by the Russian state, its nobles and the church came into the hands of the Georgian state, which had overnight become the country's largest landowner.

The main opposition parties – the Socialist Revolutionaries, Socialist Federalists and National Democrats – were united in their opposition to the new law. Agriculture Minister Noe Khomeriki, a veteran of the Gurian Republic, replied to his critics: "Our agrarian reform destroyed the principle of feudal property. … In general we neither establish nor reject bourgeois private property; this is a fact of life with which, of course, the law has to deal.[14]

Not only the opposition parties expressed concerns; peasants too complained about the implementation of the new law. As Ronald Grigor Suny wrote,

> In some districts where there were few large estates to be confiscated, the land shortages could not be alleviated locally; elsewhere the population was so dense that farmers received only tiny supplements to their small plots. In no district of Kutaisi province, for example, did the average peasant farm exceed 1.6 hectares; the situation was considerably better in Tiflis province, where the average plot ran from 4 to 7 hectares.[15]

In addition to selling land and redistributing it, the government also began to move peasant families around. Over 8,000 families were moved in the second half of 1918 to areas where more land was available. Sometimes the peasants were moved for strategic reasons as well as economic ones, to borderlands facing the Russians or disputed territories with the Armenians.

In the 1919 elections, the Social Democrats did very well among the urban voters, winning 72% of them, but even better among rural voters with 82% – which more than anything else demonstrates the popularity of the agrarian reform they had introduced.

Eighteen months after the passage of agrarian reform law, Khomeriki addressed a congress of the Georgian Social Democratic Party. He was able to report that the confiscation of land owned by nobles had been completed. Nine-tenths of that land had been turned over to poor or landless peasants. Almost 5,000 estates had been affected.

Nobles often wound up with more land than their peasant neighbours, but not much more, and the poorest peasants did the best from the reform. The state, meanwhile, retained control of the pasturelands, forests and waterways. As Suny put it,

> The extent to which the confiscation and redistribution was actually carried out was quite extraordinary, given the fact that the Georgian lands had not been surveyed, that the ministry had few qualified people to carry out the technical aspects of the reform, and that the whole operation was largely completed in two years while the government was fighting off external enemies and internal rebellions.[16]

Though the Georgian Social Democrats had achieved their aims with the agrarian reform, it was not without its critics. Karl Kautsky for one was concerned that the reforms kept in place a system of inefficient small-scale farms. He hoped that over time the existing village cooperatives would grow and cultivate larger areas.

Historian Teodor Shanin, who wrote approvingly about the agrarian reform, noted that few peasants played leading roles in the Social Democratic Party, or in Georgia's parliament. "Little was done to mobilise the peasantry politically or militarily. The privatisation of land without any collective projects attached or considered led, if anything, to the peasants' political demobilisation." As a result of this, he wrote that

Nothing like the Red Guria of 1905-07 was called into being in the Georgian republic, with significant results for its fate. ... The peasant majority which gave its loyalty to the revolutionary leaders of 1903-07 was told to stay at home, till its land, vote once in a while and leave politics to the hegemonic classes of the bourgeois stage of history.[17]

Shanin links this "demobilisation" of the radicalised peasantry to the occasional outbreaks of peasant unrest that took place between 1918 and 1921, including in places where ethnicity was not an issue, noting that these were put down by force.

The motivation of the Social Democrats for carrying out the land reform in the manner they did was not specifically to thwart the risk of an "Asiatic restoration," as Plekhanov had warned. Instead, it was a practical measure to reduce the risk of peasant rebellion, while also ensuring that the nobles, whose lands were expropriated without compensation, were also not turned into irreconcilable enemies. The land reform was a success in that sense, as there were not large-scale peasant uprisings, and the nobles quietly accepted that the old ways of doing things were gone forever. If the reform didn't contribute to big improvements in productivity or reduce rural poverty, that may have come over time. Unfortunately, this was time which the Georgian Republic did not have

The Bolsheviks were the harshest critics of the Social Democrats. They were furious that nobles were allowed to keep some of their property, arguing that the allotments given to the nobles were so large that they could still employ hired labour. Furthermore, they could game the system by dividing up their families to claim additional lands, and once the buying and selling of land became legal again, wealthy nobles could snap up even more land. Above all the Bolsheviks were furious that while the nobles had paid a price, they still remained intact as a privileged landowning class.

While in Georgia the Social Democrats took the existing agrarian reform first proposed in 1917 and carried it through to the end, resulting in widespread peasant landownership, in Russia the country passed through several different periods. "War communism" was, in essence, a civil war between the Bolshevik regime based in the cities and peasants in the countryside. It was a disaster for all concerned and was finally ended by Lenin with the proclamation of the "New Economic Policy" (NEP) in 1921. The NEP, which brought an end to the food crisis that had gripped the Soviet regime from the beginning, had certain similarities with the Georgian agrarian reform. But it was replaced within a few years by Stalin's programme of forced collectivisation, a monstrous policy that caused millions of deaths and unimaginable human suffering. Forced collectivisation also had the effect, predicted by Plekhanov during the 1906 debate, of providing the social basis for an "Asiatic restoration," in the form of the Stalin regime. In Georgia, the agrarian reform was one aspect – probably the most important one – of the new society the Social Democrats were creating. But it was not only in rural areas that the Georgian Mensheviks were distinguishing themselves from the Bolsheviks. Georgia's small urban working class was also to learn the difference between authoritarian and democratic socialism.

8

THE INDEPENDENCE
OF THE TRADE UNIONS

The trade union movement in Georgia in 1918 was a very young one. The first unions had really only emerged during the 1905 revolution, and these were "mercilessly suppressed," according to Kautsky. The repression was worse in Georgia than in Russia, as the country was seen (correctly) as a hotbed of resistance to tsarist rule. "Only after the March Revolution of 1917," Kautsky wrote, "was it possible for Trade Unions to be formed again in Georgia."[1]

The first unions to emerge after the revolution were the printers, followed by the commercial employees. At the very end of 1917, the first Trade Union Congress was held in Tiflis. There were forty-one trade unions represented there with a combined membership of 29,000. This number was soon to soar. The second congress of the unions held in 1919 showed twice as many affiliated unions. By the end of 1920, there were 113 unions in the country with 64,000 members – out of an estimated 100,000 wage workers.[2]

The trade unions were officially politically neutral, but an estimated 95% of their members belonged to the Menshevik party. The party, with 80,000 members, actually had *more* members than the unions. This would have been quite unusual in most other countries, but it made sense in Georgia because the party included peasants and intellectuals as well as industrial workers.

The new Georgian unions born during the revolution of 1917 were organised by industry, not vocation – though this was not rigidly applied. In some countries, including the United States, this was a major point of contention in the labour movement, with first the Industrial Workers of the World and later the Congress of Industrial Organizations challenging the traditional craft unionism of the American Federation of Labor.[3]

The unions as well as the party controlled a number of newspapers. The party had four dailies, five weeklies and two monthlies. The unions had two newspapers for the whole movement. Most of the publications appeared in both Georgian and Russian editions. In addition to owning newspapers, the newly formed unions owned their own buildings, including a theatre and a meeting place called the Plekhanov House, named after the founding father of Russian Marxism.

The railway workers union played an important role in the early Georgian labour movement, and continues to do so even today. It had a special building of its own in Tiflis and two newspapers. "The wage workers in the large undertakings are quite steeped in modern ideas," observed Kautsky, and "above all, the railway workers who are the proletarian élite in economically backward countries, where Capitalism has commenced to penetrate."[4]

The railway workers union in Russia also played a pivotal role in the revolution. Shortly after the Bolshevik seizure of power in November 1917, the railway workers' union rejected the one-party state and demanded that Lenin bring other socialist parties into his government. Though the union initially had a great deal of leverage, in the end the Bolsheviks prevailed and a single-party dictatorship was established.

In Georgia, throughout the first couple of years of revolution, strikes were common. In late June 1918, the port workers in Poti regularly walked out, demanding increased pay, which seriously hindered the export of manganese to Germany. Manganese was essential to the war effort and the Germans were not at all happy with the Poti port workers and their incessant strikes. Other Georgian exports including tobacco, wool and copper were affected as well, as were imports of much-needed food supplies including flour.

The workers in Georgia's other port, Batumi, were also causing trouble and in 1919, when the British had displaced the Germans occupying the country, Mr. Stevens, a British diplomat, complained about continuing industrial action in the two ports. "Workmen demand enormous increase on already high rate of daily wage," he wrote.[5]

But by early 1919, strikes had become rarer. During that year, only 2,427 workers across the entire country participated in strikes. What had happened?

Probably the most important reason was the creation in May 1919 of a Board of Wages (*tarifnaia palata*) under the Ministry of Labour. The employers and the workers each got to send ten members to this board, whose president was the minister of labour. The board tried to keep wages in line with rises in the cost of living. But it had other tasks as well, including discussion of collective bargaining agreements and acting as a mediator in industrial disputes. As Kautsky summarised its work:

This office has hitherto succeeded in averting the outbreak of any open conflict. Since it began to function in May, 1919, the Trade Unions of Georgia have not found it necessary to declare a single strike, although they were not hindered from doing so by no prohibition, as is the case in Bolshevist Russia. In this respect Georgia is unique.[6]

Another reason is that the Social Democratic government asked the unions to help increase production. The country was in a state of permanent economic crisis and the last thing Georgia's economy needed was more days lost to industrial action. During the three years of Georgian independence, the country was isolated from its neighbours and from the West. This had a devastating effect on industry. Internal economic relationships had also broken down. As Ronald Grigor Suny wrote, "Soviet scholars estimate that coal production fell nearly 50 percent from 1913 to 1919 and manganese dropped to about 13 percent of prewar production by 1920. The shortages of raw material caused reductions in industrial output; only about 60 percent of Georgia's largest plants managed to operate steadily."[7]

Because of the very close relationship between the organised workers and the ruling party, this appeal did not fall on deaf ears, and unions were willing to cooperate. The Georgian trade unionists Kautsky met in late 1920 painted a picture of a loyal and responsible trade union movement which was willing and eager to do all it could to strengthen the country's economy. Strikes were therefore not on the agenda.[8]

As Kautsky pointed out, the Georgian trade unionists he met "regard the strike as the sharpest weapon in the proletarian class struggle. How highly they esteem it is shown by the fact that they demand the establishment of the right to strike in the

Constitution. But they are quite clear on the point that this formidable weapon is only to be used in case of direct need."[9]

The legal right of workers to form independent trade unions was never in doubt in Georgia. According to Article 35 of the draft constitution, "The citizens of the Georgian Republic have the right to form professional or other societies without previous authority of the government, provided that their object is not forbidden by law. The dissolution of such societies is only possible by order of a court of law."[10]

According to a Georgian government publication in 1919, "The Employers, Administrators and any persons preventing a member of a Union or a Union itself from exercising their rights are liable to imprisonment. Unions enjoy complete liberty with regard to the realization of their aims, provided that these latter are not prohibited by the Law."[11]

Though the right of workers to join and form trade unions is today generally regarded as a basic human right, the right to strike remains somewhat more controversial even now. The International Labour Organisation now acknowledges that "the right to strike has been recognised internationally as a fundamental right of workers and their organizations and as an intrinsic corollary to the right to organize."[12] But not all governments and not all employers accept this. In Georgia, long before most countries even recognised the right of workers to form unions, workers had a legally protected right to strike.

Not only did the Georgian union leaders choose to waive their right to strike, even after forcing the Constituent Assembly to enshrine that right in the new constitution, they went on to make further concessions, including allowing piece-work and a system of bonuses in the workplace. In exchange for these concessions, they demanded and received more than just goodwill and fine words from their Social Democratic leaders.

In spite of the ongoing economic crisis, workers could buy essential goods such as bread and salt from the government at lower than market prices, while the rapidly growing cooperatives also allowed them buy products at wholesale prices.

In addition, many of the unions' demands were met – including the adoption of an eight-hour workday. Overtime work was permitted only in special cases and workers doing overtime received double the normal rate of pay. Child labour was made illegal. Insurance schemes were established to ensure that workers continued to receive an income when unemployed or ill. New rules were adopted regarding the hiring and firing of workers. Night work was forbidden for women and adolescents. Adolescents were not allowed to work more than a six-hour day.

Though the government tended to avoid any large-scale nationalisation of industry, in August 1919 it established a state monopoly on manganese export followed by a general monopoly on all foreign trade. The local Bolsheviks pushed for more radical measures aiming for the abolition of capitalism, which the Social Democrats rejected. Other opposition parties, including the Socialist Revolutionaries and Socialist Federalists, also argued for more extreme measures, hoping that these could help undermine the Bolsheviks. But the Bolsheviks had little influence inside the country's unions. At a trade union conference in April 1919, a Bolshevik proposal that unions should pursue political rather than economic ends was ignored.

The trade unions' decision not to use the "sharpest weapon in the proletarian class struggle" was, in Kautsky's view, a sign of their strength, not weakness. He wrote: "The wage workers are the only organised and resolute class in Georgia. They know exactly what they want. They know not only their special interests, but also the common interests of the community, which they allow to guide them."[13]

They were strong not only because they organised two-thirds of the country's workers, but because of their unique relationship with the intellectuals who provided much of the Social Democratic leadership. In Lenin's view, the working class needed to overcome a narrow, "trade union" view of the world in order to carry out a socialist revolution. Intellectuals were therefore needed to provide a vanguard to lead the class and his Bolshevik party was unashamedly a party led by intellectuals, providing leadership to a class which did not and could not understand its own historic role.

The Mensheviks, and particularly the Georgian Social Democrats, presented a somewhat more complicated picture. "Among the one hundred and two members of the Social-Democratic Party in the Constituent Assembly," observed Kautsky, "are thirty-two workers, the rest being intellectuals; twenty teachers, fourteen journalists, thirteen lawyers, seven doctors, three engineers and thirteen officials."[14] In Kautsky's view, the workers were able to influence the intellectuals. Other writers, though, disagree.

"What Kautsky fails to understand is that the proletariat did not lead but was rather led by the intellectuals," wrote Kazemzadeh. "The Menshevik Party leadership was full of former nobles, merchants, lawyers, graduates of Church seminaries, and children of priests."[15] The secret of the Mensheviks' success, he believed, was their being an all-inclusive, multi-class party representing the whole nation. And yet the Social Democrats did have their own special relationship with one of those classes – the workers. "It is a fact that labour received more attention from the Government than any other social class," he wrote. "The socialist ideology of the Mensheviks and their connections with the workers made them the champions of the proletarian cause, though, by their own admission, they were building a capitalist society as the only one from which a socialist society might ultimately emerge."[16]

Kautsky pointed out that twenty years of Social Democratic agitation among the Georgian working class established a level of trust between the workers and the intelligentsia. When local Bolsheviks argued that shortages of goods were due to Georgia's separation from Russia, Labour Minister Giorgi Eradze persuaded a mass meeting that independence had saved Georgia from the horrors of such things as forced requisitioning from the peasantry.

In another example, when municipal workers in Tiflis went on strike to protest at unpaid wages, they were opposed not only by the Social Democratic party leaders, but by the Tiflis soviet and even the council of trade unions.[17]

The Georgian Democratic Republic was developing a strong civil society, with trade unions at its core. Those unions were independent and powerful, winning the right to strike, which became increasingly unnecessary as the government bowed to key union demands. The Social Democrats were "careful to maintain and nurture their special relationship with the small and variegated working class," wrote historian Ronald Grigor Suny. As a result, "workers showed restraint in their protests" and "class antagonisms in Georgia were not nearly as deep as they were in central Russian cities or even in Baku."[18] Innovative new institutions such as the Board of Wages ensured that workers received their basic needs even as the country passed through a period of enormous economic difficulties. The relationship between workers, their unions and the broader society foreshadowed similar developments that took place decades later in Western Europe.

The Georgians also provided an alternative model to the one pursued by the Bolsheviks in Russia, where the "trade union question" was the subject of fierce debate at the time. In Russia, the civil war was winding down. Trotsky, who had led the Red Army to victory on many fronts, began to turn his attention to post-war reconstruction. Russia faced many of the same problems Georgia did, cut off from foreign trade, facing high unemployment and shortages of essential goods. In addition, there was considerable unrest among the urban working class, with periodic waves of strikes.

In Trotsky's view, the military discipline that had worked so well in the Red Army should be applied to civilian life as well. Towards the end of 1920 he proposed that the "chatterboxes" who ran the trade unions be replaced, and that the unions forfeit their independence and become appendages of the state. Using unusually sharp language, and anticipating accusations that workers would become little more than slaves, Trotsky publicly defended compulsory labour.

"Is it true that compulsory labour is always unproductive?" he asked. "This is the most wretched and miserable liberal prejudice: chattel slavery, too, was productive ... Compulsory serf labour did not grow out of the feudal lords' ill-will. It was [in its time] a progressive phenomenon."[19]

Trotsky's biographer Isaac Deutscher commented: "Carried away by his desire to justify the measures he sponsored, he, the rebel *par excellence*, the expounder of permanent revolution, came very near to talking like an apologist for past systems of coercion and exploitation."[20]

The most outspoken opponents of these proposals came from outside the Bolshevik ranks, and the Mensheviks experienced a surge of support among industrial workers as they fought against Trotsky's plan to militarise labour. One of the Russian Menshevik leaders, Abramovich, famously commented that "You cannot build a planned economy in the way the Pharaohs built their pyramids."[21]

Trotsky's contempt for the "miserable liberal prejudice" proved to be ahead of his time. Lenin for one thought that unions deserved a small measure of autonomy, if for no other reason than to allow workers to let off steam. He was supported by Zinoviev and Stalin, who made the case to the Bolshevik Party.

Ultimately, the "trade union debate" revealed a great deal about how Trotsky and other Bolshevik leaders viewed the urban working class in whose name they governed. Trotsky accused the Workers' Opposition, a group of Bolshevik dissidents, of using "dangerous slogans" in that debate. His response to them is worth quoting at length:

> They have made a fetish of democratic principles. They have placed the workers' right to elect representatives above the party, as it were, as if the party were not entitled to assert its dictatorship even if that dictatorship temporarily clashed with the passing moods of the workers' democracy. ... It is necessary to create among us the awareness of the revolutionary historical birthright of the party. The party is obliged to maintain its dictatorship, regardless of temporary wavering in the spontaneous moods of the masses, regardless of the temporary vacillations even in the working class.[22]

The trade unions were seen as representatives of the "passing moods" of the workers, of their "temporary vacillations," and were therefore dispensable.

Trotsky's extreme views, calling for full militarisation of labour, and suppression of existing unions, were rejected at the time. But like other ideas he advocated, his views on the unions eventually came to be adopted under Stalin's leadership. Unions in the Soviet Union, and later in all other Communist countries, came to be arms of the state, with no independence whatsoever.

For decades to come, until the birth of *Solidarnosc* in Poland in the 1980s, the Communist Party's domination of the working class and the suppression of trade unions went unchallenged. *Solidarnosc* (Solidarity) was the independent, democratic trade union that grew out of the wave of strikes that began among shipyard workers in the port city of Gdansk in 1980. Under the leadership of Lech Walesa, it forced the Polish government to grudgingly accept the right of workers to join trade unions that were free of Communist Party control. By the time shipyard workers in Gdansk made the first cracks in the wall that would eventually come tumbling down, the Georgian experiment with its powerful, independent trade unions had long been forgotten.

9

THE RISE AND RISE
OF THE COOPERATIVES

Writing about Georgia after his visit in 1920, Karl Kautsky naturally had to address the question of the cooperative movement in the country. But in a book which is overwhelmingly positive about what the Georgian Social Democrats had accomplished, he showed little enthusiasm for the producer and consumer cooperatives that had sprung up across the country. Kautsky began by acknowledging that many socialists were sceptical about cooperatives. This was due "to the fact that they are represented by the advocates of harmony as a panacea to cure the evils of Capitalism." Kautsky rejected that positive view of cooperatives, writing: "This is nonsense."[1]

Before looking into what was going on with the Georgian cooperatives and the role they played in the social democratic society being built there, it is worth pausing to consider what Marxists at the time thought of cooperatives. Jules Guesde, one of the founding fathers of the socialist movement in France, was an uncompromising firebrand and looked the part, with his massive, unruly black beard and tiny, nearly rimless glasses. Guesde savaged his rival, Jean Jaurès, among others, for "compromising" with bourgeois parties, and was one of the French Marxists that Noe Zhordania had met during his exile in Europe in the 1890s. Guesde's purist and fanatical politics are believed to be the cause of Karl Marx's famous deathbed outburst, "*je ne suis pas Marxiste.*" If that was Marxism, Marx wanted no part of it.

Guesde gave an example of his Marxist fundamentalism in his view of the cooperative movement. In July 1910, the sixty-five-year-old Guesde delivered an impassioned address to a congress of French cooperatives in Paris. "It is impossible to attach any socialist value to co-operation in itself," he told the delegates. "It does not even prepare the elements of the new society, prepared as they have been for a long time, both as material and as organization, by capitalist concentration which preceded co-operation by far and in proportions which it will never equal."[2]

Despite having no intrinsic socialist value, cooperatives did have their uses for Guesde. That is, they could bankroll socialist politicians like him. Guesde could not be more blunt about it: "The co-operatives' only value is to coin money, to furnish the workingmen's party with arms and ammunition. It is not the duty of the party to help the co-operatives, but it is the strict duty of the co-operatives to help materially the party with all of their strength," he proclaimed. He considered anyone who suggested otherwise to be a Utopian.[3]

Marx had a rather different take on the subject. In his 1864 Inaugural Address to the First International, Marx wrote: "But there was in store a still greater victory of the political economy of labour over the political economy of property. We speak of the co-operative movement, especially of the co-operative factories raised by the unassisted efforts of a few bold 'hands'. The value of these great social experiments cannot be over-rated."[4]

Marx took it further, writing that:

By deed, instead of by argument, they have shown that production on a large scale, and in accord with the behest of modern science, may be carried on without the existence of a class of masters employing a class of hands; that to bear fruit, the means of labour need not be monopolised as a means of dominion over, and of extortion against, the labouring man himself; and that, like slave labour, like serf labour, hired labour is but a transitory and inferior form, destined to disappear before associated labour plying its toil with a willing hand, a ready mind, and a joyous heart.

Marx never laid down a blueprint for the new society he advocated. His magnum opus, *Das Kapital*, described the existing society, capitalism, and had little to say about the society which Marx expected would succeed it. As a result some socialists believed that a powerful, centralised state should assume control over the entire economy, while others imagined a looser federation of autonomous cooperatives.

As for Guesde, his ultra-leftism only lasted a few more years. In August 1914, with the outbreak of the First World War, he rediscovered his French patriotism, supported the war, abandoned his socialist colleagues and joined the government. Among those who condemned him for this betrayal was Trotsky, who asked, "How is it possible for an honest socialist not to fight you?" In an open letter to Guesde, now a minister in the French government, he added that the former leftist had "transformed the Socialist Party into a docile choir which accompanies the choir-masters of capitalist brigandage in an epoch when bourgeois society –

whose deadly enemy you, Jules Guesde, used to be – has disclosed its true nature to the very core."[5]

Nevertheless, Guesde's "Marxist" view of cooperatives continued to be quite influential, while Marx's own view (and there many positive quotes from Marx on the subject of cooperatives) was largely forgotten. This becomes clear when we look at Karl Kautsky's comments on the cooperative movement in Georgia.

Cooperatives were not forerunners of a socialist society, in the eyes of Kautsky, who shared the widespread socialist disdain for cooperatives that Guesde had expressed. Nevertheless, Kautsky acknowledged that "in those spheres where the monopolistic character of capital has scarcely made itself felt, the production carried on by organisations of consumers can create socialistic conditions of production, if these consumers' organisations are dominated by the socialist outlook, and thus are in the hands of proletarians conscious of their part in the class struggle."[6]

In other words, if cooperatives are in the hands of socialists, they may be of some value. In Georgia, dominated by the Social Democrats, that was certainly the case. Still, Kautsky was not carried away with enthusiasm. Cooperatives, even if led by class-conscious proletarians, were useful only in certain underdeveloped societies. "The consumers' co-operative societies," he wrote, "may become of special importance in countries where industry is as yet underdeveloped, but where a class conscious proletariat already exists."[7]

In countries like Georgia, such cooperatives could theoretically involve peasants, and as the country's capitalist economy was only beginning to emerge, such organisations might contribute to "building up the co-operative industry which will arise in competition with the capitalist industry" which could in turn "restrict and moderate the influence of the latter over workers and consumers." Whilst not exactly embracing the idea that cooperatives were some kind of embryonic socialist societies growing inside the capitalist womb, Kautsky acknowledged that they *might* "assume unsuspected importance for the proletarian class-struggle, and the establishment of Socialism."

Kautsky's scepticism notwithstanding, the story of the Georgian cooperatives is an important one, and yet most histories of the country have barely touched on them. Some have focussed extensively on tiny organisations like the Bolshevik party, while ignoring the hundreds of thousands of Georgians whose lives were changed by the cooperative movement, or for that matter the trade unions. This may have to do with historians' generally focussing more on politics and war, and less on social movements. But it may also have to do with the fact the Kautsky, Trotsky and others had very little say about the cooperatives.

The first cooperatives in Georgia were established in 1867, fifty years before the overthrow of the Romanov regime. By the 1880s, pamphlets about the ideas of Robert Owen and Charles Fourier, early socialists and founding fathers of the cooperative moment, appeared in Tiflis.[8]

Robert Owen is today largely forgotten, but in the nineteenth century he was a pioneering advocate both of the cooperative movement and of trade unionism. Marx and Engels were among his admirers. In his view, cooperatives were a building block of the future socialist society, and he was being read in Georgia long before there were Marxists in the country or trade unions had emerged. Of the three great pillars of the labour movement the cooperatives came first, with the trade unions and Social Democratic Party following much later.

The first agricultural cooperative, a silk-worm factory, was founded in 1899 in Kutaisi. In eastern Georgia, which then, as now, was a wine-growing region of some renown, cooperatives flourished, purchasing grapes from their grower-members, manufacturing the wine and selling it. They also supplied their members with various appliances and chemicals.

Credit cooperative societies also began growing quickly and by 1917 there were more than 300 with a membership of 150,000. The fastest-growing cooperatives were for consumers, and these were founded by 1900 in the major working class population centres in Tiflis, Batumi and elsewhere. By 1916 there were 126 of these throughout Transcaucasia – the bulk of them in Georgia – and they formed a central organisation.

In spite of their growth over the preceding half century, it was only after the overthrow of the tsarist regime and under the rule of the Georgian Social Democrats that the cooperative movement really took off in the country. Before that, especially during the First World War, the Georgian cooperatives fell on hard times. In parts of Georgia which had been overrun by invading armies, such as Batumi, which had been in the hands of the Turks, little was left of the pre-war cooperatives, their property having been plundered.

But the cooperative movement in Georgia revived after 1917 – and then grew dramatically. In 1916, on the eve of the overthrow of the tsarist regime, there were just 199 consumer societies. By 1919, that number had grown to 989. A year later, nearly a third of those societies owned their own buildings, an indication of growing success.

In 1919, the Georgian cooperatives re-organised themselves into *Tsekavschiri*, the Central Cooperative Union of the Republic of

Georgia, while across Georgia, regional cooperative organisations were founded. *Tsekavschiri* was dominated by consumer co-operatives and grew rapidly in value and membership. In 1920 there were many cooperative congresses, representing (among others) wine growers, tobacco growers and sheep farmers.

Though consumer cooperatives continued to dominate, Kautsky noticed a change when he visited the country in 1920. Producers' cooperatives were growing stronger. "The Union of Co-operative Societies began to produce on its own account in 1919," he wrote. "A silk factory is established, a sausage factory, engineering works, which turn out agricultural implements; then vegetable and fruit preserving factories, and finally a printing-press. None of these undertakings works at a loss, and most of them yield a surplus."[9]

In addition to those, by 1919 there was a cooperative soap boiling works, a glassware factory, workshops to produce smaller agricultural implements, a power station, an electric mill, a saw mill, a couple of carpenters' shops, a boot factory, and three tile and brick works. The movement was growing up and expanding beyond consumer and farmer cooperatives.

One of the most promising developments in the Georgian cooperative movement took place in 1920 with the founding of the Cooperative Bank, which had first been decided upon several months earlier at a congress of cooperatives from across Transcaucasia, held in Tiflis It was agreed to create a management committee consisting of representatives from the Georgian cooperatives, and the bank's basic capital was set at 5 million roubles. Initially it struggled to link up to existing cooperative credit societies, but eventually became hugely popular with the population. Many worker and peasant organisations trusted the Cooperative Bank with their money.

In addition to traditional bread and butter economic work, the cooperatives had a social and educational agenda as well. The regional cooperative unions had departments to cater for "popular instruction" and these controlled bookshops, public reading rooms, theatres and cinemas. In Zugdidi, a town in western Georgia, the regional cooperative union opened more than ten bookshops.

The cooperative movement also had funds for teacher training, workers' sick funds, and the maintenance of sanatoria. There were also cooperative restaurants, with reports that western Georgia had ten "fairly well organised" cooperative eateries.

Unlike traditional businesses, the cooperative movement was driven by a set of values, among these "self-help, self-responsibility, democracy, equality, equity and solidarity," and these needed to be taught to the members.[10] *Tsekavschiri* created an education department in 1920 which engaged in research and encouraged the discussion of "practical questions." It was also tasked with spreading the ideas of cooperation. "The people," wrote J. Tsagareli in his 1922 book on the cooperative movement in Georgia, "have been taught by their own experience and practice what Co-operation is capable of achieving, and what it was able to accomplish under the most trying conditions."[11]

As the Georgian experiment was nearing its end, Karl Kautsky looked at what the Georgian cooperatives had done in just three years and was delighted not only by how much they had achieved, but also at the measured pace of their progress. "It is all to the good that the co-operative societies have proceeded slowly and cautiously in laying the foundations of their productive activities," he wrote. "The stormy movement, which corresponds to the revolutionary temperament and is in place when hostile positions are to be captured, is not advantageous in the founding of economic organisation."[12]

Georgia's experience with cooperatives under Social Democratic rule was not unique. In other countries where socialist movements were strong, or achieved state power, cooperatives were often quite strong as well, and their growth was encouraged by public policy. For example, the Israeli government during the thirty years of Labour Party rule gave strong support, including financial support, to the socialist kibbutzim and the moshavim (cooperative farms).

All of this growth of the Georgian cooperatives was taking place at a time of economic crisis in the country when private businesses struggled to make a profit. As a result, cooperatives were growing and private businesses starting to disappear. In one survey, it was discovered that private trading establishments in Georgian villages had declined from 2,071 to 1,479, as cooperatives moved "to take the places vacated by private capital." By 1920, only 19% of Georgian workers were employed by the private sector. A majority – 52% – were employed by the state and a further 18% worked for municipal or cooperative enterprises.[13]

The cooperative movement had decided not only to combat speculation and reduce rivalry between different cooperatives and private companies, which were its previous targets, but according to a 1919 report, "it hopes to become a powerful regulator, and in time *the only regulator*, of all market prices."[14]

As a result, Georgia's economy was slowly transitioning from one based on production for profit to one resembling Robert Owen's vision of a cooperative commonwealth.

10

ACHILLES HEEL: GEORGIA'S NATIONAL MINORITIES

The Georgian Social Democrats believed in the rights of ethnic minorities. Article 129 of the constitution made this very clear: "It is forbidden to bring any obstacle to the free social development, economic and cultural, of the ethnical minorities of Georgia, especially to the teaching in their mother language and the interior management of their own culture. Everybody has the right to his mother tongue in writing, printing and speaking."[1]

Over the course of eight more articles in the constitution, the Georgian leaders laid out their vision of ethnic and linguistic minorities with full rights. In this they were not only acting in accordance with socialist principles, and in particular what they had learned from the pre-war Austrian Marxists, but with the *zeitgeist* of the post-war era, particularly US President Woodrow Wilson's Fourteen Points. Everyone, including Lenin and the Bolsheviks, now seemingly supported the rights of peoples to self-determination, and the rights of national minorities within multinational states.

But the multicultural paradise proposed by the Georgian Constitution was not to be, as it clashed with a very different reality on the ground. It was not only that the peoples of the Transcaucasian region had a long history of conflict, which would have been difficult enough. In addition, they were also not alone in determining their relationships with one another, as other powers (and Russia in particular) had an interest in exploiting inter-ethnic conflicts to gain influence in the region. What is extraordinary is the *persistence* of these conflicts, which played an important role in the three years of Georgian independence and continue even today. Historian Emil Souleimanov wrote of this period:

> A greater security threat to the new republic [than that coming from Denikin] was the Bolshevik incitement of separatism among the South Ossetians and Abkhazians ... The civil war that broke out in Georgia's ethnic peripheries and cost thousands of lives, was partially instigated by the Bolsheviks who, after the defeat of Denikin's troops at the end of 1919, concentrated their efforts on regaining control over the South Caucasian region.[2]

If in 1918-21 we can detect the hand of Russian Bolsheviks in some of the ethnic unrest that plagued Georgia, there are striking parallels to the situation today. Souleimanov wrote:

> During the most recent period of Georgia's national history, the mosaic-like (sub) ethnic map of the Georgian region ... has proven to be an effective tool for intervention by outsiders: and this factor has indeed become the central nightmare of Georgian intellectuals and statesmen striving for the territorial and ideological-political cohesion of the country. Thus, Georgian statesmen have become especially sensitive to the efforts - if

sometimes only perceived – of foreign powers to take advantage of Georgia's ethnic and territorial fragmentation.[3]

In this chapter, we'll look at the relationship between the Georgian Social Democrats and four minorities who lived within the borders of their republic – the Abkhazians, Ajarians, Ossetians and Jews.

ABKHAZIA

Abkhazia is the region along the Black Sea coast stretching up to the Russian frontier. In 1917, with the fall of the tsarist regime, the Abkhazians were quick to assert their national identity, establishing a local parliament, the Abkhazian National Council, which drafted a constitution for the new country. But their dreams of independence or autonomy were not to last. In March 1918 Russian Bolshevik troops reached Sukhumi, the Abkhazian capital on the Black Sea coast, prompting the Abkhazians to turn to Georgia for help, though some were suspicious of Georgian intentions.

The Georgians sent troops and the Bolshevik forces were pushed back north. On 24 July, the Georgians and Abkhazians signed a treaty by which the district of Sukhumi became a part of Georgia – temporarily, with the Abkhazian National Council continuing to govern the area until a national assembly could make the final decisions.[4] Abkhazia was one of three autonomous districts – the other two being the areas around Batumi and Zakhatala – which could determine their own affairs, according to Article 107 of the Georgian Constitution.

Unfortunately, the Bolshevik attack on Abkhazia in 1918 was not the last Russian intervention in that country. Less than a year later, General Denikin, then commanding a powerful Volunteer

Army that threatened to topple the Bolsheviks, set his sights on Abkhazia. He sent a telegram to his British allies claiming that the Georgians – who had been invited into the region to defend it against Russian aggression – were oppressing the local population. They had dispersed the existing Abkhazian government, according to Denikin, and were forcing new elections to ensure that the local leadership remained pro-Georgian. As Kazemzadeh wrote:

> The Abkhazian people, Denikin declared, had addressed to him a plea to stop the election, remove the Georgians from Abkhazia, and assure peace and safety from Georgian violence. In the opinion of Denikin the continued occupation of Abkhazia by the Georgians, whom the local population hated, would necessitate military intervention on his part for the sake of restoring order.[5]

There is no question that the Georgian government had fallen out of favour with at least some of the Abkhazians. There had been a failed landing of Abkhazian rebel forces in Sukhumi, several local rebellions, and a failed military coup. Zhordania explained this in the following way: "There was no similarity whatever to a peasants' revolt. What happened here was that some local landowners (counter-revolutionaries) tried to gain power with the help of Turkish detachments who attempted to land. We naturally opposed this attempt and, by force, drew away the detachment."[6]

The Georgians decided on a policy of repression. Abkhazia's autonomous status was suspended and separatists were jailed. Abkhazian separatists welcomed help from Denikin's forces in 1919 and, two years later, from the Red Army. Having previously welcomed the Georgians as their protectors against the Russians, many of them had switched sides. The Georgians saw them as taking the side of the Russians who had never accepted Georgian independence, and felt threatened.

Georgian historians today blame Russia for Abkhazian separatism, then and now. Mariam Lordkipanidze, for example, writes that the tsarist regime promoted Abkhazian separatism before the revolution, while understanding that the region was "a natural, inalienable part of Georgia." With Georgian independence in 1918, "Abkhazia formed its integral part" and this was recognised by the Russians.[7] Abkhazian separatism was, in her view, entirely the product of Russian Bolshevik agitation: "In the years of the existence of the Georgian Democratic Republic, Georgian Bolsheviks backed by the government of the Russian Federative Republic, tried by every means available to weaken the Georgian Democratic Republic. … The risings in Abkhazia against the Georgian Democratic Republic were the result of the action of these forces."[8]

There can be little doubt that historians like Lordkipanidze are putting history at the service of current Georgian politics. Faced with an ongoing Russian military threat, including a decades-long occupation of Georgian territory by foreign armies, this is understandable. But simply blaming Russia – under the tsar, under the Communists and today under Putin – for Abkhazian separatism denies Georgia any role in possibly having provoked it, as well as denying the Abkhazians the same right to self-determination that Georgia itself claims.

Today, Abkhazia is a breakaway region, occupied by Russian troops and recognised diplomatically by only a handful of countries. The official website of the "Republic of Abkhazia" summarises their view of the history of this period. "In May 1918 the new Georgian Democratic Republic occupied and annexed Abkhazia," it states. "From 1918 until 1921, Abkhazia fought a liberation war against Georgia, backed by Caucasian regional organizations."[9]

The views of nationalist Georgian historians today and those of the Russian-sponsored Abkhazian regional government are mirror images of each other. For some Georgians, Abkhazia has always been a part of Georgia, and only the nefarious activities of Russian agitators have stirred up conflict. For the Russians, and their supporters in Abkhazia, Abkhazia is a country in its own right, which Georgia is trying to control. Both views reflect the passions stoked by a long history of conflict, climaxing in a bloody war in the early 1990s which caused the Georgians to speak bitterly of "ethnic cleansing," as ethnic Georgians were expelled from the region.

In comparing the relationship between Georgia and Abkhazia under the Mensheviks with the situation in the early twenty-first century, it seems clear that the Mensheviks were on to something. They did acknowledge Abkhazia's right to self-determination in their constitution. And early on they came to the aid of the Abkhazians when Denikin's forces invaded the country. But they, like Georgian leaders a century later, struggled to accept Abkhazian claims of a right to national self-determination, and blamed any unrest on the Russians, which in turn probably fuelled the conflict. That conflict seems no closer to resolution today than it did a century ago.

ADJARA

South of Abkhazia along the Black Sea coast, in the south-western corner of Georgia, lies the region of Adjara, the largest city of which is Batumi. Much further away from Russia than Abkhazia, separatist tendencies in the region could not really be blamed on the Russians, or on Denikin or the Bolsheviks.

(Though the Bolsheviks did have some influence in Batumi itself.) The Russians, though, were not the only players in the region.

In his book *The Struggle for Transcaucasia*, Kazemzadeh wrote at length about this region in a sub-chapter entitled "Georgian Imperialism." Whether such a term is a fair characterisation of the Georgian Social Democrats' actions is worth examining, in part because Kazemzadeh's book remains after many decades the definitive work in English on this period.

In the chaos following the fall of the tsarist regime and the final months of the First World War, Batumi fell into the hands of the Turks, who remained the most powerful military force in the region. The Turks (and Azerbaijan) felt a special connection with the local population, the majority of whom were Muslims. Local residents proclaimed an independent republic and appealed for recognition from the great powers. They "granted equal rights to all its citizens irrespective of national origin, religion, or social standing, *though the Armenians were excluded*."[10] Surrounded on all sides by more powerful neighbours, including both Georgia and Armenia, the "South-Western Caucasian Republic" seemed unlikely to last. Azerbaijan appealed to the British, who now occupied the region, to help out, and the British promised to maintain the status quo. But as Kazemzadeh admitted, it "soon it became clear to the Allies that the South Western Republic was a creature of the defeated Turks, who were attempting to preserve a foothold in Transcaucasia."[11]

By February 1919 the Georgians were ready to begin moving into some parts of Adjara, with Zhordania claiming this was in accord with an agreement with Turkey to end the war. But when Georgian forces arrived, they encountered the opposition

Head of the German mission in Georgia, General Friedrich Freiherr Kress
von Kressenstein is visiting the head office of the newspaper *Imereti* in
Kutaisi. From the left: K. Dateshidze, Major of Kutaisi D. Kalandarashvili,
General Dateshidze, Kress, General T.Vashakidze, Kress's Adjutant Baron
Gamm, famous Georgian writer David Kldiashvili. Kutaisi. 30 January 1919.

Photo by A. Mikhailov. A402/96

Delegation of the Second International in Georgia. Thomas Shaw, member of the British parliament, speaking at a meeting in Tiflis, 1920. Photo by E. Klar. A402/15

Delegation members of the Second International in Georgia in the small town of Dusheti, 1920. In the photo: Valiko Jugeli, head of the People's Guard, B. Chkhikvishvili, Tom Shaw, Camille Huysmans and others. Note the banners in French welcoming the leaders of the world's proletariat. A402/17

Delegation members of the Second International at the Tiflis Railway
Station. Georgian leader Noe Zhordania in standing in the centre, wearing
the white hat. A402/18

French socialist leader Alfred Inghels addressing a meeting of workers in
Tiflis, 1920. A402/21

British Labour Party leader Ramsay MacDonald, Belgian socialist Emile Vandervelde, A. Lomtatidze, K. Gvarjaladze and others. 1920. A402/22

A feast held for the delegation members of the Second International in Georgia, 1920. A402/25

Noe Zhordania.

Official meeting with the delegation of the Second International at
Noe Zhordania's office, 16 September 1920. A402/26

First session of the Constituent Assembly of Georgia. On the right
are members of the government: Noe Zhordania, Noe Khomeriki,
Grigol Lortkiphanidze, S. Mdivani and others. 12 March 1919.

Photo by Evtikhi Zhvania. A402/33

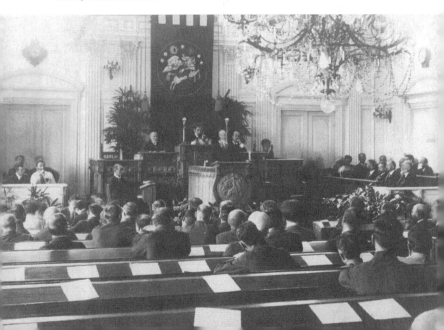

Members of the People's Guard. Commander Valiko Jugeli is first on the right. 1918–1920. A402/61

Members of the People's Guard on motorcycles, 1920. Photo by V. Grinevich. A402/75

Armed group of the People's Guard, 1920. Photo by V. Grinevich. A402/76

The 11th Red Army enters Tiflis, February 1921. A402/104

of the Turkish-backed Adjarian separatists. Disorder and clashes became increasingly serious until the British occupying forces decided to put a stop to it. They disbanded the local government and took responsibility for maintaining order. Whether or not the "South-Western Caucasian Republic" had a future would be decided, the British announced, by the Peace Conference then taking place in Paris.

Meanwhile, Armenian forces moved on the city of Kars, while the Georgians advocated for their right to Batumi, the country's most important port. Batumi was at that time a rather lawless place, and one of the few strongholds of Bolshevism in the region. The British treated the Bolsheviks ruthlessly, jailing many of their leaders and breaking the back of the organisation, while the Georgians blamed the disorder in Batumi on the local Russian bureaucrats who remained in place. Eventually, the British accepted the Georgian arguments and when their forces left Batumi in July 1920, with their permission, the Georgian Army assumed control of the city.

That almost didn't happen, as the local Bolsheviks – who hated the Georgian Social Democrats even more than they hated the British imperialists – blew up a railway bridge hoping to block the Georgian troops and prevent them arriving. They failed. The Georgians successfully took control of the city, but the local population remained restless, and their army was threatened with repressive measures.

OSSETIA

Ossetia is a region that straddles two countries: North Ossetia is part of the Russian Federation, and South Ossetia has (mostly) been part of Georgia. The origin of its present conflict with Georgia dates back to the first Georgian Republic in 1918.

Like most regions in Transcaucasia, following the fall of the tsarist government the local population formed an Ossetian National Council. The Bolsheviks quickly gained control of the council, resulting in it not demanding independence, but rather annexation to Russia. Though the Russian Bolsheviks were clearly involved in causing unrest in the region, the roots of the conflict – which included uprisings in 1918, 1919 and 1920 – were primarily based on class, with an ethnic component as well.

At first the discontent was focussed on the Georgian government's economic policies. These were seen by many South Ossetians as supporting the interests of the big landowners, most of whom were ethnic Georgians. After some time, the discontent turned into armed struggle. What had been a class struggle became an ethnic one.

The reaction of the Georgian government was to send troops to quell the unrest, but they were met with fierce resistance. The rebels were able to take control of the region's capital, Tskhinvali, and fought the Georgians to a standstill. Hundreds of South Ossetian civilians were reported to have been killed by Georgian troops in revenge attacks, and the Georgians stood accused of a kind of "ethnic cleansing" (even if the term itself would not be used for another several decades). The People's Guard formed a major part of the Georgian forces involved in the suppression of the South Ossetian revolts and they were charged with carrying out a particularly brutal counter-insurgency. As Kazemzadeh wrote:

> The Mensheviks were well aware of the Bolshevik inspiration
> of the uprising, as the newspaper, *Ertoba*, pointed out. The Head

of the People's Guard, Jugeli, wrote in his diary: "The Oset nationalists are our worst and most relentless enemies … Last year, they helped Denikin and now they are at one with the Bolsheviks." Jugeli put the number of the insurgents at several thousand. "These traitors," he added, "should be cruelly punished. There is no other way."[12]

The furious South Ossetians turned to Soviet Russia for help, which was forthcoming (though covert). But the Georgian forces prevailed, and nearly 20,000 South Ossetian civilians fled to Soviet Russia while an estimated 3,000-7,000 were killed in the fighting. By mid-1920, following the signing of the Russian-Georgian peace treaty, the Russians began to withdraw their support for the South Ossetians. Still, the separatists went on to proclaim the "Rokskaya Soviet Republic" near the Russian border and continued to dream of being annexed by Russia.

By the time the Russians had re-established their rule over the region in 1921, supported by South Ossetian volunteers, they realised that to ensure peace between the various ethnic groups in Georgia it would be necessary to re-write the history of those years in South Ossetia. There was little discussion of rebellion and ethnic cleansing. But despite the best efforts of the Soviet authorities, the bad blood between Ossetians and Georgians persisted, and their shared history came back to haunt them following the collapse of the Soviet Union, when fighting broke out in Abkhazia and South Ossetia. The Georgians and South Ossetians fought a short war in 1991-92 in which an estimated 2,000 people were killed. A year later, a similar war broke out in Abkhazia, resulting both in thousands of casualties and charges of "ethnic cleansing" as Georgians were expelled from the break-away province. Issues in both regions remained unresolved until

2008 when war broke out between Russia and Georgia, leading to a Georgian military defeat. Today South Ossetia is occupied by Russian troops, "independent" like Abkhazia, but its statehood not recognised by anyone except for Russia and a handful of allies.

THE JEWS

If the Abkhazians and South Ossetians grew to resent Georgian independence, one ethnic minority in the country celebrated it: the Jewish community.

Georgian independence raised great hopes for the country's Jews, who had suffered under the tsarist regime and who saw the Social Democrats as being sympathetic to their cause. They also knew that Georgia, almost alone among European countries, had no history of anti-Semitism and was a country where Jews had lived happily for many centuries. Thus, a Jewish community which had been largely inward-looking suddenly took an interest in public affairs. David Baazov, a leader of the Georgian Jewish community, participated in a Zionist congress held in Baku in August 1917. He gave a speech calling for the establishment of Jewish educational and cultural institutions in Georgia, and the congress resolved to support this. The Zionist movement took the lead, inspired by the British government's issuance of the Balfour Declaration and the British army's conquest of Palestine during the First World War. They founded a school in Tiflis which became a centre for Zionist activity and launched the first Zionist newspaper in the Georgian language in Kutaisi. It had a large circulation, appearing bi-weekly.

But the Jewish community was divided, and its divisions became quite public in the run-up to the February 1919 elections to the Constituent Assembly. The Jewish community was allocated three seats: one for the Russian Jews living in Georgia and the other two for local Jews. The election committee sanctioned only the non-Zionist candidates who supported the Social Democrats, causing bitter disappointment for the Zionists. But as a result of the election, two Jewish leaders – Moshe Davarashvili, representing the anti-Zionist and orthodox religious *Agudat Yisrael* party and Yosef Eligoulashvili, a merchant and economist and lifelong Social Democrat - were able to sign the Declaration of Independence. The former focussed on defending the rights of the Jewish community and ensuring the dominance of orthodox religion, while the latter eventually became deputy minister of finance, trade and industry and travelled to Europe as a commercial representative of the Georgian Republic.

Meanwhile, the Zionists, excluded from the mainstream of Georgian political life, focussed on the promotion of emigration to British-occupied Palestine. As two Israeli historians have put it: "The conquest of Georgia by the Red Army in 1921 delivered a heavy blow to the hopes of both the Zionists and their opponents, and exposed the Jews of Georgia to dangers such as they never known before."[13]

There is little doubt that the Georgian Social Democrats were well-intentioned when it came to dealing with national minorities, and were prepared to concede a considerable amount of autonomy to Georgia's various ethnic groups. They were not, however, willing to concede their right to independence. Here is how Zhordania put it:

We know that the border areas differ from the centre as far as culture is concerned. There history has worked out completely different relationships and customs. We take this into consideration, the Government having resolved to grant autonomy in internal affairs to these border areas, on one condition – the preservation of the historical and economic integrity of Georgia. We can accept all their demands of autonomy, no matter how extensive they be. We cannot accept only one thing, separation from us.[14]

Like many young countries, Georgia felt unsure about its existence and had good reason to fear its neighbours. The republic was born as the Turkish army made an attempt to grab Batumi; Russians, both Reds and Whites, seemed eager to reassert their control over the newly independent country; even little Armenia tried to bite off a chunk of Georgia in 1918. The Georgians insisted that their country, though newly independent as a republic, was actually continuing the sovereign tradition of the Georgian kingdom which had existed until the early nineteenth century.

As Zhordania would later write in response to Trotsky, "Georgia had no need to invent a desire for independence; for two thousand years she was independent and only at the end of the 18th century, under pressure of enemies – Turks and Persians – she, by virtue of a special agreement, joined Russia."[15] Restoring Georgian independence, and then fighting off attempts at invasion, also meant a strong commitment by the Georgian government to holding on to all the territory that historically belonged to Georgia during its 2,000 year history as an independent state.

In this they differed from the Bolsheviks, who under Lenin's leadership conceded that the right of self-determination meant the right of peoples to secede. But while the Bolsheviks had the better slogan, in practice they were no more willing to let go of historically Russian territory than the Georgian Social

Democrats. Where Russia let go of some territories (such as Poland or Finland) it was because it was compelled to do so.

As we have seen with the South Ossetians, what began in some cases as a class struggle (between peasants and nobles) changed into ethnic conflict when the classes were ethnically homogenous. The ethnic conflicts that tore at Georgia throughout the years of independence were not always the continuations of ancient rivalries.

The treatment of Georgia's Jewish community shows that the Social Democrats could get it right, too. Leaving aside the question of the ban on Zionists running for the Constituent Assembly, the Georgian Jewish community benefited from the new republic, where they had full political and civil rights, and later suffered terribly under Soviet rule. The latter brought about the destruction of trade, which was how most Georgian Jews earned their living, and systematically attacked their religion. The Soviet government also suppressed the Zionist movement and blocked most Jewish emigration to Israel.[16]

But the Georgian Social Democrats sometimes got it horribly wrong, most notably in South Ossetia. While some might argue that unleashing the terror of the People's Guard on South Ossetian villages was understandable behaviour given the context of the era, they would be completely wrong. For all its achievements, the Social Democratic government was tarnished by its crude and brutal attempts to suppress some of Georgia's ethnic minorities. Memories of those years have lingered long in the collective memory, and contribute to ethnic conflict even today in Abkhazia and South Ossetia.

Kazemzadeh was harsh in his evaluation of what he called "Georgian imperialism":

In a year or two Georgia had traversed the long road from a colony of Russia to a small empire of her own. The difference between the Georgian attitude toward Abkhazia, or Ajaristan, and the attitude of Russia toward Georgia, or Armenia, was not one of principle but of scale. In their own backyard the Georgians proved to be as imperialist as the Russians. The beautiful phrases of socialist solidarity of nations, self-determination, etc., were forgotten and buried.[17]

While he has a point, it is not the whole story. As he admits, Adjara was a Turkish client state, Abkhazia was a pawn in the hands first of Denikin and then the Bolsheviks, and the Bolsheviks were highly influential in South Ossetia, campaigning not for independence, but for annexation to Russia.

The Armenians, Turks and Russians all tried, with varying degrees of success, to stir up the ethnic minorities in Georgia. The Georgian Social Democrats did not always handle the issue well, and in some cases were responsible for horrific crimes. But, from their perspective, they were fighting for national survival, rather than attempting to create "a small empire," and retaining the breakaway regions formed a key element of this struggle.

FIFTH COLUMN

During the Spanish Civil War, one of Franco's generals boasted to a journalist that Madrid would fall not only to his four columns of troops then converging on the city, but also to a "*quinta columna*" based inside the Spanish capital. The phrase "fifth column" entered our language at that point, but fifth columns had existed long before 1936.

Prior to 1917, the Bolsheviks represented an insignificant force both in Georgia and throughout Transcaucasia, with the popularity of the Social Democratic Party over many years ensuring that no significant rivals emerged on the left. When Zhordania and his comrades took the side of the Mensheviks in the dispute within the Russian party, they took all of the Georgian Social Democratic Party with them.

There were, though, some Georgian Bolsheviks, among them Stalin. Stalin took Lenin's side in the party split and over a number of years tried without great success to build Bolshevik organisations across the region. In late 1898, the twenty-year-old Stalin had gone to speak with Zhordania in order to ask his advice about quitting the Tiflis Theological Seminary and devoting his life to becoming a full-time revolutionary. Zhordania interrogated him and concluded that the young man's knowledge was superficial and that he would benefit from another year in the seminary. According to historian Robert Conquest, Stalin "seems to have taken some offence at this rebuff, and was heard making a heated attack on Zhordania to a group of students."[1] Zhordania remembered that Stalin was not a good speaker and could only recite speeches as if he were giving lessons in school, and used vulgar language for rhetorical effect.[2] Furthermore, Stalin was plagued during his whole career as a revolutionary in Transcaucasia with accusations of improper conduct, including charges that he colluded with the tsarist police.

Stalin's possible role as a tsarist police spy was first raised by people who knew him during his long years in the Social Democratic underground in Transcaucasia. Many accusations were made about him by Georgian Menshevik leaders, including the assertion that he revealed the location of the secret party printing press in the Tiflis neighbourhood of Avlabar in 1906, or that he betrayed the location of a safe house used by the famous Armenian Bolshevik Stepan Shaumian. Some of Stalin's former comrades insisted that he was the subject of a party "court of honour" at one point, and that he may even have been expelled from the party or ordered to leave the region. Early biographies of Stalin included many such stories. But the most important evidence about his possible secret involvement with the tsarist police appeared in 1956, three years after his death.

The American mass-circulation magazine *Life* published two major articles in the same issue on the subject. One, by Soviet secret police general Alexander Orlov, who had defected to the West several years earlier, told a story he had heard about a secret file that had been discovered in the tsarist police archives in the

1930s. According to Orlov's account, when Stalin learned of this discovery, he began the wave of purges of Communist officials, some of whom may have been conspiring to topple him from power using that file.

The other article, by Isaac Don Levine, an American journalist who had published the first biography of Stalin in English in the 1930s, revealed the existence of the "Eremin Letter," a document that appeared to come from the tsarist Department of Police and which named Stalin as a paid police agent, who spied on the Bolsheviks. The American diplomat and historian George F. Kennan, who inspected the Eremin Letter at the request of the State Department in the 1940s, wrote that it was "one of those curious bits of historical evidence of which it can only be said that the marks of spuriousness are too strong for us to call it genuine, and the marks of genuineness are too strong for us to call it entirely spurious."[3]

Today most historians dismiss the charge that Stalin was a tsarist police spy, though Edward Ellis Smith's 1967 book *The Young Stalin* raises important questions about the future dictator's early career that are rarely addressed. Though he dismissed the Eremin Letter as a forgery, Smith was convinced that a mountain of circumstantial evidence pointed to Stalin's collaboration with the police.[4]

Regardless, after several short periods of prison and exile, Stalin was finally sent away to Siberian exile on the eve of the First World War and there he remained until the revolution of March 1917. Finally free to resume his political activity, he returned not to his Georgian home but to the Russian capital, Petrograd. He did not set foot in Georgia again until it had been occupied by Soviet troops in 1921.

By the time the tsarist regime collapsed in March 1917, there was practically no Bolshevik organisation left in Georgia. The few Bolsheviks in the country put their factional differences with the Mensheviks behind them, and established a joint party committee with their formal rivals. But developments on the battle front with Turkey gave Lenin's party an unexpected opportunity.

As the First World War dragged on, Bolshevik agitators worked tirelessly among soldiers and sailors on every front, demanding Russia's withdrawal from the conflict. Other left-wing parties, including the Mensheviks, were divided in their attitude towards the war. Some Mensheviks had been sympathetic to the Allied cause, Zhordania among them. Others, most notably Julius Martov, led a faction of the party known as "internationalists" who shared the Bolshevik opposition to the war. As a result, the Bolsheviks had considerable success among ordinary soldiers, who have been described as "peasants in uniform," with such successes taking place not only on the fronts where the Russian army had suffered military setbacks. The Bolshevik organisations inside the armed forces grew throughout 1917, during the period of the Provisional Government. They were helped by the Provisional Government's decision to honour Russia's commitment to supporting the Allies, and by their refusal to enact a land reform programme. The war dragged on, and of all the blunders made by the Provisional Government, its continued support for the conflict was surely the greatest. It cost the administration the loyalty of the army and in the end ensured the victory of the Bolshevik coup in November of that year.

The bungled "Kerensky offensive" in July 1917 was a turning point. The offensive against Austria-Hungary and Germany, which marked a renewal of the Russian war effort, lasted barely two weeks and revealed the weakness of the Russian army, which had lost the will to fight. The Tiflis Soviet had passed a resolution offering lukewarm support for the war effort on 22 June, not long before the offensive began. The next day, a huge meeting of radicalised soldiers took place in the Aleksandr Garden in Tiflis, adopting a resolution put forward by the Bolsheviks condemning the offensive. And the day after that, the Bolsheviks decided to make a show of strength by holding a protest march. The Mensheviks attempted to take over the demonstration, but their speakers were shouted down, and some 10,000 soldiers voted again to condemn the offensive and to demand a government of the Soviets. It was a high-water mark for the Georgian Bolsheviks.

During this entire period, right up until the Bolshevik coup in November 1917, there was still some hope that the Bolsheviks and Mensheviks across the former Russian empire could be united in a single party, as seemed to be the case in Tiflis. It was not until Lenin's arrival at Petrograd's Finland Station in April that the Bolsheviks began to be pulled away from the other revolutionary parties and to strike out on their own. Zhordania's old comrade Pilipe Makharadze returned from the April 1917 Bolshevik Party Congress in Petrograd firmly convinced that with Lenin's return to Russia and his fierce opposition to any reconciliation with the Mensheviks, the split within the party was now permanent.

In Georgia, the Bolsheviks initially controlled the only Social Democratic newspaper published in the Russian language, *Kavkazskii rabochii* (Caucasian Worker) and it was not until May that the Mensheviks began publishing their own, *Bor'ba* (Struggle). Finally in June 1917 the Bolsheviks in Georgia formed their own independent party – which was a branch of the Russian Bolshevik Party.

In Georgia, the Bolsheviks had little success recruiting followers among the peasants who made up the vast majority of the population, and even less success among industrial workers in the major cities. But they did manage to win over a not inconsiderable number of demoralised soldiers, most of them Russians, hungry for peace and a chance to go home. In addition to winning over Russian soldiers, the Bolsheviks had some success with Russian workers living in Georgia as well.

Those radicalised soldiers, persuaded by Bolshevik promises of an end to the war and land reform, were what allowed Lenin's relatively small party to seize power in the Russian capital Petrograd, and were the mainstay of Bolshevik rule in the first years of the revolution. But while the liberals and moderate socialists in the Russian capital were easily overcome by Bolshevik soldiers and sailors – both at the time of Lenin's seizure of power and again in January 1918 when the Constituent Assembly was dispersed by the Bolsheviks – the Georgian Mensheviks were determined not to allow this to happen on their home turf.

They reacted to the Bolshevik challenge by setting up the People's Guard, and entered into a fierce competition with the Bolsheviks to win the loyalty of the army garrison in the city. As Ronald Grigor Suny put it, "It was also a struggle for power in the city, and its outcome would determine whether the Georgian working class or the Russian soldiery would decide the political fate of central Transcaucasia."[5]

In the end, the Georgian working class won. They seized the Tiflis armoury from Russian Bolshevik soldiers and, now well-armed, were able to maintain order in the Georgian capital even when threatened by armed Russian soldiers who were passing through the country.

Early in 1918, the Bolsheviks made several efforts to cause unrest in Transcaucasia, to no avail. On 10 February, the day of the opening of the Transcaucasian Sejm (parliament), a Bolshevik protest meeting was again held in the Aleksandr Gardens in Tiflis, but this time it was dispersed by gunfire.

The Menshevik leaders, including Zhordania and Tsereteli, were trying to learn the lessons from Lenin's coup in Petrograd three months earlier. Tsereteli, who had been in the Russian capital, told the Transcaucasian leaders that the Kerensky government had been excessively timid in its dealings with the Bolsheviks. This was a mistake not to be repeated. Trotsky later quoted a Georgian representative's comment to the Americans regarding the Bolsheviks: "We have successfully suppressed them. The proofs are self-evident: out of the former territory of Russia, Georgia alone is free from Bolshevism."[6] (Which was something of an exaggeration, as whole regions of the former Russian empire remained free of Bolshevik rule for several more years.) Bolshevik newspapers were suppressed in Georgia, many Bolsheviks were arrested, and the party went underground, where it stayed for two long years.

The strong reaction by the government to the Bolshevik protests, and the successful seizure of the arsenal a few months earlier, persuaded the Georgian Communist leaders that they would need a new strategy, which included stirring up revolt among the peasants. Their efforts focussed for a time on western Georgia, scene of the earlier Gurian Republic, but the People's Guard was usually able to put a stop to these efforts, often using brutal force.

The Georgian Bolsheviks never accepted the idea of independence for the three breakaway Caucasian republics, and always fought to reunite them with Russia. In fact, when the Transcaucasian Sejm voted on 22 April 1918 to break away from Russia, the Bolsheviks joined the Russian Socialist Revolutionaries and the Kadets (Constitutional Democrats) in opposing the move. This must be one of very few examples of Bolsheviks and Kadets, which was seen as the quintessential liberal party, working together in common cause.

A month later, the Bolsheviks were among a small minority of Georgians who did not celebrate the country's declaration of independence when the Transcaucasian Federation fell apart. Despite Georgia's declaration of independence, the local Bolsheviks insisted on calling themselves the Georgian branch of the *All-Russian* Communist Party (Bolsheviks) and only adopted the name "Communist Party of Georgia" several years later, for reasons which will be become clear.

The Russian Bolsheviks had already instructed all the young Communist parties then springing up around the world to form both legal and illegal sections. One would work legally, where possible, spreading propaganda, recruiting new members, forming factions in the trade unions, participating in elections to parliaments and so on. The other section would work underground, secretly preparing the party for the day when it would need to lead an armed insurrection to overthrow the existing government. In the view of the Bolsheviks at that time, based on their experience in tsarist Russia, there was no peaceful, parliamentary road to socialism. In the end, the working class would come to power in each country under the leadership of a disciplined vanguard party, and the seizure of power would be a violent act.

In countries like Georgia, Armenia and Azerbaijan, bordering on Russia and once part of its empire, the Communists (as the

Bolsheviks now styled themselves) had an additional task, which was to challenge the legitimacy of the country's independence, and campaign for its reintegration into a Russian – now Soviet – empire. In some cases, as in the Transcaucasian republics, this eventually meant providing assistance to the Russian Red Army when it crossed the frontiers.

After November 1917, and following their failure to seize power when other Bolshevik groups were doing so across the Russian empire, the local Bolshevik groups in Georgia worked feverishly, trying to exploit peasant rebellions that took place sporadically across Georgia, with considerable success. They exploited peasant discontent with the existing land reform in northern regions of the country including Dushei, Racha, Tianeti and Lechkhumi. Many of the Bolsheviks were former soldiers and they organised armed detachments of peasants, in one case mounting an assault on the town of Zugdidi, which failed.[7] The Bolsheviks also had success with some South Ossetians. Zhordania challenged the Bolshevik narrative that they had taken part in genuine peasant revolts, claiming there were just three events over the course of the three years of Menshevik rule:

> In all these three cases, events developed along the same lines: armed Bolshevik bands from time to time crossed the frontiers of the Republic and attempted, each time, by bribery, threats of violence, to win over some members of the local population; they even made demagogical endeavours to play on the feelings of the local separatists, of the more backward sections of the populations of Abkhasia [sic] and Ossetia.[8]

But he also acknowledged that "there were instances of excesses towards the local inhabitants who had been incited by the Bolsheviks and the punishment of marauders by martial law."

Trotsky, in his critique of the Georgians, found quotations from People's Guard commander Jugeli that confirmed how terrible those "excesses" were in practice. But Zhordania would have none of it, writing that those quotes "show how heartrending it was for our comrades in the ranks of the Peoples Guard to have to resort to such excesses."

One of the reasons why the Bolsheviks were unable to seize power in Georgia at that time was the presence of the German army from mid-1918 until the end of the year. Another was the departure of the Russian soldiers who were the Bolsheviks' main source of support in the country. As a result, the party was forced to relocate its Regional Committee (*Kavkraikom*) from Tiflis to Vladikavkaz, in the northern Caucasus. Two leading members of the *Kavkraikom* found themselves in Baku, cut off from the others. Now based outside of Georgia, the Bolsheviks tried to maintain control through a small bureau in the Georgian capital headed by Mikha Tskhakaia. But the main leadership was cut off from the country by the mountains, and Georgian troops effectively sealed their border with Russia.

Probably the main reason for the Bolshevik failure in Georgia, however, then and in subsequent years, was the enormous popularity of the Social Democrats, who were seen as a party representing the whole nation, with overwhelming public support. And while the Provisional Government in Russia had failed to carry out agrarian reform, which weakened them just as their continuation of the war had done, the Georgian Social Democrats did carry out their promise to redistribute land to the peasants.

The departure of the Germans at the end of 1918, following their defeat in the world war, opened up new possibilities for the Bolsheviks. The *Kavkraikom* returned to Tiflis not a moment too soon, for with the advances of General Denikin's counter-revolutionary White forces, the exiled Bolsheviks in the North Caucasus were driven back into Georgia. Leading Communists including Sergo Ordzhonikidze hid out in Tiflis. They "began to publish a newspaper, *Volna* (The Wave)," reports Kazemzadeh. "Organisational work was resumed, with special attention payed to the trade unions and the army. The army was given importance because it consisted of peasants, who could easily be influenced, while the proletarian People's Guard staunchly adhered to Menshevism."[9] They also began preparations for the armed overthrow of the hated Social Democratic government.

Communist youth groups were organised across Transcaucasia, and by September appeared to have recruited up to 1,800 members. At a conference in Baku, they adopted the name used by Communist youth across Russia: *Komsomol*. These young Communists were destined to play a critical role in the Bolshevik plans to wrest control of Georgia from its elected government.

Kazemzadeh, relying on Soviet sources, speaks highly of their efforts.

> When it was necessary to print some proclamations, the Komsomol members would go at night to the press rooms of *Borba* or *Ertoba*, the two leading Menshevik newspapers, bribe the janitor and the lonely guard and take them to the nearest tavern, while others would enter the building and print thousands of copies of their leaflets and pamphlets. On every piece they printed the following inscription was to be found: "Printed at the Press of the Regional Committee of the Russian Communist Party." The Menshevik police looked everywhere for the clandestine press, except, of course, in the building of *Borba* and *Ertoba*. The Komsomol repeated this operation several times before the trick was discovered.[10]

The story has a familiar ring. In pre-revolutionary Georgia, Stalin boasted that he too was able to use someone else's press to produce illegal Bolshevik propaganda – the press of the tsarist police. That story was one of several that led Georgia's Mensheviks to distrust the young revolutionary.

In the late summer of 1919, the Bolsheviks held secret party meetings across Georgia, and at the one held in Tiflis it was decided the time was ripe to strike and bring an end to Menshevik rule in the country. In their view, the economy was in crisis, the Social Democratic government was tottering on the brink of catastrophe, and it would be relatively easy to seize power.

The Georgian Bolsheviks organised a military staff and set the date for the revolution: 7 November, the second anniversary of the Bolshevik *coup d'état* in Petrograd. Later the date was moved up by a couple of days. The *Komsomol* was given the task of scouting around the Georgian capital, determining where the government troops were, drawing up plans of government buildings to be taken over, and so on.

Georgia's "November Revolution" was due to be led not by industrial workers, but by disgruntled soldiers, with the former remaining stubbornly loyal to the Menshevik government and forming the core of the People's Guard. The reliance on mutinous soldiers had worked for Lenin two years earlier, and the Georgian Bolsheviks opted for a time-tested formula.

On the eve of the planned insurrection, twenty-two Bolsheviks who served in the Georgian army met to make last-minute plans. They were the general staff of what would have been declared a "proletarian revolution," even if the actual proletariat wanted nothing to do with it. The only problem with the conspiracy was that it was a conspiracy. All it took was for just one of the soldiers to break ranks and inform the government, which is precisely what happened. The Mensheviks knew all the details of the plot, and sent a special detachment of loyal men to arrest the conspirators.

As a result, the Communist Party leadership called off the revolt. However, not everyone in the ranks of the Georgian Bolsheviks had heard the news, and in some rural areas, local Communist cells rose up and attempted to bring down the government. Their efforts were easily suppressed by the People's Guard and the army.

A British journalist, C.E. Bechhofer, happened to be visiting Georgia that month, and had the opportunity to interview Noe Ramishvili, who was then minister of war and the Interior. Ramishvili, he wrote, "offered me an explanation of the risings which had disturbed the country a week or two before. They were, he said, entirely due to Bolshevist propaganda from Moscow. The Bolshevists, after their defeats at Kursk and Orel, wanted to establish a new front in Denikin's rear, and decided to attempt to capture Georgia for the Bolshevist cause."[11]

The Russians had invested some 87 million roubles in the coup attempt, the money mainly intended to produce pro-Bolshevik propaganda.

According to Bechhofer's account, Ramishvili told how the Georgian government learned about the planned uprising and stopped it, but added:

As for the outbreak that had actually taken place, it had been manned almost entirely by criminals and deserters, led by Russian and Chinese Bolshevists; the peasants took no part in the rising whatever. The trouble had now been satisfactorily liquidated; the Constituent Assembly had permitted the institution of courts-martial, and some thirty of the leaders of the rising had already been shot. Altogether during the past year several hundred Bolshevists and their supporters had been executed; and there was no longer any possibility of a renewed outbreak.[12]

Bechhofer was a Russophile and not particularly sympathetic to the Georgian Social Democrats. He did not at all approve of the new nation's parliament speaking Georgian. He believed that Ramishvili was convinced that the executions of Bolsheviks "would go down well with English papers. Curiously enough, Mr Ramsay Macdonald, passing through Georgia about ten months later, has stated (of course, on information received from the Georgian Government) that no 'reprisals' have been resorted to against the Bolshevists." Bechhofer neglected to point out that by the time MacDonald visited Georgia, the Communist Party had been legalised, its prisoners all freed from the jails, and was operating above-ground. Bechhofer added that lists of the "Bolsheviks" (he put the word in quotation marks) who were executed appeared in Tiflis newspapers and "there were no Chinamen among them."[13]

Reading Bechhofer's account of his conversation with Ramishvili today, what stands out is not that the blood-thirsty and hypocritical Mensheviks abandoned their pledge to be humane democrats, but that what they approved was "the institution of *courts-martial.*" In other words, the men who were arrested and faced a death sentence were serving soldiers in the Georgian army. Whatever one thinks of the decision to enforce the death penalty in this case, it was not unusual for a government to treat an armed mutiny by its own soldiers in this way, and the Georgians had re-introduced the death penalty for treason back in June 1918.

Writing decades later, historian Vera Broido in her book *Lenin and the Mensheviks*, challenged Bechhofer's account. "The new country was beset on all sides by hostile forces, but its worst enemy proved to be within: Georgian Bolsheviks recognised only one fatherland and one government and that was Lenin's Russia," she wrote. "These Bolsheviks fomented discontent and rebellion among disbanded soldiers and other unstable elements. In November 1919 they staged an abortive coup, after which almost a thousand of them were imprisoned by the Georgian government. Like their Russian counterparts, the Georgian Mensheviks had scruples about using violence against their opponents."[14]

We don't have to rely simply on Broido's account – the Georgian Menshevik leaders, Zhordania first and foremost, denied Bechhofer's account of his conversation with Ramishvili, as I will make clear later. Bechhofer's bias against the Georgian Mensheviks is very apparent. His account of the conversation, which is the only source for the figure of thirty Bolsheviks being executed, cannot be accepted without question.

The charge that the Georgian Social Democratic government was treating the local Communists brutally was taken up by Trotsky following the Russian invasion of Georgia in 1921. The Red Army leader blasted Kautsky for his assertion regarding the "complete liberty of action" for the Georgian Bolsheviks. "It would have been sufficient had he said that it had some liberty," Trotsky wrote. "But, as we already know, if he speaks of neutrality, then it is the strictest, if of liberty, it is the fullest; he does not speak merely of good relations, but 'the very best possible.'"

Referring to the various socialist leaders who visited Georgia in 1920, Trotsky added that

> It is amazing, above all, that neither Kautsky nor Vandervelde,
> nor Mrs. Snowden herself, nor the foreign diplomats, nor the
> journalists of the bourgeois press, nor the faithful guardians of
> liberty – *The Times*, nor the most upright Temps, in a word, none
> of those who bestowed their benedictions upon the democracy
> of Georgia ever noticed there the presence of … the Special
> Detachments. Yet such did exist.[15]

Trotsky wasn't upset that there was a kind of political police (the special detachments) operating in the country. Instead, he compared it to the Bolsheviks' own secret police, the Cheka. "The Special Detachments, if you please, is the Menshevik Cheka," he wrote. "The Special Detachment seized and imprisoned and shot all those that were active against the Menshevik democracy." Trotsky boasted that the Bolsheviks themselves did exactly the same thing with the Cheka.

"The Special Detachment in its methods of terror in no way differed from the Extraordinary Commission of Soviet Russia," he wrote. "Where it did differ was in aim. The Extraordinary Commission protected the Socialist dictatorship against the agents of capital; the Special Detachment protected the bourgeois regime against the Bolshevik "anarchy." But it was for this very reason that the respectable people who cursed the Cheka, did not notice the Georgian Special Detachment."[16]

Trotsky believed that creating a secret police force and executing one's opponents was perfectly alright. What he objected to was the assertion that the Georgian Social Democrats were somehow better than this.

Zhordania rejected Trotsky's comparison entirely. "To compare them [the special detachments] with the Soviet 'Tchekas' who have the right of life or death over the inhabitants, who are not bound by any laws and are responsible to no one, is possible only by an entire disregard of the truth."[17] He insisted that these detachments were unable to launch an enquiry or legal proceedings, and were not independent in any way.

There can be little doubt that the Georgian Social Democrats used force to put down Bolshevik coup attempts, just as they did when dealing with separatist ethnic groups such as the South Ossetians. The question is whether they had any choice and if their response to violent attacks was proportionate.

The Georgian Bolsheviks operated as a conspiratorial organisation dedicated to supporting Russian attempts to bring the country back into the Russian fold. They were not simply a group of dissidents, a political party with a different view of how Georgia should be run, even if many of the party's adherents joined for perfectly good reasons and had no particular loyalty to Soviet Russia. The party was very much an arm of the Soviet state, and particularly of the Red Army, as became clear in 1921 when they helped invading Russian troops into their country.

As a group with utter contempt for democratic norms, the Bolsheviks could not be treated the way the Georgian Social Democrats treated all the other opposition parties, which operated quite freely and whose leaders were not jailed. The Georgian Mensheviks were deeply affected by the failure of the Provisional Government in Petrograd to defend itself in 1917 when the Bolsheviks seized power with relative ease, and were grappling with issues that would come up again within a decade in Weimar Germany, where once again Social Democrats found themselves employing repressive measures against the Nazis and Communists – though again without sufficient force.

The Georgian Social Democrats were dealing with something that had not been anticipated by the founding fathers of the modern socialist movement. Totalitarian political parties were a new phenomenon, conspiratorial in nature, committed to the violent overthrow of elected democratic governments. Democracies needed to find ways to defend themselves against this threat.

The debacle of the November 1919 coup attempt put a damper on further efforts by the Bolsheviks. But the dream of overthrowing the Social Democrats by force, backed up by the Russian Red Army, remained. And it took less than six months for the Bolsheviks to try again.

The Komsomol sent out an appeal to anyone in Russia who would listen – including the All-Russian Central Executive Committee, the Council of People's Commissars, the Comintern, the Red Army, and the Central Committee of the Russian Young Communist League – asking for help against "the oppressive governments of the Mensheviks and the Dashnaks."

The Georgian Komsomol forced its youngest members into something called the "Young Communist Guard." On 17 April 1920, this group issued "Order No. 3" which said: "Those who have been mobilized should immediately be organized into fighting groups of ten men each. These groups should be of two types: first, those who know how to use weapons; second, reserve groups."[18] The Komsomol began to buy and store arms, to prepare for yet another attempt to seize power.

Meanwhile, in neighbouring Azerbaijan, the Bolsheviks were taking steps to put an end to the country's existence as an independent state. At noon on 27 April 1920, the local Communists presented an ultimatum to the Azerbaijani government demanding that it hand over power within twelve hours. The ultimatum was a ploy as it had already been decided that the Red Army would invade. For propaganda purposes, however, the Russians wanted it to appear as if there had been a local uprising.

While the Azerbaijani parliament debated how to respond to the ultimatum, and long before the twelve hours were up, Red Army forces crossed the border and seized a couple of railway stations. They began their advance on Baku, meeting hardly any resistance along the way. Most Azerbaijani soldiers were too busy fighting the Armenians for control of Karabagh, a disputed region (then and now), to have mounted a real defence of the capital. Seeing no alternative, the parliamentarians voted to dissolve their government and hand over power to the Bolsheviks.

Telegrams were then sent to Moscow by the Azerbaijani Communists asking for the assistance of the Red Army in support of their "revolution" – as if that army hadn't already invaded. As Kazemzadeh summed it up, "it was the might of a resurrected Russia which destroyed the Musavatist Government of Azerbaijan."[19] There was no international outcry when Azerbaijan lost its independence and was absorbed into the Russian Soviet system. The time therefore seemed ripe to stage a similar coup and invasion in Georgia.

Three days after the fall of Baku, on the morning of 1 May 1920, Communist demonstrators marched toward the centre of Tiflis. According to one young Communist eyewitness, "Our trucks were thundered by big crowds, calls for an uprising and the thunder of applause were heard. Hundreds of thousands of leaflets were distributed."[20] Workers loyal to the Social Democrats chose to fight back, together with the police, and the demonstration was broken up. Many arrests were made.

The coup was scheduled for the following day, 2 May 1920. Soviet historians would later question why the Bolsheviks didn't make their bid for power a day earlier, on International Workers' Day, when Communists were leading their supporters in the streets. As a result of the provocative character of the Bolshevik demonstrators on May Day that year (they were, after all, aware that they were only hours away from a planned armed insurrection) the Menshevik government arrested a number of Communist leaders.

The Bolshevik plan this time was to arrest the entire leadership of the Menshevik party, who would be attending a meeting of the Tiflis soviet on the night of 2 May. Presumably, the Bolsheviks had intelligence that the Mensheviks would not be protecting themselves, and would be vulnerable to a bold strike, just as the Provisional Government had been in Petrograd in 1917.

As it turned out, the Mensheviks had little to fear. The Georgian Bolsheviks, emulating their Russian heroes, decided on a plan that would begin with a cannon shot fired from the Tiflis arsenal. In this, they were attempting the recreate the shots fired by the cruiser *Aurora* in Petrograd which signalled that the Bolshevik revolt there had begun in November 1917. The would-be Georgian Lenins, however, were unable to re-enact the successful seizure of power in Petrograd. They had given the task of reporting on when the Mensheviks had begun their meeting to a group of Young Communist girls. The girls, however, arrived late. The Mensheviks had held their meeting and gone home. The cannon did not fire. The revolt had to be cancelled.[21]

As in November 1919, a small part of the Communist Party didn't get the news and went ahead with the revolt – a single detachment of the *Komsomol*. It turned out to be no match for the People's Guard or the police. Some of the Communist rebels were killed while others fled. An attempted revolt in South Ossetia which was supposed to take place at the same time also collapsed.

While the coup attempt in Tiflis failed because the Komsomol girls showed up late, it was probably doomed from the start. As Kazemzadeh summed it up, "the Georgian Bolsheviks were far too weak to overthrow a well-established Government enjoying popular support. The May revolt was a useless adventure."[22]

The Georgian Bolsheviks were very upset that the Red Army did not come to their assistance, especially given just days earlier the Soviets had occupied Baku. But a bigger shock was to follow when, five days after the failed coup, on 7 May 1920, Soviet Russia and Georgia signed a peace treaty in which the Russian Bolshevik government formally recognised independent Georgia. In a *quid pro quo*, the Georgian government made the Communist Party fully legal and agreed to release all the jailed Communists.

The Georgian Bolsheviks and their comrades in Armenia and Azerbaijan were furious. "We, the toiling masses of all Trans-caucasian peoples, proclaim … before the international proletariat that we despise the slogan of 'independence' announced by a minority of the Caucasian population through our oppressors and ravishers, the 'governments' of Georgia, Azerbaijan and Armenia," they declared.

As Kazemzadeh wrote, "But what was the use of denouncing independence when it was solemnly and 'unequivocally' recognized by the Soviet Government in Moscow? For a brief moment the Georgian Communists felt deserted. The Party, which was small and weak to start with, yet capable of waging battles by the sheer power of its enthusiasm, lost its heart."[23] It was this legal, though weakened, Communist Party that Kautsky, MacDonald and the other visiting socialists encountered during their trip to Georgia four months later.

The two failed revolts in November 1919 and again in May 1920 were evidence that the Georgian Bolsheviks had no intention of being a genuine opposition political party. They also proved that the party had little if any public support and armed insurrection was not on the cards. The only way the Georgian Bolsheviks would ever come to power would be if the Red Army could be persuaded to invade the country.

Legalisation proved to be a mixed blessing for the local Bolsheviks. "The only purpose which animated the Party was, as one of its leaders said, the organization of armed uprisings for the overthrow of the Government," wrote Kazemzadeh.[24] A decision was taken to maintain the underground party as well as the newly legal and above-board version. Armed robberies which had been used to fund the party were stopped, but weapons and other equipment were to be kept well hidden.

Following legalisation, the local Bolsheviks needed to re-name their party. They were now the Communist Party of Georgia, but they still referred to themselves as the "forward detachment of the Russian Communist Party." They and the newly formed Communist Parties of Armenia and Azerbaijan continued to see themselves as part and parcel of the Russian Communist Party. They took advantage of their new-found freedom by organising a new, provisional Central Committee and launched two legal party newspapers – *komunisti* in Georgian, and *Kommunist Gruzii* in Russian.

In addition to legalising the Communist Party, the Georgians had agreed to release any jailed Bolsheviks, which, according to Trotsky, amounted to 900 Communists. As Zhordania pointed out, many of these may have been Russian agents who crossed the border into the country, with their illegal weapons and sacks of cash. And while 900 Communists may seem like a large number, it pales in comparison to the size of the Menshevik Party, which had 80,000 members in Georgia. Nevertheless, it does indicate that some support for the Bolsheviks did exist in the country.

The Russians took advantage of the new relations with Georgia to send an ambassador to Tiflis, Sergei Kirov, who would go on to become a very prominent figure in the Bolshevik Party, eventually becoming party leader in Leningrad. His assassination in 1934 marked the beginning of Stalin's Great Purge. (It is today widely believed that Stalin orchestrated the assassination himself.) Kirov's job was not only to represent Russian interests in dealings with the Georgian state, but also to personally direct the Georgian Communist Party in its ongoing efforts to seize political power. For this purpose, he had access to a very considerable amount of money, and an embassy staff in Tiflis with hundreds of employees. They were often picked up by Georgian police for their subversive activities but quickly released due to their diplomatic immunity.

The signing of the peace deal did not prevent the Russian Bolsheviks from trying to spark local insurrections in various parts of Georgia, as they had done in the past. In July 1920, for example, a Bolshevik conspiracy was uncovered in Abkhazia. Local Communists had been in touch with both the Russian Military Command and officials employed by Kirov's Russian diplomatic mission in Tiflis.

Also, according to a report in a British newspaper, in August 1920 a former minister in the Azerbaijani government, Hassan Agayeff, was murdered by Bolshevik agents in Tiflis. "Attempts on the lives of Georgian Menshevist politicians are also reported," it added.[25]

Meanwhile, Armenia was coming under increasing threat of a Soviet invasion. Though its local Communists proved to be even less popular than those in Georgia, the Dashnak government foolishly embroiled the country in a war with Turkey which it could not win. The Turks easily defeated the Armenians and by 18 November 1920 an armistice was proclaimed which formalised the Armenian defeat. This was followed just ten days later by the arrival of Communist troops crossing over from Azerbaijan.

As they had done when conquering Azerbaijan, the Russian Red Army again tried to paint this as a revolt by the "toiling masses of Armenia." The Dashnak government decided not to resist, having no army left after the defeat at the hands of Turkey. Their capitulation was an odd one, cloaked in an effort to create an alliance between the Dashnaks and the Communists while welcoming the Russian troops. That "coalition" lasted only a few days before the Bolsheviks established a firm grip on power. Communist rule with its repression, its failure to feed the local population, and its inability to push back against the Turks, made the regime deeply unpopular from the outset.

In Georgia, despite the Bolshevik Party's best efforts over several years, the working class – especially the urban proletariat – proved resistant to the Communists' allure. In Petrograd in 1917, the Russian Bolsheviks had managed to win over a considerable number of urban workers, and possibly a majority, to their cause. But their Georgian comrades remained a small sect on the fringes of Georgian politics.

Karl Kautsky was an eyewitness to this. "The Communists boasted, from time to time, that they were recruiting their ranks from the Georgian proletariat. But, whenever an opportunity arose it revealed their insignificance," he wrote.

> Thus they commenced a great agitation among the railwaymen. A brilliant result was to be achieved. Just as I was departing, a Congress of Railwaymen was held in Tiflis which was going to demonstrate that the confidence of the railway workers in the Government had been completely shattered. The Communists expected to dominate the conference. Behold, when the delegates were counted, one single Communist was found among them. All the others, and there were over eighty, were Social-Democrats.[26]

Kautsky said that the same experience repeated itself at other union meetings.

The Communist Party, now legal and funded with vast sums by the Russians, did not thrive. Some members were lulled into a false sense of security and revealed their membership, allowing the Georgian police to more accurately gather intelligence on the party. The moment the party tried any subversive activity, the government reacted forcefully, jailing and exiling some leaders. In an honest appraisal of the state of the party, an internal report admitted that most Georgian workers were "contaminated with the poison of Russophobia" and followed the Mensheviks.[27] Even so, they persisted in their plans to overthrow the Georgian government, and on 20 September 1920 the Georgian Communist leaders met in the safety of Soviet-occupied Baku. There, they decided to strengthen their party, to imbue it with a new sense of discipline, knowing that an uprising would eventually come.

The Menshevik government, meanwhile, fought the Bolsheviks with every means at their disposal. Trotsky's account reads like an indictment, claiming that from the beginning the Georgian Menshevik leaders made "the ruthless suppression of Bolshevism" an essential plank of their programme. … Communist newspapers were suppressed, meetings dispersed by gunfire, revolutionary villages led by Bolsheviks were burnt down. The Special Detachment conducted wholesale shootings of leaders. The Mskhet [prison] was crowded with imprisoned Communists, Bolshevik refugees were handed back into the power of Denikin. During one month, October, 1919, in Georgia, according to a statement by the then Minister for the Interior, over 30 Communists were shot.[28]

These are serious allegations, and the Menshevik leaders rejected them. For example, Zhordania, writing in a 1922 manuscript entitled "Imperialism Behind the Mask of Revolution," insists that Trotsky's mention of the execution of thirty Communists in October 1919 "is sheer invention." What surprised the Georgian president, he wrote, "is that Mr. Trotsky put forward so modest a figure as 30 men; he might with equal truth say that we shot 300 or 3000 Bolsheviks."[29]

Zhordania also rejected Trotsky's insistence that the Bolshevik Party in Georgia was illegal from 1918 to 1920. "This is not true," he wrote. "The party existed openly, but its party organs which called on the people to revolt and attacked the idea of the independence of Georgia were, it is true, very often suppressed by us, and its agents were arrested and exiled to Russia for having prepared plots."[30]

Zhordania also addressed the issue of arrests of large numbers of Georgian Communists. He said that following the May 1920 peace treaty with Soviet Russia, the Georgian Communist Party was not only made fully legal, but was even offered a building for its use by the Menshevik government. However, the Georgian leaders were well aware of the Communists' ongoing subversive activities. The country, he wrote, was "inundated by agents from Soviet Russia. They crossed our frontier daily, by the score, bringing with them arms and sacks of paper money (for propaganda). We often succeeded in laying our hands on many of them." To Trotsky's assertion that Georgia imprisoned large numbers of Communists, Zhordania answered: "I would ask Mr. Trotsky one thing: what would happen if one of the neighbouring states of Soviet Russia sent agents into its territory to prepare plots, revolts, etc., and if these agents were caught by the Soviet authorities? I ask whether their lives would be spared, and their freedom restored."[31]

Zhordania's rebuttal of Trotsky is, I think, an effective one. While the Georgian Mensheviks did not offer complete freedom of operation to the Bolsheviks, as they did for all other opposition parties, it was because the Bolsheviks (unlike all the other parties) served as agents of a powerful foreign country, and worked constantly to violently overthrow Georgia's elected government. And even under those circumstances, the Georgian state's repression of the Communist Party was infinitely more humane and less brutal than the Soviet Communist treatment of opposition groups in Russia, including the Russian Mensheviks.

Even in its new-found role as a legal (and extremely well-financed) party, old habits died hard. By early January 1921, according to a report in a London newspaper which may not be entirely reliable,

the Russian Bolshevists are in a position to overwhelm the country at any moment, but are holding their hand for some reasons unknown. The Georgian Government, taking advantage of this circumstance, have dealt in a drastic fashion with the extensive Communist organization which has sprung up during the last few months. Thousands of Communists have been arrested and imprisoned, expelled from the country, or sent into exile. The *Kutais*, a Communist paper published in Tiflis, has been suppressed. Thus for the time being, at least, the interior menace has been staved off, but the external danger is still imminent. The Georgians are resolved to keep out the Bolshevists if possible.[32]

In hindsight, with a Russian invasion only months away, it was probably foolish of the Georgian government to give the local Communists freedom of operation, but that was the price for Soviet recognition of Georgian independence. Of course that recognition soon turned out to have been worth very little, though the Georgians did not know that at the time.

From the moment the Bolsheviks seized power in Petrograd in November 1917, the Georgian Mensheviks grappled with the question of how to deal with the local Leninists. Tiny in number, with little influence over workers or peasants but with some support in the army, the Bolsheviks represented a security threat of considerable magnitude from the very beginning. Their willingness to use violence to achieve their goals, and their subservience to the Russian state, meant that they were like no other opposition group the Mensheviks had to deal with.

In the long run, it didn't really matter whether the Georgian government treated the local Bolsheviks with velvet gloves or an iron fist. The fate of the country was not decided by the amateurish attempts by local Communists to re-enact the conditions of Petrograd in November 1917. Georgia faced a far greater threat from across its northern borders.

EUROPE'S SOCIALIST LEADERS COME FOR A VISIT

By mid-1920, the situation of democratic Georgia had settled into a relative calm. The peace treaty signed with Soviet Russia put an end to the imminent threat of a Red Army invasion. The Communist Party of Georgia, previously busy with periodic attempts at armed insurrection, was now legal and above-board, and would not be making another attempt at an armed insurrection anytime soon. Though Azerbaijan had fallen to the Soviets, neighbouring Armenia retained its independence. The British forces were on their way out and Georgian diplomats were working feverishly to secure recognition from the great powers and the newly formed League of Nations. For the Social Democratic leaders of the country, this seemed to be a good time to show off Georgia's accomplishments to sympathetic leaders. They turned to the Second International.

The Second International had collapsed during the world war as most of its most important member parties took the sides of their own countries. Once the war had ended, it was formally revived at a congress in Geneva in 1920. There was a Georgian delegation to that congress consisting of six delegates, among them Irakli Tsereteli, a former minister in the Russian Provisional Government and a leader of the Petrograd Soviet, who was already quite well-known among European socialists from their pre-war congresses. The Georgians invited representatives of the relaunched International to visit Tiflis.

At the end of August 1920, Karl Kautsky, Emile Vandervelde and Camille Huysmans, who had met six years earlier in Brussels in a failed attempt to stop the world war, met up in Paris and set out on a journey of over 6,000 kilometres to Georgia. That they would choose to travel to Tiflis rather than to Moscow showed the extent of the rift between the socialists and the newly formed Communist parties. Georgia, not Russia, was seen as a model democratic socialist society, one worthy of study – and deserving of solidarity.

According to a report in *The Times* (London) on 4 August 1920, "A Socialist Delegation will leave for Georgia on September 1, at the invitation of the Georgian Government, to investigate political and social conditions there. The delegation is composed, as nearly as possible, of the Socialists who recently visited Bolshevik Russia, so that they may be able to compare the situation of the two countries."[1]

Kautsky, Vandervelde and Huysmans were joined by some of the best-known socialists of post-war Europe.

James Ramsay MacDonald was a leader of the British Labour Party, though he was no longer an MP, having lost his parliamentary seat in the 1918 elections. MacDonald would soon win back his seat and four years later led Britain's first Labour Party government. Despite his astonishing electoral success, MacDonald ended up demonised by his own party, reviled for having broken ranks by forming a coalition with its opponents. But that came much later.

Tom Shaw was a Labour MP from Preston who had served as the party's Junior Whip. Shaw was also an experienced figure in the international socialist and trade union movements, and was secretary of the International Federation of Textile Workers.

Ethel Snowden was the only woman on the trip in her own right. Like MacDonald and Shaw, she was a leader of the Labour Party and served on its National Executive Committee. Snowden was an experienced foreign traveller, having visited Palestine, the United States and a number of European destinations. Early in 1920, she joined a joint Labour Party–Trades Union Congress delegation to Russia. She was not pleased with what she saw, and published a book (*Through Bolshevik Russia*) that was highly critical of Lenin's regime. As *The Times* reported, she was one of those who was competent to "compare the situation of the two countries."

The French members of the delegation to Georgia included Pierre Renaudel, Adrien Marquet and Alfred Inghels. Renaudel was a French socialist leader, like Ramsay MacDonald temporarily out of parliament. He was close to Jean Jaurès and witnessed his murder in 1914. Marquet went on to become the socialist mayor of Bordeaux and later turned to the far right, serving in the Vichy government under Pétain and Laval. Inghels was described by Mrs. Snowden as "the typical bluff and substantial Trade Union leader, a representative of the textile workers."[2]

The Belgian delegation consisted of Emile Vandervelde and his wife Lalla, Louis de Brouckère and Camille Huysmans, accompanied by his wife Marthe and daughter Sara, who acted as secretary to the delegation.

We have detailed accounts of this visit because many of the participants wrote about it, in particular Ethel Snowden and Sara Huysmans.

MacDonald noted in his diary that he left London on Monday, 30 August 1920 for Paris, where he met up with the others.[3] The delegates were hosted by Tsereteli, who was in Paris with the Georgian delegation to the peace conference.[4]

"All of them were really looking forward to the trip," Sara Huysmans wrote. "They were vaccinated against the plague – except for Mrs Snowden, who categorically refused vaccination – and boarded a train which took them via Paris and Rome to Taranto, in southern Italy. Kautsky, who had developed a high fever, was to stay in Taranto and only two weeks later were he and his wife to arrive in Georgia."[5] Though the sixty-six-year-old Kautsky came later than the other delegates, accompanied by his wife Louise and his secretary, he stayed in Georgia much longer, enabling him to write his book detailing his experiences there.

The socialist travellers did not have an easy time of it. As Sara Huysmans remembered: "One piece of luggage (a crate) was stolen on the way – it was actually replaced by another, empty crate, cleverly put among the rest of the luggage. An alert porter made a remark about it, saying that 'somebody must have felt that if someone takes along so much luggage others may well have their fair share of it'."[6]

MacDonald noted in his diary that when they arrived in Rome, he saw the Coliseum in the moonlight, and visited the Vatican on the following day.

Sara Huysmans described the rest of the journey.

After an ultimate passport control, the party sailed for Constantinople (Istanbul), having been joined in the meantime by one Russian and seven Georgians. Clearly, Istanbul was overwhelming at first sight, for everybody, whether sick or healthy, was on deck at daybreak – only wearing pyjamas or a nightdress: nobody wanted to miss out on the view. Camille waxed lyrical about Istanbul in his travel letters in *The Volksgazet* (Flemish socialist newspaper), a city which was unknown to him. The party managed to do some hasty sightseeing. When they set out without a guide, trying to find their way around Istanbul, they had to ask for it. They did so in French: no response. In English: even less. Finally, they tried in Dutch. And they were lucky! A Turkish carpet merchant, who did some business in Brussels, Ostend and Amsterdam, showed them the way.

The ship was now heading for Batoum, the largest port city in Georgia. The delegation had no trouble filling its time with planning and scheduling meetings, reading, discussing and singing. Watching the dolphins swimming along with them also proved to be a nice pastime.

While the socialist leaders were singing and talking, keeping an eye out for dolphins in the Black Sea, the Georgians were preparing an unforgettable welcome for them in Batumi. Two weeks after leaving Paris, they finally arrived. According to Ethel Snowden, no fewer than 5,000 people greeted them.

"They were welcomed by a large delegation, sailing towards them, with flags attached to the boat," Sara Huysmans recalled.

People were waving banners on shore, thousands of people, children with flowers, playing music, under triumphal arches … There was no time to leave their sea legs behind, they were immediately taken to the town hall to speech! And there were more speeches to come: in the people's house! And cheers! Lunch was served in a special train and off they were to visit a tea factory. There they enjoyed an open air dinner and then again there were speeches, toasts … and toasts, singing and dancing.

Ethel Snowden, who had previously been to Bolshevik Russia and could therefore make comparisons, has provided us with a very detailed account of the visit, including that first day in Batumi. It gives a real flavour of how the international socialist delegates were greeted by the Georgians. She recalled what it was like for her to visit Bolshevik Russia.

> In Georgia it was different. The experience in Batoum was the same everywhere. There was no compulsion to meet us. The people came because they wanted to come. They moved freely amongst us, without restraint of speech or manner, laughing, shouting, singing. The brown-eyed children climbed into our laps. They shyly played with our watches or examined our clothes. In all those merry faces turned up at us on the balcony I saw not one look of bitterness, no tightening of thin lips, no burning hate in the eyes. One jolly giant, whose curly grey-black hair waved a head's breadth above the crowd, led the cheering, which was caught up by the crowd in unmistakable sincerity. They ran by the side of our carriages, flinging red roses into them and blowing kisses to us as we gathered up the roses and pinned them to our coats as the red emblem of international solidarity.[7]

They stayed only one day in the port city. Sara Huysmans was sad to leave Batumi:

> The party was delighted … but had to move on, boarding the train again and sleeping in solid hammocks, on its way to the Georgian capital Tbilisi. Unfortunately, they did not enjoy a good night's rest … At every station in which the train halted the delegation had to hear out the local variant of The International and greet an enthusiastic crowd. It went on all night!

Ethel Snowden recalled that their train

> had been a royal train. It was replete with every comfort. There were bathrooms even, and an excellent kitchen. The food department was in the hands of a Russian family, a widowed

mother and three children. They were a family of good birth whose fallen fortunes had been relieved in this way by the Social Democrats as a reward for saving the life of the President, always in danger from the violent extremists of both sorts.

They finally arrived in Tiflis. "It seemed very odd," wrote MacDonald.

> There we were, having left for some days all that seemed to be of the West, having gone through the Bazaar and the mosques of Constantinople and proceeded far beyond towards the rising sun, and, at our journey's end at last, we were being received by a President of the Republic of Georgia in a waiting room at the Tiflis railway station, covered with the most glorious Oriental rugs, but hung with the portraits of Karl Marx and his best known disciples.

Snowden described the cheering crowd that awaited them before they left for their quarters in the former residence of the American commissioner. According to Sara Huysmans, "The welcome they were given in Tbilisi was even more splendid than in Batoum. There were speeches again, and cheers and toasts, but now they had to get down to business. "

That business included, according to MacDonald, a meeting with the Social Democratic Party's Central Committee followed by a visit to the opera. Snowden wrote that the delegation's "first business in Tiflis was to attend the special session of Parliament called in our honour, to hear a speech of welcome from each of the eight political parties represented in that Parliament."

After three days in the capital, they were taken around the country, accompanied by journalists and even someone with a movie camera. According to Sara Huysmans, "the delegation worked long hours, from 7 a.m. to 2 a.m." Her father proposed concrete measures to intensify cooperation between the Belgian labour movement and the Georgians. "Huysmans had ambitious plans to establish solid cooperation with Belgium," she wrote. "He would arrange for the shipping of Georgian vegetables and fruit to Belgium, and of course to Antwerp in particular. Belgian cooperatives could sell them to their customers. Well-trained Belgian technicians had to be sent to Georgia urgently to share their expertise in order to make production more efficient and improve technical education."

MacDonald described visiting "the heart of the Caucasian mountains, surrounded by the wildest and the gayest rout of untamed mountaineers armed with sword, shield, and rifle" and then standing reverently "whilst an old priest by the light of altar candles guttering in the wind read to us an address of welcome which ended with 'Long live the International.'"[8]

"In every one of the numerous villages which I visited," he wrote, "and from the still greater number of peasant deputations that came offering us wine and bread and salt, I heard of nothing but satisfaction, nothing but hope."

Ethel Snowden described hearing MacDonald speak to the Georgians at that church:

> The old church in which the address of welcome was to be delivered was too small for the company assembled. We held the meeting in the churchyard and spoke to the people from the top of a broad wall. I never heard Mr. MacDonald speak better than he did to those grim but simple mountain warriors, reminiscent as they were of the shaggy Highlanders of his native Scotland three centuries or more ago.

A number of the visiting Socialists commented on the way in which the local nobility had acquiesced in the Social Democratic reforms. "I met Princes who gloried in their new-found civic equality," recalled Ramsay MacDonald. Ethel Snowden "met landlords who submitted cheerfully to the new system and noble ladies who rejoiced in their new-found economic liberties." Sara Huysmans wrote that "large landowners had been disinherited with little difficulty." They found none of the bitter class warfare that had torn Russia apart in the years following the Bolshevik coup in 1917. This was partly due to the specific character of the landed nobility in Georgia. Many of the local Georgian aristocrats were hardly richer than their peasant neighbours, and many had been resentful of the Russians, welcoming Georgian independence. Some of the Georgian Menshevik leaders were themselves descended from the nobility, Zhordania included. This, and the broadly pro-peasant policies of the Georgian Mensheviks as compared to the Russian Bolsheviks' focus on the urban working class, contributed to the different results in each country.

Snowden recalled travelling to Guria to meet Zhordania's mother in their modest family home. "She was dressed in the native woman's dress," she recalled. "This tiny old lady of lovely and hospitable spirit could not understand or appreciate a subdivision of land which robbed her loved son of a large part of his patrimony." Zhordania explained "with gentle firmness" that the agrarian reform law "was for all alike, the rich as well as the poor, and that those who had more must give to those who had none."

"Those who had more must give to those who had none" – this was the Georgian socialists' core principle which guided their policies, and it expressed their vision of a new society.

The socialist delegates were then taken to Zhordania's family garden, where in they were shown "a sacred spot where a loved child lies buried. It is beautifully kept, and a garden seat facing the west is placed near the grave. We bent our heads at this sacred family shrine in a common feeling of sympathy and understanding."

Sara Huysmans' recollection of the final day of the "fascinating and passionate tour" ended when her father

> was asked to give a critical farewell speech. Obviously, there was still a lot of – ideological – work to be done, because the speech amounted to something like this: "You have already achieved a lot, but now you must also learn to work. You introduced the eight-hour working day: now you are expected to really work eight hours a day! Production has to increase continuously and better skills will enable you to reduce the number of working hours in the near future."

Huysmans' patronising tone was fortunately not echoed in what the socialist visitors told journalists back home. Ethel Snowden, for example, was interviewed by *The Times* on her return to London. She gave an entirely positive account. "Georgia," she said, "has had experiences of warfare with Turks, Armenians and Bolsheviks. Prices are still very high, and the exchange is heavily against her. But the people are full of hope and determination. They have set up what is the most perfect Socialism in Europe."

As *The Times* had earlier reported, one reason why Snowden was on the delegation was to compare her experiences in Bolshevik Russia with Georgia. One cannot help but be struck about how naïve some of this sounds today. Snowden and her comrades were completely won over by the Georgians, and unlike Kautsky (who had some critical words to say about the Menshevik government in his book), their glowing praise for the Georgians reads almost exactly like what some "revolutionary tourists" would say first about Soviet Russia and later about the various other totalitarian regimes that emerged in the twentieth century. This does not mean that she and the others were wrong. But it does mean that some of what they say needs to be read critically.

"I was immediately struck by the difference between the appearance of the people in Georgia and in Russia," Snowden said.

> The constant sight of misery in Russia was intolerable. The Georgians were in a physical condition infinitely superior to the Russians. They looked well fed and well clothed, and, above all, genuinely happy. There was no terror in their faces. There were no demonstrations arranged by military order.
>
> As we went from town to town and village to village the people who had been told we were coming came in the friendliest way to welcome us. They brought us gifts of fruit and wine and – according to their traditions of hospitality – bread and salt. They danced their national dances for us, but it was all spontaneous and natural.[9]

Ramsay MacDonald too was interviewed by the *Manchester Guardian* upon his return.[10] As the newspaper summarised the interview, the Labour leader described "a happy country under a Socialistic regime." MacDonald told the journalist that he was "delighted with his visit to Georgia. It is, he said, a beautiful country and small as it is – its population is about four millions – he believes it to have a great future. The Georgian Republic, as he reminded me, is Socialist, and, as a member of the Government had said to him, the aim of the Government is to organise it on I.L.P. [Independent Labour Party] lines."

MacDonald explained what he saw in Georgia. "The land system is much the same as that of Bolshevik Russia. The holdings are limited and remain the property of the peasants only as long as they themselves till the land," he said. Following upon the peace treaty with Soviet Russia, MacDonald noted that "the

Georgians are intensely anti-Bolshevik and also anti-Russian, but there is active Bolshevik propaganda which is not interfered with, as there is complete liberty of opinion."

The newspaper reported MacDonald's description of the rest of the Georgian economy.

> The largest coal mine … is run by the State, but the important manganese mines are still in private hands. All the forests belong to the State. Most of the few factories are still in private hands, but schemes for socialising the mining and other industries are under consideration. Much is being done to promote co-operative production, and a plan has been made for putting tobacco growing, which is an important industry, in the hands of associations of producers. Georgia is a most productive country. Its wine is of very high quality. The country is prosperous on the whole, and there is plenty to eat. Of course … the Socialist regime is only beginning and it will take a long time to develop it.

MacDonald was a firm believer in the need for the three Transcaucasian countries to reunite in a new federation. Armenia had not yet been taken over by the Red Army, while Azerbaijan had recently fallen under Soviet control, but MacDonald believed that its inhabitants were hostile to the Russian Bolsheviks and would "get rid of them when they can," thus opening the door to renewed cooperation between the three countries.

Finally, MacDonald urged the British government to recognise Georgia. He was very critical of the British attitude so far. "We have behaved very badly to Georgia," he said. "We have tried to force the Georgians to support Denikin, and when they refused the British military authorities seized Georgian guns and munitions and handed them over to Denikin, who used them against Georgia." He noted that the Georgians feared attacks from Baron Wrangel, Denikin's successor commanding White armies in southern Russia, and were ready to defend themselves against aggression from his forces.

Not everyone was enthusiastic about the delegation's visit, even among the Georgians. One of the critics was Zourab Avalishvili, a Georgian diplomat who was highly critical of the Social Democrats. He considered the delegation to be a waste of time, and he wrote contemptuously of the socialist visitors, referring to "prominent European Socialists – including the three 'ladies-in-waiting' of the 2nd International (Mrs. Kautsky, Mrs. Vandervelde and Mrs. Snowden), gazing with curiosity at 'that charming picturesque Georgia'." He also expressed disgust at how they were welcomed by the Georgian government. They were greeted "with official honours, to which they were not so accustomed at home," which was true at the time. But Avalishvili could not have known that two of the delegates (MacDonald and Huysmans) would go on to become prime ministers of their countries. He considered the delegation to "be of no importance at all: it even created or stimulated more untimely illusions with regard to the support of the 'Western democracies'" He may have had a point here. Avalishvili argued that the Georgian people had no idea of "the comparative importance for Georgia's independence in 1920 of the 'Supreme Council of Allied Powers' and the 'Amsterdam International'," referring to the socialists.[11]

The sharpest criticism of the visiting Socialists came not from Georgians who stood to the right of the Mensheviks, but from the Bolsheviks. Trotsky was scathing. He begins his pamphlet on the Georgian question with this description of the Socialist mission to the country:

Hearing of this righteous land, several pilgrims of the Second International, known for their piety – Vandervelde, Renaudel, and Mrs. Snowden - immediately booked a direct passage to it. Immediately after them followed Kautsky, bent with age and wisdom. All these, like the apostles of old, conversed in tongues they did not understand and saw visions which they afterwards described in articles and books.[12]

In the end, as it turned out, neither the Second International nor the Allied Powers could do much for Georgia when Stalin and his comrades decided it was time to put an end to the Menshevik experiment.

13

THE STATE THAT NEVER WAS

The Georgian Constitution of 1921 described a society which never came into existence. The work drafting the document began in 1918 and ended just as the Russian Red Army was completing its successful invasion and occupation of the country. The significance of the constitution lies in the fact that it lays out in considerable detail how the Georgian Mensheviks imagined the democratic socialist republic would function.

Though Karl Marx had left little in the way of specific instructions about the shape of a future socialist society, his life-long partner Friedrich Engels was slightly more forthcoming. Writing in 1891, after Marx's death, he said that "If one thing is certain it is that our party and the working class can only come to power in the form of the democratic republic. This is even the specific form for the dictatorship of the proletariat."[1] The famous sentence in *The Communist Manifesto* – "the first step in the revolution by the working class is to raise the proletariat to the position of ruling class to *win the battle of democracy*" – indicates that Marx was likely to have agreed with Engels.[2]

According to George Papuashvili, the president of the Constitutional Court of Georgia, writing in 2012, the 1921 Georgian Constitution "can unquestionably be considered as one of the most advanced and perfect supreme legislative acts oriented towards human rights in the world for its time."[3] As Papuashvili points out, despite the Georgians having had no legal and constitutional experience during their century under autocratic Russian rule, the Social Democrats "managed to create such a legal act which stood out among the post-World War I constitutions in terms of its uniqueness and consistency." He highlights several key elements of the new constitution including local self-government, abolition of the death penalty, freedom of speech and belief, universal suffrage (including votes for women), trial by jury and a ban on unlawful detention.

Work on the Georgian Constitution began in the very early days of the independent republic, in June 1918, with a Constitutional Commission established, consisting of representatives of several political parties. S. Japaridze, a Social Democrat, was the first head of this commission.

In the summer of 1918, Noe Zhordania addressed a party meeting and discussed the importance of democracy. Social Democrats, he said,

> set a certain bright goal for the state – transformation of society on social grounds. But when we chase this goal we must by all means negotiate certain political-economic stages. We cannot bypass these stages nor take a leap forward, history does not allow for this ... [the] Bolsheviks endeavoured to jump from the lower to the higher stage, [to] take one jump from the older regime to the realm of socialism, bypassed democracy, cheated history ... By denying democracy they achieved not socialism, but vandalism.[4]

The Mensheviks had no intention of cheating history.

The work of this commission was continued by the Constituent Assembly, elected in February 1919. Members of that body were elected by universal suffrage and the Social Democrats won by a landslide. The Constituent Assembly went on to create its own commission to continue work on the draft constitution. Like the first commission, this one too had representatives of parties other than the ruling Social Democrats, including National Democrats, Socialist Federalists and Socialist Revolutionaries. While R. Arsenidze was named to chair the commission, Japaridze remained a member.

Until there was a constitution in place, the Georgian Declaration of Independence played a legal role as a foundational document, declaring a democratic republic, respect for human rights, and so on. Though this was no substitute for a formal constitution, the act of independence was re-confirmed by the Constituent Assembly in 1919.

Members of the commission were influenced by democratic constitutions from around the world. Almost all of the existing constitutions were translated into Georgian and published in the press. Members of the commission and others, including lawyers, wrote articles reviewing these different documents. By July 1920 a draft constitution was ready, and was published for review. Four months later, the Constituent Assembly began reviewing it with an eye to formal adoption.

The articles were adopted one by one in a painstakingly slow process as time was running out for the Georgian Democratic Republic. Voting on the final article took place just four days before the Red Army entered Tiflis, and the government began its flight to the west.

The official text of the constitution was finally published in the port city of Batumi, the last refuge of the Menshevik government, by N. Khvingia, a local printer. At the Constituent Assembly's last meeting on 17 March 1921, a decree was passed temporarily suspending the brand-new constitution. And then the Georgian Republic was no more.

The Georgian Constitution expressed a very broad interpretation of the concept of human rights. It guaranteed free primary education for all children, and recognised the right of all children to clothing, hats, school supplies and meals. All citizens were to be offered employment or insurance by the state. The working week was restricted to forty-eight hours. Women and young workers were assured protection in the workplace. Violations of the labour code were made punishable by criminal law.[5]

As Papuashvili explains, "The 1921 constitution is one of the first documents in the world which reflects citizens' socio-economic rights, which is not surprising given that social-democrats were heading the government."[6] He is convinced that the Georgian Mensheviks were keen to be seen not to lag behind the Russian Bolsheviks in this regard, but there was probably more to it than that. The ideas about social and economic rights the Georgian Constitution expressed were intrinsic to the Social Democrats' vision of how a new society should work.

The constitution also limited property rights, with forceful expropriation of property or restriction of private enterprise being allowed. In case of deprivation of property, suitable compensation was to be paid, unless the law stipulated otherwise – as was the case with the agrarian reform. Papuashvili is critical of some articles which "carry a rather ultra-socialist tinge." One of these allowed "forced expropriation or restriction of private enterprise," for example.

In guaranteeing economic and social rights, the Georgian Constitution anticipated later documents such as the Universal Declaration of Human Rights (1948), even if the drafters of those documents may have been completely unaware of the Georgian experiment. This broader concept of human rights expounded by the Georgian Mensheviks in their constitution is not to be found, for example, in the United States Constitution, though more recent constitutions, including those of South Africa (1996) also embrace wider concepts of human rights.

Like many other democratic constitutions, the Georgian one guaranteed freedom of belief and conscience and separated church from state, even banning the state from financing any church. This was far more secular than the current Georgian Constitution which acknowledges a special role for the church in Georgian history. The constitution also guaranteed the rights to freedom of speech and press, the abolition of censorship and freedom of assembly. At the insistence of the powerful Georgian trade unions, it also included clauses guaranteeing the right to join and form trade unions, and the right of workers to strike.

Citizens were also protected from arbitrary rule by a series of provisions in the constitution which established the rule of law. It was forbidden to detain a person without trial. If arrested, a person had to be brought before a court within twenty-four hours, though an extension of another day was possible. Article 19 of the constitution specifically abolished the death penalty. This was highly unusual, as only a few countries had already done so by 1921, among them Colombia, Costa Rica, Ecuador, San Marino, Uruguay and Venezuela.[7]

Whatever their failures in practice, in theory the Georgian Social Democrats were committed to full equality for all national and ethnic minorities in the country, with the constitution including several articles about this. Though Georgia was declared to be a unitary state and the constitution explicitly banned the ceding of national territory, three regions were granted autonomy: Abkhazia, the region around Batumi, and Zakatala, a district which was then part of Georgia but which was given to Azerbaijan by the Bolsheviks in 1922 and remains part of that country even today. South Ossetia was not given any special status.

Among the powers given over to the autonomous rulers of Abkhazia were the following: "local finances, public education, local community and town governance, magistrate and court institutions, safeguarding individual and public order, administration, public health, roads of local importance, local budget."[8] In addition to the specific powers given over to autonomous regions, all national minorities were guaranteed the rights to use their own national languages and to establish local governments.

The constitution proposed an unusual system of government that consisted essentially of just two branches – the legislative and the judicial. There was no strong executive branch, certainly not one with equal status to the others, as was the case in some democracies.

A supreme court was to be elected by parliament and its role was to serve as a court of cassation – meaning that it was to interpret the law. A modern example of such a court is the European Court of Justice. All the other courts were declared to be independent, and their decisions could not be overturned by any other branch of government. A jury system was introduced for important cases, thus involving the general public in the administration of justice, and following up indirectly on the popular courts established back in the days of the Gurian Republic. Many of these rules were already in place before the adoption of the constitution, having been turned into law by Georgia's elected governing bodies from 1918 onwards.

The legislature was to be elected on the basis of universal, direct, secret and proportional suffrage for a term of three years. Elections were to be held in the autumn and the work of parliament would commence on the first Sunday of November. All citizens over the age of twenty were given the right to vote.

Women were granted equal suffrage with men, and voted in the 1919 elections to the Constituent Assembly, with several women elected members of that Assembly. In this matter, as in others, the Georgians were ahead of many older democracies, only a handful of which (including Australia and New Zealand) had granted women the right to vote. The constitution also confirmed that "the citizens of both sexes enjoy equal political civil, economic and family rights."

Members of parliament were elected under a strict system of proportional representation by party, and this presumed and encouraged the existence of a strong system of political parties. Parliament was to be kept under the watchful eye of the general public, and various provisions of the constitution gave the nation tools to control their representatives.

The constitution gave parliament nine specific powers: to pass laws; to direct the army and all armed forces; to declare war; to ratify treaties; to order an amnesty for prisoners; to make a budget; to take out loans; to appoint officials; and to control the executive.

That executive branch of government was the subject of considerable debate at the time. Not one member of the commission drafting the constitution supported the restoration of the Georgian monarchy. But some, particularly the National Democratic Party, did want the country to have a president. The Social Democrats strongly opposed this, and opposed a strong executive branch in general.

To an extent, this was probably a lingering reaction to the authoritarian Russian tsarist system, but it also reflected the culture of leadership which had developed over many years among the Social Democrats. Inside their party, there were many leaders and they ruled in a collegial fashion. This was one of the things that distinguished them from the Bolsheviks, whose leadership was increasingly concentrated in the hands of Lenin and later Stalin. Even Zhordania, despite being the undisputed leader of his party, strongly opposed the introduction of the post of president and his influence ensured that the constitution made no provision for such a post.

The government was to be headed by a chairman, who was elected by parliament and served as the supreme representative of the republic. The term of office was just one year, and individuals elected to this post could serve just two terms. Kautsky for one was very critical of this provision, and would have preferred a strong executive branch.

The powers of the government were quite limited, particularly when it came to the use of military force. While the government was given the responsibility to "safeguard the Republic from external dangers and to defend its independence," the armed forces could be mobilised by the government for only twenty-one days and only in "unforeseen circumstances." It required an act of parliament to extend this period, and only parliament had the right to declare war. More than fifty years later, in the wake of the Vietnam War, the American Congress found itself passing a "War Powers Act" that paralleled what the Georgians had done, strengthening the war-making authority of congress and curtailing that of the executive.

The executive branch was made fully accountable to parliament, and individual members of the government could be dismissed, though the government as a whole could not be.

The Georgians deliberately made their constitution difficult to amend, as the Americans had done before them with their constitution. To initiate any change in the constitution, a majority of members of parliament and 50,000 electors were needed. To actually enact a change, two-thirds of parliament needed to vote in favour, followed by a referendum.

The Georgian Constitution was seen as highly progressive in its time and future British Labour Prime Minister Ramsay MacDonald wrote, "I familiarised myself with its constitution, its social and economic reconstruction and what I saw there, I wish I could see in my country too."[9]

During the long years of Soviet rule, analysis and discussion of the Georgian Constitution of 1921 were forbidden. But like the Georgian Republic itself, it remained somehow in the collective memory of the Georgian people and at the very first opportunity, it re-emerged. In February 1992, the Georgian National Congress declared the 1921 Georgian Constitution to be the effective constitution of Georgia. The following year, however, Eduard Shevardnadze, who had previously led the Georgian Communist Party and then served as the Soviet Foreign Minister, called for extensive revisions of the 1921 Constitution.[10] By 1995, Georgia had a new constitution which states in its preamble that it is based on the earlier document, and includes such features as the right to form trade unions and to strike. In addition, whole sections of it are copied directly from the Universal Declaration of Human Rights.

George Papuashvili sums ups the significance of the 1921 Constitution as follows: "This document reflects the democratic aspirations of the Democratic Republic of Georgia, which could have earned our country an important place in the civilized world. Though in the conditions of occupation and following annulment the 1921 Constitution ceased to operate, it played an important role in terms of political and legal development of modern Georgia."[11]

There is something terribly poignant in the image of Georgia's Constituent Assembly holding its final meeting in Batumi on the Black Sea coast. With the Red Army only hours away, and the Georgian government rushing to board ships that would take them into exile, the Georgian Social Democrats were keen to complete their legacy. That legacy was a model constitution that laid out their vision of a society which embraced both political and socio-economic rights, that imagined a society unlike any which existed in the world at that time, or since. Perhaps they imagined that sometime they might return to govern Georgia, or that socialists in other countries would want to know the results of their deliberations over the course of three years and the conclusions that they reached. Whatever they were thinking, the document they produced remains even today a vision that socialists can learn from and embrace, a vision of a new society that is radically different from the one that Lenin, Trotsky and Stalin were creating at that time.

14

THE EXPERIMENT ENDS

In early February 1921, the time was ripe. Lenin was ill and inactive. Red Army Commander Trotsky was out on an inspection tour of the Urals. It was time for Stalin to strike.

Ironically, Friday, 11 February 1921 started out as a good day for the Georgians. The Supreme Council of the victorious Allied powers, meeting in France, had decided to extend *de jure* recognition to the Georgian Democratic Republic. Just after 3:00 that afternoon, Earl Curzon, the British foreign secretary, cabled his military representative, Colonel Stokes, in the Georgian capital, Tiflis: "You are authorised to inform Georgian Government that His Majesty's Government grant them *de jure* recognition." Just a few hours later, though, long before the good news would reach Colonel Stokes, the Russian invasion began.

In a virtual repeat of the first stages of Georgia's short war with Armenia in 1918, several Georgian military detachments were disarmed by rebels in the Lori district and Shulavery, south of Tiflis near the Armenian border. The rebels called upon the peasants to rise up and oust the Menshevik rulers. The next day, the Georgian army reported that "regular units made a surprise attack upon our advanced posts" from Armenia.

The controversy over whether this was a genuine civil war or brazen Soviet aggression had already begun. On Sunday, 13 February, the Georgian Social Democratic newspaper *Borba* reported that a full-scale revolt had broken out in the Lori-Bortchalo area, claiming that the revolt had been provoked by a foreign power, though without naming which. (The nearest foreign power was Armenia, which was already in Soviet hands.)

The population in this troublesome district had previously been disarmed, which raised the question of who was supplying the rebels with arms. Bortchalo was still a disputed area between Georgia and Armenia. Though the Bolsheviks were interested then, as later, in suppressing national rivalry in the Caucasus, in this case they benefited from Armenia's claim. The Soviet Armenian government demanded a withdrawal of Georgian forces from Bortchalo by 14 February, then proceeded to invade a full three days earlier to make certain the Georgians could not meet their deadline. Over the next several days, some 36,000 infantrymen of the Eleventh Red Army crossed into Georgia.

Colonel Stokes cabled his first report on the outbreak of war to London. But news travelled slowly and his message reached the Foreign Office only six days later. The first press reports of the invasion appeared in New York and London a full week after the outbreak of fighting.

In Moscow, the Bolshevik leaders themselves were also late to learn about what was happening in Georgia. On 12 February, as the invasion was beginning, Lenin sent a handwritten note to Trotsky's deputy commander of the Red Army, Ephraim Sklyansky, which began "Unheard-of and incredible things are happening with our communications. Stalin and I are unable to communicate with Ordzhonikidze on *the most important matters*."

Sergo Ordzhonikidze was busy at the time leading the Red Army invasion of Georgia.

Lenin was furious. In the same note, he wrote, "If this is not done, I will have those responsible here committed for trial (or will endeavour to have them dismissed and arrested). It is intolerable."

If this was not clear enough, Lenin added a PS: "This is the complete disintegration of the *top* army *command*! There are no *communications*!!! with officials like Smilga and Ordzhonikidze!!"[1]

Two days later, Skylansky replied with a message to Lenin marked Top Secret and signed "on behalf on the Central Committee" (of the Communist Party). It appears to be directed to the Red Army commanders then leading the invasion of Georgia. It begins by saying that "The Central Committee is inclined to allow the Eleventh Army to give active support to the uprising in Georgia and to occupy Tiflis provided that international norms are observed" – what an odd phrase – "and on condition that all members of the Military Revolutionary Council of the Eleventh Army, after a thorough review of all the information, guarantee success." The message concludes by ordering that "no decisive steps are to be taken before receipt of our answer to telegrams from all these persons."[2]

Lenin added a note to this in his own handwriting, saying "Have this encrypted at once *ultra-carefully, in your own presence*, keeping the original. Send it to Smilga, making sure that he is at the receiver *in person* and deciphers it *himself* (tell the C.-in-C. about it without showing it to him.) Stalin will send it himself to Ordzhonikidze. Triple caution and the utmost caution, then. It is on your responsibility."

Where was Trotsky at this time? The first sign of life from the Red Army commander was a short message to Skylansky on 21

February, ten days after the Red Army had begun the invasion of Georgia: "Please compile for me a short note on the military operations against Georgia, when those operations began, by whose order, and so forth. I need the note for the Plenum."

"By whose order?" Trotsky asked, an extraordinary question from the head of the army. Clearly the order had come from Ordzhonikidze, one of Stalin's most trusted men, and almost certainly originated with Stalin himself, though Lenin was clearly unaware of this.

Lenin issued orders that the Russian invaders should behave with respect towards the Georgians, even towards Zhordania, and should try to win their support. His orders were ignored as the Red Army faced increasingly stiff opposition – and as it became clear that there was no popular uprising taking place in the country.

Despite his lack of involvement in the invasion, Trotsky eventually felt it necessary to defend what the Soviet state and its army had done, and wrote his book rebutting Kautsky's account. Because of that book, and his role as the head of the Red Army, Trotsky was widely seen as being responsible for the attack on Georgia. It was not the first time or the last that Trotsky found himself putting loyalty to his party above all other concerns.

By Monday 14 February, battles were raging near Vorontsovka, on the Georgia–Armenia border. The Georgian army did considerably better, at first, than they did in the 1918 war with Armenia, mounting a fierce resistance and reporting the capture of a large number of Russian soldiers. The Georgians later claimed that the invasion was from beginning to end a Russian operation, with only token involvement of non-Russian troops. This was already a lesson learned from the 1918 experience with Armenia, when the Georgian government could not accept at first that a foreign country had invaded their territory.

Meanwhile in Moscow, the Politburo of the Russian Communist Party reached an important decision in principle: the Red Army would not intervene in the fighting, which as far as they knew was a local rebellion. For several days, the Russians denied all knowledge of an invasion. Lenin himself, apparently, did not actually know that Georgia had been invaded at this time. A few days after the revolt had started, a "revolutionary committee" was set up by the rebels in Shulavery, and appealed to the Russian Soviet regime for help in liberating Georgia from Menshevik rule.

The rebels in the border area had been given a few days to establish the fact of a *bona fide* rebellion or border war. Once that happened, the Russians dropped all pretence, and poured troops into Georgia from all sides. Four days into the fighting, Georgian forces counter-attacked in strength.

At Sadakhlo, on the railway line from Yerevan to Tiflis, they scored some initial successes against the invading Russian troops. The Bolsheviks attacked at Poili, south-east of the Georgian capital, and at Red Bridge, crossing the River Kura. The Georgians at Sadakhlo were forced to pull back, but they then formed a line from Kolsalo to Bolshoi Muganlo, and then westward along the River Khram.

On the night of Tuesday the 15th, just four days into the fighting, the tide turned against the Georgians. Their army fell back to a line in the foothills to the north. Hearing of this, Colonel Stokes considered for the first time evacuating British subjects from the country, while reporting that the Russian representative in Tiflis, Sheinman, still denied any Russian involvement in the fighting.

Moscow apparently ordered Sheinman to "take necessary steps" to bring an end to the war and to re-establish the conditions of peace guaranteed in the Russian-Georgian treaty of May 1920.

Incredibly, Stokes believed that "Moscow's profession of ignorance of invasion is possibly sincere." He wrote this after Russian troops had been captured in the fighting, and after reports of Russian involvement appeared in the Georgian press. But he also expected General Hekker's Eleventh Red Army, which had been pulled back from Georgian border just before the invasion, to attack shortly. He predicted that "Azerbaijan and (the) North Caucasus will certainly rise against Bolsheviks if Georgian troops advance into their territories." Stokes had no reason to expect that Georgian forces would attack Bolshevik-controlled territory as they would have a hard enough time defending Georgia. His point was that in territories like Azerbaijan, the North Caucasus and Armenia, Soviet rule was not yet firm.

Stokes saw two elements as crucial to the success of Georgia in the war. First, it was essential that the Allies reach agreement with the Turks and prevent any alliance between them and the Soviets. Second, Britain must send munitions – immediately. "Time is of extreme importance," he stressed to the British foreign secretary. However, the British government, which had now recognised Georgia, was unwilling to help.

On the 15th, the Soviet representative in Georgia, Sheinman, received an encrypted telegram from the headquarters of the Eleventh Red Army. "It has been decided to cross the Rubicon. Act accordingly."[3]

The following day, Wednesday the 16th, as expected, the Eleventh Red Army invaded in the east, from Azerbaijan, which was now in Soviet hands. While the commander of the Eleventh

Army was Hekker, he in turn was commanded by the Caucasian Bureau (Kavburo), which had been set up by Stalin's closest allies a year before the invasion of Georgia. Heading the Kavburo were Bolshevik leaders Ordzhnokidze and Kirov, both of whom were to play key roles in Caucasian and Russian politics in the years to come.

Five days into the fighting, Georgian troops were now in full retreat, blowing up railway bridges and demolishing roads in an attempt to slow down the Red Army advance towards the Georgian capital. Kazemzadeh wrote: "If up to the 16th, some people were under the delusion that this was a mere rebellion, they now knew the truth."[4]

There was plenty of bad news for the Georgians that day. The town of Salakhlu, south of Tiflis, was taken by the Bolsheviks. At night, the Red Army renewed its attacks. But there was good news too. Georgian regulars were holding their line and repelling Russian attacks. Best of all, though, there was the news from Armenia, where Soviet rule was crumbling. On February 16th, newspapers in the Armenian capital of Yerevan reported some slight trouble. By evening, gunfire could be heard in the streets, and overnight Soviet Armenia collapsed. The following day, there was more pressure on the Soviets as Haidar Bammat, the leader of a group of North Caucasian and Azerbaijani exiles living in Georgia, called upon the Georgian government to mobilise his people as allies. Given time, the Georgians, Armenians and Azerbaijanis might have been able to pull it off. But it was time they did not have.

In the early hours of the morning of 17 February, the Georgian line defending the capital was penetrated. At 3:15 in the morning, a Foreign Ministry official awakened Colonel Stokes to tell him to prepare to leave Tiflis. A train was scheduled to depart at 7:00 am to take the foreign missions out of the city, with the Bolsheviks not expected to behave kindly towards the British and French representatives, who had spent the Civil War years aiding the various White armies. Stokes arranged for the British mission's papers to be burned. At 10:30 am, most of the foreigners were evacuated from Tiflis on a special train. The Georgian capital, meanwhile, remained calm and quiet.

Noe Zhordania issued a special appeal to the people to defend the homeland. In Tiflis, the Armenian and Azerbaijani Soviet representatives were placed under house arrest. The Georgian Military School cadets fought a bloody battle in defence of the city, suffering heavy casualties.

The Georgian line held. The front was re-established and, for the moment, Tiflis was out of danger. The Russians were held at bay 13 miles south-east of the city, and their cavalry attacks repulsed.

That evening, Colonel Stokes was informed that the Georgian government had reversed its decision, and would remain in the capital. Six days into the fighting, up against Russian onslaughts from the south and east, the Georgians were mounting a stiff resistance. Georgia's diplomatic successes continued as Austria and Romania announced their recognition of the country's independence. But in Tiflis, ammunition was running low.

Though the Georgian government had decided to remain behind in Tiflis – and with it, Colonel Corbel of the French mission – Stokes left at 1:30 am on Friday the 18th in a train heading west towards the Black Sea coast. Half an hour after his departure, Russian forces attacked on both sides of the River Kura.

The main attack, on the west bank, penetrated the outskirts of the city, but the Russians were stopped by efficient Georgian artillery fire. The Georgians then counter-attacked, once again repelling the Red Army troops. Flanking Bolshevik forces, including two Armenian battalions and a cavalry brigade, took Kajuri.

That Friday, a journalist in Constantinople reported an Azerbaijani declaration of war on Georgia. "It is believed," he wrote, "that the Eleventh Soviet Army has occupied Tiflis." That report – the very first to appear in *The New York Times* about the war – was a tiny, three-paragraph story which appeared at the bottom of the newspaper's second page. So swift had been the Soviet advance that *The Times* was already summing up the war, assuming it had nearly ended.[5]

While *The New York Times* was reporting that Georgian and foreign mission officials had already arrived in the port city of Batumi on the Black Sea coast, the London *Times* lagged behind, reporting only Bolshevik advances threatening Tiflis. Theirs turned out to be the more accurate version, as Tiflis had not yet fallen.[6]

All the foreign newspapers emphasised the Allied naval vessels which were in the area or on their way. The US ships *Barker* and *Whipple* were already at Batumi, with the destroyer *Boric* on its way. Meanwhile, the *HMS Calypso* was in the area and would be joined by two battleships on their way from Constantinople.[7]

That night, with the British mission already on its way to Batumi and the Georgian army fighting furiously to defend Tiflis – up against an entire Soviet Army – Colonel Stokes' first telegram begging for help finally reached the Foreign Office in London.

On Saturday the 19th, Western reporters in Constantinople announced that Georgia had been overrun. The Georgian government, they said, had fled to Kutaisi on the way to the Black Sea coast. Three Bolshevik divisions had invaded from Armenia and others from the east.[8] The French Foreign Office announced in Paris that Tiflis had fallen, while the London *Times* reported that the Russians had hurled three divisions of the Eleventh Army, as well as the whole of the Armenian army and Azerbaijani forces, at the Georgians.

Though it was true that the Georgians were facing an ever-more-powerful Red invasion force, there was once again good news from the front. British wireless messages sent out of Tiflis on Saturday reported heavy fighting on the Poili bridge, east of the city. Georgian troops, it was said, took 4,000 Russian prisoners of war. The Russians did capture an arsenal, but were later expelled. In fighting at Ackstafa, to the east of the capital, the Georgians won a battle. Best of all for the Georgians was the wire received from Yerevan: it claimed that Bolshevik rule had been completely overthrown in Armenia.

The Red Army forces which had attacked originally from Armenia were now in the dangerous position of having the enemy both in front and behind. The war entered its ninth day with Tiflis remaining in Georgian hands, Armenia having overthrown the Soviet regime established there just a few months earlier, and with Azerbaijani and North Caucasian exile detachments joining the fight on the Georgian side.

To win the war, the Soviets would have to attack swiftly and with overwhelming force in order to avert the danger of a widening of the war and the possibility of foreign assistance to the Georgians. Moreover, they would have to pour in troops from many other directions, opening several fronts against the small Georgian army and People's Guard forces. The Armenian insurgents would be taken care of later – and ruthlessly. For now, every hour counted.

Barely a week into the invasion, conflicting reports reaching the outside world showed the Georgians either being crushed or heroically throwing back the invader. On 20 February, Associated Press's Constantinople correspondent informed readers that Tiflis had fallen the previous week. It was now cut off from the outside world, with telegraph down cut, and the wireless silent.[9]

Colonel Stokes, however, reported that though Russian forces had penetrated the city, they had been repelled. Telegraph lines to the Georgian capital were, in fact, still open. The Russian attackers had lost four guns, eight machine guns and "numerous prisoners and horses." As a result of the vigorous Georgian defence, Russian attacks on the capital ceased for a full three days.

Stokes reported that thousands of Georgian volunteers had come forward, offering to fight, but the government had no arms to give them. The Associated Press confirmed that Georgia was belatedly attempting to mobilise an army of 200,000 men to supplement the 40,000 regulars already fighting. Stokes' appeal to his government to arm the Georgians had fallen on deaf ears.

To the government in London, Georgia must have seemed to be a lost cause. Even though the British government had grown increasingly sympathetic to the Georgian cause, finally giving the Georgians the diplomatic recognition they had so long craved, providing effective military assistance at so late a stage was simply not on the cards. By early 1921, the British and the other Allies had accepted defeat at the hands of the Red Army, having backed the losing side in the Russian Civil War. They had no appetite to get involved in further fighting in the region.

At this stage of the war, some keen foreign observers already had their eye on what opportunities the future might bring. W.E. Griffith, the representative of the American Foreign Trade

Corporation was quoted as saying that "Red rule would probably improve business, as the Georgians had been making trade impossible."[10] The United States remained the only major Allied power which refused to recognise independent Georgia, and American businessmen were the first to rush in and make deals with the new Soviet Georgian government when the war ended.

Meanwhile, an American ship, the *USS Barker* had arrived at the port of Batumi.[11] There they found more than 1,000 refugees who had fled the advancing Soviet forces.[12]

Reports of Tiflis' fall continued to flow out of Georgia even during the three-day lull in the fighting. It was reported from Paris that General Budyenny, the legendary leader of Trotsky's Red Cavalry, had captured the Georgian capital after a bloody fight. But Associated Press' Constantinople reporter was already hedging his bets, reporting that in fact no news was coming out of the Georgian war. The London *Times* was the first foreign newspaper to break the big story that Georgian forces had stopped the Russian armies and that Tiflis was safe – for now.[13]

On Tuesday, the 22nd, the second day of the lull in the siege, the Georgian Constituent Assembly finally managed to adopt the republic's constitution.

Meanwhile, French warships in the Black Sea shelled Russian forces which were now heading south, down the Georgian coast, in Gagry. Of all the Allied powers, only France offered actual military help during the war, and its shelling was the only concrete military aid Georgia received.[14]

In Moscow, the Soviet government denied the persistent reports that Russian forces were involved in the war. Meanwhile, Georgian troops fighting along the Black Sea coast suffered heavy casualties as they fought off some 8,000 Red cavalry and infantry.

Following an all-day attack, the Georgians withdrew to the River Bzib. Weak Russian forces attempted to invade Georgia from yet another direction, through the Daral Pass in the north, but were repelled. Despite receiving local help, the Georgian forces holding the northern frontier were having a hard time of it, bogged down in snow.

On Wednesday, 23 February, the London *Times* reported confidently that Tiflis was now out of danger.[15] But from a new direction storm clouds gathered, with Turkey announcing demands for the cession of territories near Batumi as its price for not joining in with the Russians and squeezing the Georgians from yet another side.

Meanwhile, the Russians renewed their push in the Daral Pass. The French cruiser *Waldeck-Rousseau* was reported to be helping the Georgians fighting along the River Bzib, bringing them ammunition and reinforcements. The Russian retreat from Tiflis was reported to have been "hurried." The war was now being fought on three fronts. Stokes wired London with yet another appeal: "I hope His Majesty's Government will immediately assist Georgia in her gallant struggle which compels admiration." But His Majesty's Government was not listening.

Even as Russian forces from all directions were converging on the capital, pushing Georgian forces down the Black Sea coast, and fighting their way through the Daral Pass, Georgia continued to rack up diplomatic successes in the aftermath of the Allied Supreme Council recognition. On Wednesday the 23rd, tiny Luxembourg also recognised the Georgian Republic.

On Thursday the 24th, the battle for Tiflis resumed in earnest. While *New York Times* readers learned that day of the "Reds Defeated in Drive on Tiflis" and London *Times* readers could rest at ease over the "Red Defeat in Georgia," things were actually not going very well on the front.[16]

Rumours suddenly swept through the capital that Red cavalry had swung around to the west of the city, seizing control of the railway line out of the city. That night, the Georgian government finally decided to evacuate the city. In reality, only some 200 Russian horsemen had appeared in the Georgian rear – hardly enough to warrant the abandonment of Tiflis. The Russians themselves were therefore quite surprised at the Georgian decision to withdraw.

At 9:00 on the evening of 24 February, two weeks after the beginning of the Soviet assault (the "border incident" at Bortchalo), the Georgian government finally evacuated its capital. The fall of Tiflis was now imminent. Just before leaving Tiflis, the Georgian government sent off a hasty telegram to Lenin and Trotsky in Moscow, pleading with them to call off the attack (even though the official line of the Soviet government was that it had nothing to do with this).

The Red cavalry did briefly control the railway line out of Tiflis, but Georgian infantry counter-attacked, re-opening the link to the west and thereby allowing the escape of the Georgian leadership.

Following the departure of Zhordania and the government, riots broke out in the capital and looting took place. Georgian authorities blamed Bolshevik instigators, including one named Stark, who apparently caused a great deal of trouble. Regular Russian troops entering Tiflis, finally restored some semblance of order to the city. Ordzhonikidze cabled Moscow: "The red banner is aloft" in Tiflis. Friday 25 February was declared the day of the triumph of the Georgian Soviet revolution, and was celebrated as such for decades thereafter.

Colonel Stokes told London that the loss of the capital was "serious … but not hopeless." The Georgian army remained intact and a front line could be restored. But, just in case, he warned that 100 places on British ships would not be enough for the final evacuation, should that prove necessary.

Lord Curzon finally got through to the Colonel, conveying a clear message that was to be heard again and again, appropriately altered, in the coming decades: "Our sympathies," he stated, "are with the Georgian people, who have done well, but they must now depend on their own policy and resources."

On Saturday the 26th, the day after Tiflis' fall, the Georgian government and the General Staff were relocated to Mshket, just north of the capital. Later that day, they retreated to Gori. In Paris, the French Foreign Office reported the Georgian government even further away, in Kutaisi. In any event, the direction was clear. The Georgian government and its army were heading for the port city of Batumi, already threatened from the north by the advancing Ninth Red Army and now from the south by the Turks.

The following day, a Georgian government spokesman in Paris assured a London *Times* reporter that Tiflis was still in Georgian hands.[17] Reuters was reporting that the situation at the front was "satisfactory," according to Allied Missions in the country. But the reality by this stage was a headlong Georgian retreat with the Russians hot on their heels.

On Monday, the final day of February, the Georgian forces withdrew to a strong position at Suram. The Russians were not immediately pursuing now. In Batumi, the British chose to evacuate half of their colony to Constantinople on the *HMS Calypso*. The following day, Red cavalry reached Gori, while the Georgians consolidated their positions at Suram. Three hundred fresh Russian troops entered Georgia from the north, through the Mamison pass, advancing to Oni. The Turks invaded as well, seizing the provinces surrounding Batumi without entering the city itself. The *New York Times* reported that Hekker's Eleventh Red Army, which had taken Tiflis three days earlier, had lined up with Cossack forces which had crossed into Georgia from Vladikavkaz.[18] Allied traders and bankers were reported to be fleeing Batumi as the Ninth Red Army crossed the Kodor River, pushing Georgian forces south to Poti.

On Wednesday 3 March, three weeks into the fighting, Colonel Stokes left the relative safety of Batumi for a visit with the Georgian military and civilian leadership, now based in Kutaisi. The situation on the Suram front had stabilised. The Georgians had actually advanced and taken some prisoners.

On the Black Sea coast, though, they evacuated Sukhum, retreating to the River Mohva, while in the Oni sector, recently invaded, three Soviet regiments had been spotted and the situation was described as "dangerous." The Georgian foreign minister told Stokes that he still felt confident, and that Georgian troops had recaptured Sukhum and Gagri. Yet by Saturday 5 March, Stokes had to concede that "events ... took an unfavourable turn." The Georgian government was going to have to head toward Batumi, to join the foreign missions which had already been there for some time.

On Sunday 6 March, the government decided to withdraw from Kutaisi. Russian troops meanwhile captured Suram after a battalion of the People's Guard abandoned their positions without firing a shot. The fighting ability of the People's Guard militia, recruited from the ranks of the Social Democratic factory workers, was to be a subject of controversy for years to come.

General Kvinitadze's daughter wrote to me that "the little army fought much better than the People's Guard."[19] Historian Donald Rayfield writes that the Guard "often refused to fight, or give its armaments to the professional army."[20]

Soviet forces in the Oni district continued their advance toward Kutaisi from the north. The London *Times* reported Georgian successes under the headline "Georgian Rally" but conceded that an "apparently complete debacle" had sealed the fate of independent Georgia.[21]

Upon his return to Batumi, Stokes learned that the Georgian government had been forced to agree to a Turkish occupation of the city. The following day, the Soviet-backed "Revolutionary Committee" which now ruled most of the country invited the Georgian government to cease all military operations, recognise the new regime, and form a coalition government with it.

In order to press the Social Democrats into accepting this peace offer, the local Bolsheviks in Batumi organised an uprising against the government. The French, British and Italian refugees in the city had already boarded ships and were on their way out of what was rapidly becoming "Soviet Georgia." That very day, with independent Georgia now reduced to the enclave around Batumi port, Haiti belatedly joined the ranks of countries extending diplomatic recognition to the Georgian Republic.

Stokes met with Colonel Bey of the Turkish army on 10 March to clarify a question which now troubled him. As the Georgian Republic had virtually ceased to exist, had not Colonel Stokes' mission terminated with it? The following day, Turkish troops entered Batumi.

The Georgian government had now retired to the port city, where it presided over a much smaller army than had existed just a few days earlier, mass desertions having taken place. The entire Georgian armed forces now consisted of about 10,000 men holding the line from the Rion railway station on the River Rion, to Samtredi, along the railway line to Poti. In addition, about 5,000 reserve Georgian troops were in place in Batumi.

Under these circumstances, the Georgian government agreed on 11 March to open negotiations with the Soviet government now in power in Tiflis. The Turkish army meanwhile conceded the right of the Georgians to exercise sovereignty in the Turkish-occupied areas.

Fighting continued for a few more days along the Rion River front, north of Batumi. On 13 March, the Red Army seized Poti, the last remaining large town north of Batumi. Georgians there burned coal sheds and fled the town by steamers in a severe storm.[22]

On Monday 14 March, a twenty-four-hour armistice between Georgian and Russian forces was arranged. The Soviet regime in Moscow reportedly recognised the new Communist government in Tiflis and warned Turkey that any attack on Georgia would now be considered an attack on Russia as well.

Two Soviet submarines were seen in the Black Sea as French, British and other allied ships were removing their nationals from Batumi. Associated Press in Constantinople continued to report further Russian troop movements toward Georgia, including Red cavalry heading down from the Kuban. The following day, the armistice was indefinitely extended and Georgian representatives went to negotiate peace terms with the Bolsheviks.

On Wednesday 16 March, at its final session in Batumi, the Georgian Constituent Assembly ordered the government to withdraw from the country in order to continue the struggle from abroad. The next day, the Georgian government boarded an

Italian steamer and left Batumi. They became part of a small exile community numbering maybe 2,000 people, half of whom settled in France. The commander of the remaining Georgian forces in the city decided to side with the Soviet forces against the Turks. One of the Bolshevik prisoners released by the retreating Georgian forces, Kavtaradze, proclaimed a Revolutionary Committee which assumed authority in the town.

At first, Batumi remained quiet. Later reports in Western newspapers described fierce and bloody battles to capture the city, involving cannon and machine guns, and resulting in whole-sale slaughter.

Only two weeks had passed between the border incident with Armenia to the panicked retreat from Tiflis. A further three weeks later and the Georgian independent republic had ceased to exist. For many years thereafter, Georgian exiles debated what had gone wrong, and who was responsible.

Clearly one of the problems had been the lack of solidarity between the three Transcaucasian countries in the years leading up to the 1921 invasion. Even the Armenian rebellion against Bolshevik rule which occurred during the attack on Georgia was not in any way coordinated with the Georgians. This lesson was quickly learned by the exiled Georgian, Armenian and Azerbaijani politicians. On 10 June 1921, less than three months after Georgia had fallen to Soviet rule, a joint declaration was issued by representatives of the exiled governments, including the North Caucasus. It declared a military and economic union, and was sent to all the great powers and to the League of Nations. But it came too late to have any effect on the ground.[23]

One of the most striking errors committed by the Georgian leaders was their almost naïve belief that the Allied powers, which had just recognised Georgia, would come to its aid. Once the British forces had withdrawn from Batumi in 1920, it was unlikely they or anyone else would return, with the great powers which Georgia counted on for support exhausted after years of war. Following the defeat of the White armies in Russia, they had little appetite to continue the armed struggle against the Bolsheviks. The impotence of the newly formed League of Nations would not become apparent until the 1930s, and one might argue that the experience of democratic Georgia foreshadowed what would later happen to countries like Ethiopia and Spain which fell victim to fascist aggression whilst the League of Nations looked on and did nothing – or for that matter, the fate of Georgia when invaded by Russian forces in 2008.

Equally naïve, perhaps more so, were the repeated appeals and protests made by the Georgian government to a regime in Moscow which, while hurling whole armies at Georgia, consistently denied any involvement in the war. While it may have been the case that Trotsky was unaware that the invasion had taken place, and Lenin seemed unaware of the genuine facts on the ground (there was no popular uprising), the Georgian Mensheviks were never going to get a sympathetic ear in Moscow. Stalin and Ordzhonikidze were determined to bring an end to Zhordania and his comrades' rule in Tiflis.

And finally, Shanin adds, "The Georgian regular army and its generals proved remarkably inept and dispirited. There was no attempt to arm civilians, to offer a stubborn challenge in the streets of the main cities, to start guerrilla warfare or a systematic boycott of the invaders – in a word, to put to use the revolutionary experience and the political loyalties of the population."[24]

The collapse of the Georgian Democratic Republic, its complete military defeat, seemed to bring an end once and for all to the dream of independence. But this was not to be the case, with one more great battle still to come.

THE FINAL BATTLE

The story of the Georgian Democratic Republic did not end with the Red Army invasion in 1921. Karl Kautsky predicted that "the dictatorship of the Moscow tyrants cannot become permanent in Georgia."[1] He was both right and wrong. That dictatorship certainly struggled to retain power in occupied Georgia, and nothing made this clearer than the popular uprising of 1924. It would be many more decades, though, until Georgia regained its full independence.

The Bolsheviks certainly found it frustrating that long after capturing political power in the country they still needed to fight to keep it. This was true not only in places like Georgia, on the margins of the Russian empire which they inherited, but even in the very cities where they successfully proclaimed Soviet power in November 1917. The first few years of Bolshevik rule were marked by peasant uprisings and industrial unrest, in the context of a bloody civil war fuelled by foreign intervention that lasted for nearly four years.

Perhaps the most famous example of this unrest was the uprising by the sailors in Kronstadt, a fortress across the water from Petrograd. The Kronstadt sailors had been early supporters of the revolution, but by 1921 had grown disillusioned with Bolshevik rule. They rose up, demanding "Soviet democracy" with free elections and a multi-party system – but were savagely crushed by the Red Army under Trotsky's command.

Meanwhile, in Petrograd and other industrial centres, the remnants of opposition parties, such as the Mensheviks, showed surprising vitality in elections within trade unions and soviets so long as those remained relatively free. Eventually, though their parties were banned and their leaders arrested.

The Bolshevik response to rising discontent among the workers was to crush all opposition, but it took several more years before a totalitarian system really took hold. As late as 1921, there were still dissident factions operating within the Communist Party itself, and it wasn't until the end of the decade that Stalin's grip on power became absolute.

Defeating the Georgian army and exiling the Social Democratic government could not have been the end of the story in 1921. Though the Georgian experience of resistance to Russian Bolshevik rule was not unique (the Ukrainians, among others, were also difficult to pacify), they had something most other occupied peoples did not: a well-organised Social Democratic Party with a mass base in the country, and an intact leadership that had regrouped in exile. They also had the memory of an experiment in democratic socialist government that, whatever its weaknesses and flaws, was infinitely more humane and bearable than the authoritarian rule of the Communist Party.

Tiflis fell to the Red Army on 25 February 1921. A new pro-Russian government was then proclaimed and the Social Democratic government was forced into exile. For some countries that came under Soviet rule, that would have been the end of the story. The Red Army and Cheka left little doubt who was in charge once it had taken over a country. Very quickly the regime set up the repressive machinery that was already familiar in Russia and countries that had come under Soviet rule. Resistance to the new regime seemed futile.

But the Georgians were fiercely independent, and had been largely united around support for their elected leaders and the Social Democratic Party that had ruled their country for the previous four years. That party had enjoyed mass popular support for nearly two decades, long before the period of independence. They did not give up so easily.

One of the first to experience the sharp end of this enduring popularity was Stalin. Returning to Tiflis in early July 1921 after many years away from his native Georgia, Stalin – then one of Lenin's People's Commissars and not yet the leader of the Soviet state – addressed a crowd of more than 5,000 workers in the Nadzaladevi Theatre. He began by congratulating the workers on overthrowing the Menshevik yoke. Audience members began to shout. "Lies! There was no Menshevik yoke here! There was no Communist revolution in Georgia! Your troops have removed our freedom!" A furious Stalin responded by ordering a change in the leadership of the local Bolshevik party – and an increase of the Red Terror. This included the shooting of oppositionists at night in Tiflis' Vake Park. There was no trial. In 1923, the Cheka secret police executed ninety-two Georgians in retaliation for the murder of three policemen in Guria. Ordzhonikidze threatened to kill 1.5 million Georgians if necessary.[2]

For the first couple of years after the Red Army invasion, the Social Democrats and other opposition parties enjoyed a semi-legal existence. They published newspapers, organised cooperatives, and took part in some election campaigns. However, the Bolsheviks could not tolerate the existence of independent political forces for long, and in particular the popular Social Democrats. In August 1923, they compelled the Social Democrats to formally dissolve their party at a conference addressed by the Russian Menshevik Aleksandr Martynov, who by that time had joined the Communist Party and leading Georgian Bolsheviks. The effective banning of the Social Democrats drove their organisation underground, where they continued to publish newspapers and prepare for insurrection.[3]

The Social Democratic Party in exile protested and publicised the ongoing repression, going so far as to describe the Bolsheviks as behaving like fascists. "The persecution of our Party continues with the same vigour," they wrote. "Flogging of political prisoners and torturing of our comrades in the dark and deep dungeons of the Tché-ka continue unabated. The Communist Party and Tché-ka employ Fascist methods against the members of our Party, shooting them from behind. (Example: The murders of comrades Alpaidze and Pkhakadze in Koutais.)"[4]

Another document produced by the exiled Mensheviks ended with the phrase "Down with Red Fascism!"

Georgia's independent trade union movement was swiftly crushed. "As organs for the defence of the interests of the working classes they exist no longer," declared the Social Democrats in an open letter to a visiting German Workers' Delegation. "The Trade Unions in our country are only Government, bureaucratic institutions – neither more nor less."[5]

Without strong trade unions to defend them, the situation of the Georgian working class deteriorated quickly. "Exploitation of the Georgian working class under Soviet State capitalism does not in any way differ from the purely capitalist exploitation," wrote the Social Democrats. "The only difference that exists, however, is that the working class is now deprived of the right of demanding better working and economic conditions and of endeavouring to obtain them by means of strikes."[6]

The newly Bolshevised unions

> not only do not try to improve the lot of the working classes, but on the contrary, they oppose together with the Government the economic demands of the workers; they are bureaucratic organs pure and simple of the Government; for the working class they are nothing but a financial burden, as the workers and civil servants have to contribute for the maintenance of the bureaucracy of the Unions 3 per cent and even more from their meagre earnings.

The cooperatives were also quickly "Bolshevised." This led to a struggle within the international cooperative movement, as competing Georgian Menshevik and Bolshevik leaders demanded to be recognised. Though the Georgian Soviet regime took steps to bring the cooperatives under state control, as had occurred in Russia, the Menshevik-dominated cooperative movement put up stiff resistance. In defending Soviet practices in Georgia, P.I. Rabinovitch, a member of the Russian trade delegation in London and a former representative of Centrosoyus (the Soviet cooperative movement) in the Caucasus, wrote:

> The first co-operative congress, in Georgia, after the advent of the Soviet Government, took place in November 1921. Up to that time the old elected members of the Board of the Georgian Co-operative Union, with the exception of those who fled to Constantinople, remained in office. The arrest of Mr. Andronnikov, chairman of the Board, and a Menshevik, had, to my knowledge, no relation whatsoever to his co-operative work, but was due exclusively to the fact that he, along with other Mensheviks, was

implicated in an attempt to organise a strike of railway workers, timed for the beginning of November.[7]

In other words, it was perfectly understandable to arrest someone for attempting "to organise a strike of railway workers" – as long as it was not because of his cooperative activities.

Some led non-violent protests which were swiftly suppressed. Kristine Sharashidze, one of the handful of female members of the Constituent Assembly, organised a protest on 25 February 1922 during a celebration of one year of Soviet rule. She was teaching at the Tenth Pedagogical Institute in Tiflis and several of her students joined in the protest. She was arrested, but eventually freed.

With their political parties, trade unions and cooperatives under attack from the increasingly authoritarian regime, the Georgians had fewer and fewer legal and peaceful outlets for protest. Already in 1921, some of the defeated Georgian forces withdrew into the mountains and formed small partisan groups. Sporadic fighting continued in various parts of the country for several months.

Probably the most important example of this took place in western Georgia, in the highland province of Svanetia. A peasant rebellion broke out there in May, just two months after the Russian victory. Armed groups disarmed some units of the Red Army in September and began preparations for a march on Kutaisi. In early October, the Communist government branded the rebels "political bandits" and formed special military units to crush the rebellion. According to Soviet reports, there were about 1,600 rebels loyal to the National Democratic Party, though working in collusion with Tiflis-based Social Democrats as well. The Red Army forces managed to restrict the rebellion to Svanetia, and by the end of the year the revolt was over. Leading rebels were executed and severe repression followed.

Repression was a notable feature of the early years of Soviet rule in Georgia. Sometimes the Communist Party leadership was quite open about this, as when the official party paper announced the execution of twenty "political bandits." At that time, the Georgian Cheka declared that it would "struggle against banditry in the most merciless way." Executions of dissenters appeared to be an everyday occurrence, though according to one estimate 80% of cases went unreported, even when large numbers were killed. Reprisals were often carried out against families of victims, who could be deported or imprisoned. And as in Russia, the Georgian Cheka arrested some people for simply belonging to the "wrong" social class.

Repression intensified even as the new regime planted deeper roots in the country. By the summer of 1923, two-and-a-half years after the establishment of Soviet Georgia, the regime grew even more intolerant of opposition parties, especially the Social Democrats. Cheka agents infiltrated the opposition ranks and there were mass arrests.

The Georgian Social Democrats in exile were committed to continuing the fight against the Russian Bolshevik occupiers with every means at their disposal. In a letter to Ethel Snowden, Zhordania wrote: "The war is not yet finished in Georgia, but it has taken a new form: it is no longer the Republican army which desperately resists the invaders, it is the whole country which fights against the armies of occupation as it has formerly fought against the power of the Czar."[8]

The armed rebellions in Svanetia and elsewhere were just the tip of the iceberg. There was also considerable civil resistance to

Russian rule. For example, Georgians did not flock to join the ruling Communist Party, which apparently managed to recruit just 10,000 members. The Social Democrats the previous year had, according to Kautsky, some 80,000 members.

There were a number of reasons for the unpopularity of the new regime. Among these were Soviet decisions to cede Georgian territory to Turkey as part of the October 1921 Treaty of Kars. Georgian territory was also ceded to the sister Soviet republics of Armenia, Azerbaijan and Russia itself. This included the Zaqatala region in eastern Georgia, which was given to Azerbaijan. So much of the short history of independent Georgia had been spent defending the country against foreign encroachment. The Georgians were not going to take losing territory easily.

The Georgian Communists, like their Russian counterparts, traditionally had little support among the peasants. In Russia, the peasants had overwhelmingly supported the Socialist Revolutionary Party, not the Bolsheviks or even the Mensheviks. The Georgian peasants, who had long supported the Social Democrats, had reaped the benefits of the Mensheviks' agrarian reform. Also, while it was probably inevitable that the intelligentsia and the former nobility would oppose the Bolsheviks, the Georgian working class – which theoretically should have been the stronghold for the Communists – was also hostile to Soviet rule. A number of things contributed to that, including the subordination of trade unions and other workers' organisations to Communist functionaries. The memories of the Georgian Democratic Republic, where powerful unions and cooperatives thrived, stood in stark contrast to a "workers' state" where workers had few rights.

Finally, though not necessarily the fault of the new Soviet rulers, an outbreak of cholera and famine, which cost thousands of lives, did little to make the new regime popular among the Georgians.

Little more than a year after the Communists came to power in Georgia, in early May 1922, all the non-Bolshevik political parties in the country, with the Social Democrats taking the lead, formed Damkom – "The Committee for the Independence of Georgia." In addition to the Social Democrats, other parties playing a role in Damkom included the National Democratic Party, the Socialist Federalist Party, the Socialist Revolutionaries (SRs) and the Skhivi ("Beam") Party, a dissident Social Democratic group led by the former minister of war, Grigol Giorgadze.

Each party was given one seat on the committee, leading to the group also being known as the "Parity Committee." The Georgian opposition had learned the lesson of the defeat of the Svanetian uprising in 1921, and this time the National Democrats, Social Democrats and others would unite against the Bolsheviks. The Social Democrats were prepared to concede something in the Damkom that had always been contrary to their policy when they ruled the country: a coalition government including all the non-Communist parties.

As the largest party, the Social Democrats provided a chairman for Damkom, the first of which was Gogita Paghava, who was succeeded by Nikoloz Kartsivadze. Kartsivadze in turn was arrested by the Cheka on 16 March 1923 and was replaced with Prince Kote Andronikashvili. Damkom's secretary was a leader of the National Democrats, Yason Javakhishvili.

The Damkom kept in close contact with Zhordania and the rest of the Georgian government in exile through a bureau based in Istanbul. Some key members of the former Social Democratic government returned secretly to the country, including Noe

Khomeriki, the former minister of agriculture and father of the country's agrarian reform. Another was Valiko Jugeli, the former commander of the People's Guard.

Inside Georgia, Damkom set up a military command chaired by the retired general Kote Abkhazi. Abkhazi had served as a major general in command of artillery in the Russian army during the First World War. After the war, he was one of the founders of the National Democratic Party in Georgia, and helped establish the new university in Tiflis. He remained behind in Georgia when the Red Army took over the country and put himself at the disposal of the Damkom to lead its military operations.

While the Damkom was preparing a nationwide uprising, small-scale insurgencies continued to take place against the Russian occupiers. Early in 1922, a rebellion against the Soviets broke out in Khevsureti, a mountainous district in north-east Georgia. The Red Army was forced to deploy aircraft in its fight to prevent the insurrection from spreading, but could not completely crush it. The revolt's leader, Colonel Cholokashvili, crossed the border to Chechnya, where he continued to launch raids on Georgia. This contributed to the difficulties the Bolsheviks were having in securing the mountains of eastern Georgia. A local militia leader, Levan Razikashvili, son of a well-known poet and himself a local police officer, was captured and shot by the Bolsheviks after being sentenced to death for aiding a rebellion. When Georgian writers protested against the sentence to Ordzhonikidze, the Bolshevik leader told them that he would execute Levan's poet father himself.[9]

These local rebellions were small-scale and posed no serious challenge to Soviet rule in Georgia. According to one source, of fifty-seven active partisan detachments, the majority had either disintegrated or surrendered to the Soviets by 1923. The Soviet counter-insurgency strategy was largely intelligence driven, and at its head was the newly appointed deputy head of the republic's Cheka, Lavrentiy Beria. In the spring of 1920, Beria was transferred by the Bolsheviks from the Azerbaijani capital Baku, which had now fallen into Soviet hands, back to his native Georgia. In Tiflis, he set up a spy network, tried to recruit soldiers from the Georgian army, and ran secret couriers back and forth to Baku. He was arrested, but released under the condition that he leave the country. Instead, he went underground and became one of the many Soviet agents employed by the newly opened Russian embassy in Tbilisi. With the defeat of the Georgian Republic, Beria played a leading role in the establishment of the local Cheka. He went on to become head of Georgia's secret police, then the leader of its Communist Party, and was later brought to Moscow by Stalin to head up the secret police of the whole USSR. It was in crushing the Georgian rebellion of 1924, though, that Beria proved his credentials.

Less than nine months after the Damkom was formed, its military centre was dealt a severe blow by Beria's secret police. Following in the footsteps of the tsarist Okhrana, Beria managed to infiltrate agents into the organisation, a strategy the tsarist police had called *provokatsiya*. A student member of the National Democrats appeared to have been the Cheka's chief mole in the operation. Mass arrests followed.

Fifteen members of the Damkom's Military Centre including its leader, General Kote Abkhazi, were arrested, and shot on 20 May 1923. Abkhazi's last words were: "I'm dying with joy, because I'm given an honour to be sacrificed for Georgia. My death will bring victory to Georgia!"

The Social Democratic leaders Khomeriki and Jugeli also fell into the hands of the Cheka. Jugeli asked permission to inform his comrades that their plans had been discovered so that they could call off the revolt. But Beria had other ideas. If the revolt went ahead, it would give the Cheka to opportunity to crush the opposition once and for all. Khomeriki and Jugeli were shot.

Despite these setbacks, in October 1923, with the opposition parties now banned, the Damkom decided to continue with plans to organise an armed rebellion. There were disagreements on tactics, and the group failed to get any support from foreign powers or even allied groups elsewhere in Transcaucasia. Damkom chair Andronikashvili expressed doubts that the Georgian people were ready to join in a general uprising.

It took nearly a full year before they were ready. The revolt was scheduled for 02:00 on the morning of 29 August 1924, but not everyone got the correct date and the manganese miners of Chiatura started their rebellion a day earlier.

Despite the premature uprising in Chiatura, despite the capture of senior figures in the Damkom, despite more than three years of Bolshevik rule, the revolt did manage to rage for three full weeks across the country before it was finally crushed by the Cheka and the Red Army. The revolt was particularly strong in Guria, where the rebels held on to large swathes of territory for several days. Guria had long been a base of Social Democratic support among the peasants dating back to the Gurian Republic. But it had almost no support in Tbilisi. Thousands were killed – according to some estimates, up to 4,000. Many of these were hostages. Some rebels from Imeretia, a province in western Georgia, were stuffed into six railway carriages, taken to a place where graves were dug and there executed, some by Mauser pistols, others by machine guns. Five hundred rebels were shot in Senaki, a town in western Georgia. Nearly 1,000 men, described as "the cream of Georgia's intelligentsia and nobility," were shot on 1 September. Their sentence had been passed by a committee of Communist Party officials and Chekists (secret policemen) Even Stalin seemed shocked by the extent of the slaughter and ordered executions halted.[10]

Within a week of the revolt's launch, the Cheka tracked down the leaders of the Damkom, who were holed up in the Shio-Mgvime monastery near Mtskheta, about 30 kilometres north-west of Tiflis. Among those arrested was its leader, Andronikashvili. Beria arranged for the rebel leaders to be brought to Tiflis, and encouraged them to issue a declaration calling on the rebels to lay down their arms. The rebels agreed on the condition that Beria agree to stop the mass executions.

Beria agreed and the declarations were signed. However, Beria had no intention of stopping the repression, and the arrested Damkom leaders were killed. By mid-September the rebellion was over.

Looking back at the rebellion six decades later, Shanin noted that the Mensheviks and their allies had managed to do what they had failed to accomplish in the years of independence: they had mobilised their base of support among workers and peasants. "The customary militancy of the Georgian Mensheviks had its day once more," he concluded.[11]

The crushing of the 1924 revolt in Georgia led to an inter-national outcry, the Second International made a formal protest to the League of Nations. The Communists were not troubled by this, however, with Trotsky, among others, seemingly not bothered by the actions of Beria and his brutal slaughter of the Georgian

Social Democrats. Zinoviev, the leader of the Communist International, described the revolt as "a blend of Menshevism and nationalism" (which was true) and considered it as important as the anti-Bolshevik revolts in Kronstadt and Tambov.[12]

German Communist leader Klara Zetkin was sent to Georgia and wrote a booklet whitewashing the suppression of the revolt, claiming that "only" 320 people had been shot.[13]

While it might be expected that a loyal Communist would say that, the Georgian Social Democrats were shocked when their comrades from other countries accepted the Soviet line. In December 1924, just a few weeks after the crushing of the rebellion, a British trade union delegation visited the country. Thousands of oppositionists were in the hands of the Cheka, with executions occurring on a daily basis. But according to reports in state-controlled newspapers in Georgia, they had only kind words about the new regime, taking pains to distinguish themselves from the delegation that had visited Georgia just four years earlier. When meeting with former Mensheviks who had recently joined the ruling Communist Party, the unionists were asked about the previous delegation. One of the British trade union leaders replied that "Neither MacDonald nor Shaw nor Mrs. Snowden were representing British workers, they represented the Second International; consequently the English workers are not responsible for their words. But we, as representatives of the British workers and their trade unions, declare ourselves in favour of supporting the Soviet power."[14]

Large numbers of Social Democrats defected to the Communists in the wake of the rebellion's defeat, with many publicly recanting their views. Within a short period, the Georgian Social Democrats had ceased to be a significant force in the country. Reprisals continued, with the threat of Georgian Social Democracy used as an excuse, even though the party effectively no longer existed. During the following years, in 1925–1926, at least 500 Georgian Social Democrats were shot without trial.[15]

Nearly a decade after the fall of the Social Democratic republic, Noe Ramishvili, who had been the first prime minister of independent Georgia and then its interior minister, was hunted down and murdered in Paris on 7 December 1930.[16]

Meanwhile, Noe Zhordania's exile in France lasted for more than three decades. Zhordania died on 11 January 1953, just before his eighty-fifth birthday. His former comrade Joseph Stalin died just a few weeks later, on 5 March 1953.

Soviet rule in Georgia survived them both by a few decades, with the country finally declaring independence again in 1991. When it did so, the 1921 Constitution was revived, the anniversary of the May 1918 declaration of independence was proclaimed a national holiday, and the blood-red flag of the Georgian Mensheviks flew once again over the capital city of Tbilisi.

16

ANOTHER REVOLUTION WAS POSSIBLE

I want to conclude this book by answering three questions: What was the significance of the Georgian experiment? Why did it end? What can we learn from it today?

"In comparison with the hell which Soviet Russia represents," wrote Karl Kautsky, "Georgia appeared as a paradise."[1] He went on to call the Georgian Democratic Republic an "important social experiment" that constituted "the antithesis to Bolshevism." The other members of the international socialist mission to Georgia in 1920 made similar comments.

Stephen F. Jones sums up the achievements of the Georgian Republic in these words:

> For all Georgian democracy's flaws in these years, the First
> Republic was an outstanding achievement. Civil rights and dissent
> were recognized and, on the whole, legally protected. Society
> gained autonomy from the state. It preserved the two cardinal
> institutional guarantees of democracy – the right to participate
> and the right of public contestation – which includes freedom of
> expression, freedom to form and join organizations, the right to

vote, and the existence of free and fair elections. This was truly remarkable, given the conditions and the times.[2]

Georgia was not alone in its attempt to create a humane, egalitarian and democratic society. I have already mentioned the 1871 Paris Commune, which both Marx and Lenin studied for the lessons it might provide to socialists. At the time the Georgians were independent, other states that eventually became part of the Soviet Union were also living under democratic governments, even social democratic ones. Azerbaijan, for example, during its brief period of independence, was probably the first Muslim democratic republic.

The inter-war years provided other examples, including the experience of Social Democratic rule in "Red Vienna" and workers' rule in parts of Spain, particularly Catalonia, during the civil war.

There was also the extraordinary experience of the Israeli kibbutzim, whose existence pre-dated the state by several decades and whose survival as a radical experiment in socialism lasted for several generations. The kibbutzim took many socialist ideas much further than anything attempted by the Georgians, including raising children collectively from infancy, communal dining and laundry, and direct democracy. But the kibbutzim for all their successes were never more than a small part of Israeli society, and few ever imagined that all Israelis would someday live that way.

What makes the Georgian experiment significant is that it was run by orthodox Marxists, it covered an entire country and it lasted for several years. Obviously a longer period would have been better for the purposes of testing democratic socialist ideals, but Georgia's brief experiment will have to do.

The Georgian experiment did not end peacefully but it did not end in failure. So long as the Social Democrats held power, Georgia was a free society with an accountable government and a powerful civil society with independent trade unions and a strong cooperative movement. All this came to end not due to an internal collapse, but due to the invasion of a foreign army.

From a purely military perspective, the Georgians failed to defend themselves adequately against the Russian aggressors. Some other former Russian provinces did better, most notably Poland and Finland, when faced with similar attacks. But little Georgia had nothing like the resources of those countries. Still, it was argued by some that the Georgians invested too little in national defence when they had a chance; their army was far smaller than it needed to be, and they were therefore unnecessarily vulnerable when the Red Army crossed their borders in 1921.

They had also allowed the Bolshevik Party to thrive in the months following the peace treaty signed with Soviet Russia the previous year, as that treaty obligated them to do. That Party, now well-funded and directed from the newly opened Soviet embassy in Tiflis, played a key role in supporting the invading Russians. The Georgian Social Democrats remained committed to a multi-party democracy even when one of those "parties" was actually an arm of an aggressive foreign power. In their defence, it should be pointed out that the phenomenon of Communist parties funded by Moscow and acting as their agents was a relatively new one.

Over the course of their three years of independence, the Georgians did not manage to settle the inter-ethnic conflicts that were exploited by Russia, Turkey and others. Due in part to Georgian brutality in the suppression of local revolts, South Ossetians provided some forces to aid the Russian conquerors, and many, including the Abkhazians, welcomed the Russians when they arrived.

The Georgian state also failed because of its fundamental economic weakness. The Georgian Social Democrats and the Russian Bolsheviks both came to power in poor and backward countries, and both faced an enormous task of reconstruction just to bring the economies back up to pre-war levels. The Russians did so with the aim of skipping several stages of history and creating socialism. The Georgians understood that their role was the creation first of all of a liberal democracy - socialism would wait. In neither country had the economic crisis ended by 1921. Georgia's economic weakness was certainly a factor in its vulnerability first to Bolshevik subversion and later to military aggression.

By February 1921 the Georgians had also demonstrated an over-reliance on diplomacy, in particular regarding the great powers, as part of their survival strategy. Lacking armed forces that might be able to repel a Russian invasion, the Georgian diplomats worked at a feverish pace to secure recognition from individual countries and the newly formed League of Nations. They achieved some notable successes, but the fact remains that when the Russian armies crossed their borders, no one came to Georgia's aid. This was to be repeated several times during the twentieth century as democratic forces were crushed while no country came to help - for instance, during the 1956 revolution in Hungary.

There are three principal lessons that can perhaps be gleaned from the Georgian experiment of 1918--1921.

First, the Menshevik argument that an impoverished, backward society cannot skip historical stages and proceed to create socialism was *right*. The Bolsheviks in their hasty race to create a utopia created a hell on earth for millions, not only in Russia, but in China, North Korea, Cambodia and elsewhere. The Georgian Social Democrats during their short period in power, showed that an orthodox Marxist approach – no skipping of stages, but a patient building up of society in preparation for an eventual transition to socialism – might have worked, given time. Above all, the Georgian agrarian reform showed that a humane alternative to the Russian experience of forced collectivisation was always possible.

Second, *another kind of revolution* was possible. Many years after he wrote approving messages about Georgia while serving as a young diplomat, E.H. Carr wrote that "History is, by and large, a record of what people did, not of what they failed to do: to this extent it is inevitably a success story."[3] The Bolsheviks were the success story; but their revolution led to the nightmare of totalitarianism. The Georgians proved that this was not the only possible outcome of the 1917 revolution in the Russian empire. Their imperfect experiment showed that a socialist government could also mean a multi-party democracy, free elections and a free press, a thriving civil society including powerful independent trade unions and cooperatives, and more. Socialism did not inevitably mean the creation of the Gulag system of slave labour camps, the Cheka secret police, the show trials, the purges, or the terror-famines and forced collectivisation that followed.

Third, democracy is not one aspect of a socialist society; it is *the very soul of that society*. Karl Kautsky wrote a short book entitled *The Dictatorship of the Proletariat* in August 1918, just nine months after the Bolshevik seizure of power in Russia. This was not yet the totalitarian regime of Stalin, and yet Kautsky's criticism was sharp and unforgiving. He wrote: "Socialism without democracy is unthinkable. We understand by Modern Socialism not merely social organisation of production, but democratic organisation of society as well. Accordingly, Socialism is for us inseparably connected with democracy. No Socialism without democracy."[4]

The society the Georgian Social Democrats created was an inspiration to socialists at the time. But as the years passed, and as Soviet rule seemed to have become permanent, fewer and fewer people took an interest in what the Georgian Social Democrats had achieved.

Yet the dream of a more equal society, a fairer one, in which people could also be free, persisted. That dream found its advocates in the Hungarian Revolution of 1956 and again in the Prague Spring of 1968. It took the leadership of ordinary working men and women in the shipyards of Gdansk to turn it into a reality in Poland in the 1980s. It is a dream that continues today as people look for alternatives to capitalism while rejecting the legacy of Stalinism.

The ideals of democratic socialism, of a fairer, more equal society, in which people remain free, are still quite potent ones. But people still ask if such a society is possible. To them we can say, paraphrasing what Engels said about the Paris Commune, do you want to know what democratic socialism looks like?

Look at the Georgian experiment. *That* was democratic socialism.

ACKNOWLEDGEMENTS

I began work on this book in the mid-1980s when Georgia was still part of the USSR, and over the three decades that followed have received help and advice from a large number of individuals and organisations.

Among those who read chapters of this book, I'd like to thank Kirill Buketov, Eric Chenoweth, George Curtin, Roger Darlington, Chris Ford, Dan Gallin, Alexei Gusev, Martyn Hudson, Beka Kobakhidze, Edd Mustill, Jeremy Pine, and Stirling Smith. Thanks also to David Wenk for providing us with an excellent map.

Irakli Petriashvilil and Gocha Aleksandria at the Georgian Trade Union Confederation and Anton Vacharadze at the National Archives in Tbilisi were very helpful to me in Tbilisi. In the UK, I'd like to thank the Georgian Ambassador H.E. Tamar Beruchashvili and members of the British Georgian Society, including Robert Scallon.

I am in debt to the librarians and archivists at the London Library, the British Library, the International Institute for Social History in Amsterdam, the New York Public Library, the Marx Memorial Library in London, the National Archives in Kew, and the Peoples History Museum and the John Ryland Library in Manchester.

Finally, the inspiration for completing the writing of this book belongs to Cindy Berman, who was persuaded in 2010 to come with me on my first visit to Georgia, and who willingly gave up on a holiday in the Greek isles for a chance to explore this wonderful country. I think we can take that Greek holiday now.

NOTES

PROLOGUE

1 Julius Braunthal, *History of the International, 1864–1914*, Volume I (London: Nelson, 1966), p. 351.

2 V.I. Lenin, *The International Socialist Congress in Stuttgart* (1907), https://www.marxists.org/archive/lenin/works/1907/oct/20.htm

3 John H. Kautsky, *Karl Kautsky: Marxism, Revolution and Democracy* (London: Transaction Publishers, 1994), p. vii.

4 Barbara Tuchman, *The Guns of August* (London: The Folio Society, 1995), p. 110.

5 Professor David Stevenson, "World War One And The 'Short-War Illusion'", http://news.sky.com/story/world-war-one-and-the-short-war-illusion-10394372

6 Angelica Balabanoff, *My Life as a Rebel* (New York: Harper & Brothers, 1938), p. 115.

7 See, for example, https://en.wikipedia.org/wiki/Hugo_Haase

8 Cited in Janet Polasky, *The Democratic Socialism of Emile Vandervelde: Between Reform and Revolution* (Oxford/Washington, DC: Berg, 1995), p. 113.

9 https://www.marxists.org/archive/debs/works/1918/canton.htm

10 Hansard, 3 August 1914, http://hansard.millbanksystems.com/commons/1914/aug/03/germany-and-belgium

11 Rosa Luxemburg, *The Junius Pamphlet*, Chapter 1, https://www.marxists.org/archive/luxemburg/1915/junius/ch01.htm

12 Ethel Snowden, cited in The Times, 14 October 1920, p. 7.

CHAPTER 1

1 Batumi is the current preferred name of the city sometimes spelled as "Batoum".

2 Zhordania is sometimes spelled "Jordania" and that is the spelling preferred by the family today, according to Redjeb Jordania, Noe's son. However, nearly all recent works on Georgia use the Zhordania spelling, which is what I will use here.

3 Redjeb Jordania, *All My Georgias – Paris–New York–Tbilisi* (Tampa, FL: Driftwood Press 2012). Kindle edition, loc. 1364. Redjeb is quoting from his father's memoir.

4 Tiflis is what the Georgian capital was called until 1936, when it was renamed Tbilisi. I will be using Tiflis through the book.

5 Cited in David Lang, *A Modern History of Georgia* (London: Weidenfeld and Nicolson, 1962), p. 124.

6 Cited in ibid., p. 124.

7 Ibid., p. 123.

8 Firuz Kazemzadeh, *The Struggle for Transcaucasia, 1917–1921* (New York: Philosophical Library, 1951), p. 14.

9 Cited in Lang, *A Modern History of Georgia*, p. 124

10 The Social Democratic Party later became closely identified with the Menshevik wing of the Russian Social Democratic Party. As a result, I sometimes will refer to Georgian Mensheviks and sometimes to Social Democrats; in this context, they mean the same thing.

CHAPTER 2

1 The best accounts of the Gurian republic that we have today come from Professor Stephen F. Jones. One is his 1989 article in the *Slavonic and East European Review*, "Marxism and Peasant Revolt in the Russian Empire: The Case of the Gurian Republic" (Vol. 67, No. 3, July 1989) and the other is his 2005 book, *Socialism in Georgian Colors: The European Road to Social Democracy 1883–1917* (Cambridge, MA: Harvard University Press, 2005). The best first-hand account we have of the Gurian republic is by Italian journalist Luigi Villari. His book, *Fire and Sword in the Caucasus*, was published in London by T.F. Unwin in 1906.

2 Karl Marx's *Civil War in France*, a collection of articles and addresses he wrote at the time, remains the outstanding critical account of the Paris Commune written by a contemporary.

3 Engels' comment appears in a new introduction he wrote to Marx's *Civil War in France*.

4 Lang, *A Modern History of Georgia*, pp. 142-143.

5 Teodor Shanin, *Russia, 1905–07: Revolution as a Moment of Truth* (Basingstoke: Macmillan, 1986), p. 104.

6 The much-quoted phrase is from the Communist Manifesto.

7 Jones, "Marxism and Peasant Revolt in the Russian Empire", p. 418.

8 V.I. Lenin, *Account of the Second Congress of the R.S.D.L.P.*, https://www.marxists.org/archive/lenin/works/1903/sep/15a.htm

9 Alexandra Kollontai, "On the History of the Movement of Women Workers in Russia", in Alexandra Kollontai, *Selected Articles and Speeches* (Moscow: Progress Publishers, 1984), https://www.marxists.org/archive/kollonta/1919/history.htm

10 Luigi Villari, *Fire and Sword in the Caucasus* (London: T. Fisher Unwin, 1906), p. 93.

11 Ibid., pp. 93-94.

12 Ibid., p. 94.

13 Ibid., p. 94.

14 Ibid., p. 97.

15 Jones, "Marxism and Peasant Revolt in the Russian Empire", p. 423.

16 Villari, *Fire and Sword in the Caucasus*, p. 93.

17 Ronald Grigor Suny, *The Making of the Georgian Nation* (Indiana University Press, 1988), p. 166.

18 Jones "Marxism and Peasant Revolt in the Russian Empire", p. 413, citing T. Zhghenti, *Revoliutsiia 1905–1907 v Gruzii* [Revolution of 1905-1907], Sbornik dokumentov (Tbilisi: n.p., 1956), p. 749.

19 Villari, *Fire and Sword in the Caucasus*, p. 98.

20 Lang, *A Modern History of Georgia*, pp. 150-51.

21 Cited in ibid., p. 152.

22 Adam Ulam, *Stalin: The Man and His Era* (New York: Viking Press, 1973), p. 74.

23 Jones, *Socialism in Georgian Colors*, p. 150.

24 Lang, *A Modern History of Georgia*, p. 156.

25 *Great Soviet Encyclopedia*, Volume 24 (New York: Macmillan, 1983), p. 475.

26 See Fred A. McKenzie, *From Tokyo to Tiflis: Uncensored Letters from the War* (London : Hurst and Blackett, 1905), cited in http://foreigners-georgia. blogspot.co.uk/2015/02/frederick-arthur-mckenzie-from-tokyo-to. html

27 Jones, "Marxism and Peasant Revolt in the Russian Empire", p. 429. His source is a Soviet-era (1956) book, *Revoliutsiia 1905–1907 v Gruzii*, cited above.

28 Cited in Jones, "Marxism and Peasant Revolt in the Russian Empire", p. 429.

29 Cited in Jones, *Socialism in Georgian Colors*, p. 155.

30 V.I. Lenin, *State and Revolution* (London: Communist Party of Great Britain, 1925), p. 159.

31 Ibid., p. 158.

32 Cited in Villari, *Fire and Sword in the Caucasus*, p. 85.

CHAPTER 3

1 Donald Rayfield, *Edge of Empires: A History of Georgia* (London: Reaktion Books, 2012), p. 323.

2 Kazemzadeh, *The Struggle for Transcaucasia*, p. 33.

3 Karl Marx and Friedrich Engels, *The Communist Manifesto*, https:// www.marxists.org/archive/marx/works/1848/communist-manifesto/ ch02.htm

4 Cited in Kazemzadeh, *The Struggle for Transcaucasia*, p. 36.

5 Cited in ibid., p. 37.

6 Ibid., p. 55.

7 L.G. Protasov, Vserossijskoe, *Uchreditel'noe sobranie: istoriya rozhdeniya i gibeli* [All-Russian Constituent Assembly: the history of its birth and death] (Moscow: ROSSPÉN Politicheskaia éntsiklopediia, 2014), p. 164.

8 Valery Silogava and Kakha Shengelia, *History of Georgia: From the Ancient Times through the "Rose Revolution"* (Tbilisi: Caucasus University Publishing House, 2007), p. 207.

9 Alexander Mikaberidze, *Historical Dictionary of Georgia* (Lanham, MD: Scarecrow Press, 2007), p. 258.

10 Vasili D. Dumbadze, *The Caucasian Republics: The Little Democracies The World Forgot* (New York: F. Hubner & Co.,1925), pp. 47-8.

11 Wladimir S. Woytinsky, *Stormy Passage: A Personal History Through Two Russian Revolutions to Democracy and Freedom* (New York: The Vanguard Press, 1961), p. 412.

12 Wikipedia: https://en.wikipedia.org/wiki/Georgian_parliamentary_ election,_1919, based on D. Nohlen, F. Grotz, and C, Hartmann, *Elections in Asia: A Data Handbook*, Volume I (Oxford: Oxford University Press, 2001), p. 382.

13 See http://www.feminism-boell.org/en/2014/01/12/kristine-chito-sharashidze and also http://archive.security.gov.ge/sharashidze_eng.html

14 Ethel Snowden, *A Political Pilgrim in Europe*, http://archive.org/stream/ politicalpilgrimoosnowuoft/politicalpilgrimoosnowuoft_djvu.txt

15 "Camille Huysmans on a Mission to Georgia", PDF downloaded from AMSAB-ISG, http://www.amsab.be

16 Letter from Nina d'Abo to the author, 20 February 1986.

CHAPTER 4

1 Quoted in Suny, *The Making of the Georgian Nation*, p. 193.

2 Noe Zhordania, *Imperialism Behind a Mask of Revolution*, 23 April 1922, typescript, p. 3.

3 Rayfield, *Edge of Empires*, p. 326.

4 Ibid., p. 327.

5 Cited in Kazemzadeh, *The Struggle for Transcaucasia*, p. 147. From Ludendorff's *Own Story*, Volume II (Freeport, NY: Books for Libraries Press, 1971), p. 302.

6 Kazemzadeh, *The Struggle for Transcaucasia*, pp. 126-127.

7 Leon Trotsky, *Between Red and White: A Study of Some Fundamental Questions of Revolution with Particular Reference to Georgia* (London: Communist Party of Great Britain, n.d.), p. 47.

8 Ibid., p. 29.

9   Ibid., p. 28.

10 Ibid., p. 46.

11 Karl Kautsky, *Georgia, a Social-Democratic Peasant Republic. Impressions and Observations*, Translated by H. J. Stenning and revised by the author (London: International Bookshops, 1921), pp. 88–89.

12 Ibid., pp. 88–89.

13 Rayfield, *Edge of Empires*, p. 329.

14 Georgian National Committee, *Georgia and the Georgian Race: Restoration of Independent Georgian State after 117 Years Domination by Russia* (London: Georgian National Committee, 1919), p. 13.

15 Rayfield, *Edge of Empires*, p. 330.

16 Ibid., p. 330.

CHAPTER 5

1   The most detailed accounts of the Armeno-Georgia war of 1918 can be found in Richard G. Hovannisian's book, *The Republic of Armenia, Volume I, The First Year, 1918–1919* (Berkeley, CA: University of California Press, 1971) and Andrew Andersen and George Partskhaladze, *Armeno-Georgian War of 1918 and Armeno-Georgian Territorial Issue in the 20th Century* (2015), http://www.academia.edu/10176756/Armeno-Georgian_War_of_1918_and_Armeno-Georgian_Territorial_Issue_in_the_20th_Century

2   Kazemzadeh, *The Struggle for Transcaucasia*, p. 176.

3   Hovannisian, *The Republic of Armenia*, p. 116.

4   V.I. Adamiia, *Iz istorii angliiskoi interventsii v Gruzii (1918–1921)* [From the history of the British intervention in Georgia] (Sukhumi: n.p., 1961), pp. 73–74, cited by Hovannisian, *The Republic of Armenia*, p. 117.

5   Suny, *The Making of the Georgian Nation*, p. 202.

6   Hovannisian, *The Republic of Armenia*, p. 109.

7   Kazemzadeh, *The Struggle for Transcaucasia*, p. 181.

8   Ibid., p. 182.

9   Trotsky, *Between Red and White*, p. 28.

CHAPTER 6

1   Ibid., pp. 16-17.
2   Wladimir S. Woytinsky, *Stormy Passage: A Personal History Through Two Russian Revolutions to Democracy and Freedom: 1905–1960* (New York: The Vanguard Press, 1961), p. 425
3   Ibid., pp. 425-426.
4   Cited in Lang, *A Modern History of Georgia*, p. 216.
5   Ibid.
6   Suny, *The Making of the Georgian Nation*, pp. 203-204.
7   http://www.jewishvirtuallibrary.org/text-of-the-balfour-declaration
8   This material and much other comes from the National Archives in Kew, FO 608/195/2.
9   FO 608/195/2.
10 For a full account of Ghambashidze's mission, see Beka Kobakhidze, "David Ghambashidze: Representative of the First Georgian Republic to His Britannic Majesty's Government (1918-1921)", *Oaka*, Vol. 8, No. 15 (2013), pp. 151-168.
11 FO 608/88/1. The armed forces being referred to are presumably General Denikin's Volunteer Army.
12 FO 608/88/1.
13 Kautsky, *Georgia*, pp. 89-90.
14 Zhordania, *Imperialism Behind a Mask of Revolution*, p. 7.
15 Lang, *A Modern History of Georgia*, pp. 218-219.
16 Deborah McDonald and Jeremy Dronfield, *A Very Dangerous Woman* (London: Oneworld, 2016), p. 124.
17 FO 608/275/9.
18 Lang, *A Modern History of Georgia*, p. 219.
19 Ibid., pp. 218-219.

CHAPTER 7

1   Karl August Wittfogel, *Oriental Despotism: A Comparative Study of Total Power* (New Haven, CT: Yale University Press, 1957), p. 391.

2 A good summary of Wittfogel's views on Russia is available in the article
"The Marxist View of Russian Society and Revolution", *World Politics*, Vol.
12, No. 4 (July 1960), pp. 487-508, also available online: http://marcuse.
org/herbert/booksabout/60s/60WittfogelMarxistViewRussianSociety.
pdf

3 Wittfogel, *Oriental Despotism*, p. 391.

4 Ibid., p. 391.

5 V.I. Lenin, *The Agrarian Programme of Social-Democracy in the First
Russian Revolution, 1905–1907*, https://www.marxists.org/archive/lenin/
works/1907/agrprogr/ch04s1.htm

6 Wittfogel, *Oriental Despotism*, p. 391.

7 Kautsky *Georgia*, p. 38.

8 Ibid., p. 38.

9 "Agrarian Reform", *Bulletin of the Georgian Information Bureau*, Thursday,
28 August 1919, pp. 3-4.

10 Suny, *The Making of the Georgian Nation*, p. 196.

11 Kautsky, *Georgia*, p. 39.

12 Trotsky, *Between Red and White*. https://www.marxists.org/archive/
trotsky/1922/red-white/ch03.htm

13 Kautsky, *Georgia*, p. 40.

14 Suny, *The Making of the Georgian Nation*, p. 198.

15 Ibid., p. 198.

16 Ibid., p. 198.

17 Shanin, *Russia, 1905–07*, pp. 272-273.

CHAPTER 8

1 Kautsky, *Georgia*, pp. 33-34.

2 Ibid., p. 34.

3 Ibid., p. 34.

4 Ibid., p. 36.

5 Telegram from Mr Stevens, 14 March 1919. FO 608/88/1.

6 Kautsky, *Georgia*, p. 35.

7 Suny, *The Making of the Georgian Nation*, pp. 200-201.

8   Kautsky *Georgia*, p. 35.

9   Ibid., p. 35.

10 http://matiane.wordpress.com/2012/09/04/constitution-of-georgia-1921/

11 *Bulletin of the Georgian Information Bureau*, London, No. 12, 20 November 1919, p. 4.

12 Freedom of association and the effective recognition of the right to collective bargaining, ILO website, http://www.ilo.org/declaration/principles/freedomofassociation/lang--en/index.htm

13 Kautsky, *Georgia*, p. 36.

14 Ibid., p. 36.

15 Kazemzadeh, *The Struggle for Transcaucasia*, p. 195.

16 Ibid., p. 196.

17 Suny, *The Making of the Georgian Nation*, p. 201.

18 Ibid., pp. 200-201.

19 Cited in Isaac Deutscher, *The Prophet Armed: Trotsky, 1879–1921* (London: Oxford University Press, 1970), p. 500.

20 Ibid., p. 501.

21 Ibid., pp. 499-501.

22 Cited I, ibid., pp. 508-509.

CHAPTER 9

1   Kautsky, *Georgia*, p. 42.

2   Jules Guesde, *Co-operatives and Socialism*, https://www.marxists.org/archive/guesde/1910/dec/cooperatives.htm

3   Ibid.

4   Quoted in Bruno Jossa, "Marx, Marxism and the Cooperative Movement", *Cambridge Journal of Economics*, 29 (2005), pp. 3–18.

5   From Trotsky, "An Open Letter to Jules Guesde, The War and the International", https://www.marxists.org/archive/trotsky/1914/war/part3.htm#open

6   Kautsky, *Georgia*, p. 43.

7   Ibid., p. 43.

8   J. Tsagareli, *The Co-operative Movement in the Republic of Georgia* (London: The Co-operative Printing Society, 1922).

9 Kautsky, *Georgia*, p. 43.

10 These are the cooperative movement's values according to the International Co-operative Alliance, http://ica.coop/en/whats-co-op/co-operative-identity-values-principles

11 Tsagareli, *The Co-operative Movement*.

12 Kautsky, *Georgia*, pp. 43–44.

13 Shanin, *Russia, 1905–07*, p. 271.

14 *Bulletin of the Georgian Information Bureau*, 4 September 1919, p. 4 [emphasis added].

CHAPTER 10

1 Constantin Kandelaki, *The Georgian Question before the Free World: Acts, Documents, Evidence* (Paris: Impr. De Narre, 1953), translated from the French by Kandelaki, p. 207.

2 Emil Souleimanov, *Understanding Ethnopolitical Conflict: Karabakh, South Ossetia, and Abkhazia Wars Reconsidered* (London: Palgrave Macmillan, 1993), p. 77.

3 Ibid., p. 72.

4 Kazemzadeh, *The Struggle for Transcaucasia*, p. 233.

5 Ibid., p. 238.

6 Zhordania, *Imperialism Behind a Mask of Revolution*, p. 9.

7 Mariam Lordkipanidze, *Essays on Georgian History* (Tbilisi: Metsniereba, 1994), p. 203.

8 Ibid., p. 203.

9 See http://mfaapsny.org/en/

10 Kazemzadeh, *The Struggle for Transcaucasia*, p. 199.

11 Ibid., p. 200.

12 Ibid., p. 192.

13 Rachel Arbel and Lily Magal (Magalashvili), editors, *In the Land of the Golden Fleece: The Jews of Georgia – History and Culture* (Tel Aviv: Beth Hatefutsoth, The Nahum Goldmann Museum of the Jewish Diaspora and Ministry of Defence Publishing House, 1992), pp. 58–59.

14 Kazemzadeh, *The Struggle for Transcaucasia*, p. 203, citing Zhordania, *Za dva goda* [For two years], pp. 201–202.

15 Zhordania, *Imperialism Behind a Mask of Revolution*, p. 2.

16 Arbel and Magal, *In the Land of the Golden Fleece*, p. 59.

17 Kazemzadeh, *The Struggle for Transcaucasia*, p. 203.

CHAPTER 11

1 Robert Conquest, *Stalin: Breaker of Nations* (London: Weidenfeld and Nicolson, 1991), p. 25.

2 Quoted in Alex de Jonge, *Stalin and the Shaping of the Soviet Union* (London: Collins, 1986), p. 45.

3 George F. Kennan, *The Historiography of the Early Political Career of Stalin*, Proceedings of the American Philosophical Society, Vol. 115, No. 3 (17 June 1971), pp. 165-169, http://www.jstor.org/stable/985975

4 See Eric Lee, "The Eremin Letter: Was Stalin an Agent of the Tsarist Okhrana?", *Revolutionary Russia* and online: http://www.j-bradford-delong.net/movable_type/refs/Safari_Scrapbook2/Was%20Stalin%20an%20Agent%20of%20the%20Tsarist%20Okhrana%3F.html

5 Suny, *The Making of the Georgian Nation*, p. 189.

6 Trotsky, *Between Red and White*, p. 47.

7 Suny, *The Making of the Georgian Nation*, p. 198.

8 Zhordania, *Imperialism Behind a Mask of Revolution*, p. 8.

9 Kazemzadeh, *The Struggle for Transcaucasia*, p. 205.

10 Ibid., p. 206.

11 Carl Eric Bechhofer, *In Denikin's Russia and the Caucasus, 1919–1920: Being a Record of a Journey to South Russia, the Crimea, Armenia, Georgia, and Baku in 1919 and 1920* (London: W. Collins Sons & Co., 1921), p. 55.

12 Ibid., p. 55. Bechhofer got the date of the planned coup wrong, giving it as 4 October, not 5 November.

13 Ibid., p. 55.

14 Vera Broido, *Lenin and the Mensheviks* (Aldershot: Gower, 1987), p. 50 [emphasis added].

15 Trotsky, *Between Red and White*, pp. 46-47.

16 Ibid., pp. 46-47.

17 Zhordania, *Imperialism Behind a Mask of Revolution*, p. 9.

18 Kazemzadeh, *The Struggle for Transcaucasia*, pp. 207–8.

19 Ibid., p. 285.

20 Ibid., p. 208.

21 Ibid., p. 209.

22 Ibid., p. 209.

23 Ibid., p. 210.

24 Ibid., p. 315.

25 *The Times*, 10 August 1920, p. 9.

26 Kautsky, *Georgia*, p. 72.

27 Kazemzadeh, *The Struggle for Transcaucasia*, p. 316.

28 Trotsky, *Between Red and White*, p. 49. Actually, Trotsky is probably referring to the shooting of about thirty mutinous soldiers following the failed coup attempt of November 1919.

29 Zhordania, *Imperialism Behind a Mask of Revolution*, p. 9.

30 Ibid., p. 9.

31 Ibid., p. 9.

32 "Red Ferment in Georgia", *The Times*, 8 January 1921, p. 9.

CHAPTER 12

1 "British Socialists to Visit Georgia", *The Times*, 4 August 1920.

2 http://archive.org/stream/politicalpilgrimoosnowuoft/politicalpilgrimoosnowuoft_djvu.txt

3 The diary is part of the Ramsay MacDonald Papers in the John Rylands Library at the University of Manchester. Unfortunately, it is cryptic in the extreme, containing very little of interest.

4 Ethel Snowden, "A Political Pilgrim in Europe", http://archive.org/stream/politicalpilgrimoosnowuoft/politicalpilgrimoosnowuoft_djvu.txt

5 The document is entitled "Camille Huysmans on a Mission to Georgia" and was downloaded from http://www.amsab.be/images/pdf/tento/Camille%20Huysmans%20on%20a%20Mission%20to%20Georgia.pdf, but is no longer available there.

6 Ibid.

7   http://archive.org/stream/politicalpilgrim00snowuoft/politicalpilgrim 00snowuoft_djvu.txt

8   Ramsay MacDonald, "A Socialist State in the Caucasus", *The Nation*, 16 October 1920, pp 64-66.

9   *The Times*, 14 October 1920, p. 7.

10 "A Promising Russian Border State", *Manchester Guardian*, 12 October 1920, p. 8.

11 Zourab Avalishvili, *The Independence of Georgia in International Politics, 1918–1921* (London: Headley Brothers, 1940), pp. 266-267.

12 Trotsky, *Between Red and White*, https://www.marxists.org/archive/trotsky/1922/red-white/ch01.htm

CHAPTER 13

1   Friedrich Engels, "A Critique of the Draft Social-Democratic Program of 1891", http://marxists.anu.edu.au/archive/marx/works/1891/06/29.htm

2   Karl Marx and Friedrich Engels, *The Communist Manifesto* (London: George Allen and Unwin, 1959), p. 144.

3   George Papuashvili, "The 1921 Constitution of the Democratic Republic of Georgia: Looking Back after Ninety Years", *European Public Law*, Vol. 18, No. 2 (June 2012), pp. 323-350.

4   Ibid., p. 336.

5   http://matiane.wordpress.com/2012/09/04/constitution-of-georgia-1921/

6   Ibid., p. 338.

7   Amnesty International has a full listing of which countries have abolished the death penalty and when: https://www.amnesty.org/download/Documents/ACT5038312016ENGLISH.PDF

8   Papuashvili, "The 1921 Constitution of the Democratic Republic of Georgia", p. 345.

9   MacDonald, "A Socialist State in the Caucasus".

10 Armenia, Azerbaijan and Georgia Country Studies, Federal Research Division, Library of Congress, edited by Glenn E. Curtis, Research Completed, March 1994, p. 218.

11 Papuashvili, "The 1921 Constitution of the Democratic Republic of Georgia", p. 349.

CHAPTER 14

1 Leon Trotsky, *The Trotsky Papers*, edited and annotated by Jan M. Meijer, Volume II, *1920–1922* (The Hague: Mouton, 1971), p. 375.

2 Ibid., p. 377.

3 Georgia Committee, London, *The Bolshevik Invasion of Georgia* (London: G. MacDonald, 1922), p. 3.

4 Kazemzadeh, *The Struggle for Transcaucasia*, p. 319.

5 *The New York Times*, 19 February 1921, p. 2.

6 *The Times*, 21 February 1921.

7 *The New York Times*, 19 February 1921, p. 2.

8 *The New York Times*, 20 February 1921.

9 *The New York Times*, 21 February 1921.

10 Ibid.

11 The US Navy history of the *Barker* says nothing about its role in evacuations in Batumi in 1921: https://www.history.navy.mil/research/histories/ship-histories/danfs/b/barker-i.html The *USS Whipple*, also in Batumi, may or may not have evacuated refugees, but there is nothing on the official naval history about this either: https://www.history.navy.mil/research/histories/ship-histories/danfs/w/whipple-ii.html

12 *The New York Times*, 22 February 1921.

13 *The Times*, 24 February 1921, p. 10.

14 *The New York Times*, 24 February 1921.

15 *The Times*, 23 February 1921.

16 *The New York Times*, 24 February 1921; *The Times*, 24 February 1921.

17 *The Times*, 28 February 1921.

18 *The New York Times*, 1 March 1921.

19 Letter from Nina d'Abo to the author, 20 February 1986.

20 Rayfield, *Edge of Empires*, p. 337.

21 *The Times*, 8 March 1921.

22 *The New York Times*, 15 March 1921.

23 Dumbadze, *The Caucasian Republics*, pp. 33–34.

24 Shanin, *Russia, 1905–07*, p. 274.

CHAPTER 15

1 Kautsky, *Georgia*, p. 9.

2 "La Géorgie sous la domination des armées bolchévistes" [Georgia under the domination of the Bolshevik armies], *Edition de la Présidence de l'Assemblée Constituante de la République Géorgienne*, October 1921. See also Rayfield, *Edge of Empires*, p. 342.

3 Jones, "Marxism and Peasant Revolt in the Russian Empire", p. 632.

4 Foreign Bureau of the Social-Democratic Labour Party of Georgia, *Documents of the Social-Democratic Labour Party of Georgia* (London: Foreign Bureau of the Social-Democratic Labour Party of Georgia, 1925), p. 10.

5 Ibid., p. 30.

6 Ibid., p. 8.

7 P.I. Rabinovitch, "Soviet Regime in Georgia: A Reply to Victor Serwy", *International Co-operative Bulletin*, November 1922.

8 Snowden, *Pilgrim*.

9 Rayfield, *Edge of Empires*, p. 342.

10 Ibid., p. 345.

11 Shanin, *Russia, 1905–07*, p. 275.

12 Cited in Stephen Jones, "The Establishment of Soviet Power in Transcaucasia: The Case of Georgia 1921-1928", *Soviet Studies*, Vol. 40, No. 4 (October 1988), pp. 616-639.

13 See Amy Knight, *Beria: Stalin's First Lieutenant* (Princeton, NJ: Princeton University Press, 1993), citing *Na osvobozhennom kavkaze* [In the liberated Caucasus], 2nd revised edition (Moscow: Izdat. "Staryi Bol'shevik", 1935), p. 38.

14 *The British Trade Union Delegation in Georgia (According to Bolshevist Newspapers in Georgia)* (London: Foreign Bureau of the Social-Democratic Workers Party of Georgia, 1924), p. 9.

15 Knight, *Beria*, p. 35.

16 His killer was a Georgian Social Democrat, Parmen Tchanoukvadzé, who was captured but later released, and declared to be mentally unstable. It was widely assumed that he was manipulated by Stalin's secret police to carry out the murder. Tchanoukvadzé reportedly left France shortly after his release and went on to study medicine.

CHAPTER 16

1 Kautsky, *Georgia*, p. 71.
2 Stephen Jones on the 90th anniversary of the Democratic Republic of Georgia, https://matiane.wordpress.com/2009/08/30/stephen-jones-on-the-90th-anniversary-of-the-democratic-republic-of-Georgia/
3 E.H. Carr, *What is History?* (London: Macmillan & Co. Ltd, 1961), p. 120.
4 Karl Kautsky, *The Dictatorship of the Proletariat* (Ann Arbor, MI: Ann Arbor Paperback, 1971), pp. 6–7.

INDEX

ABOUT THE AUTHOR

Eric Lee is a journalist and historian who has spent over thirty years researching independent Georgia, and has himself been active in trade union and political struggles in both the US and UK. His previous works include *Saigon to Jerusalem: Conversations with Israel's Vietnam Veterans* (1993) and *Operation Basalt: The British Raid on Sark and Hitler's Commando Order* (2016).

www.ericlee.info/theexperiment